Mentors

Digest

OVERCOMING
OBSTACLES

Compiled by

Linda Forsythe

Dr. Surya Ganduri

and the

Village of Abundance

Foreword by

Bob Proctor

Mentors Digest Publishing
Chicago, Illinois

$\mathscr{S}$age Advice By Dan Kennedy

There are three principles I've lived by, that can be helpful
whenever confronted with calamities

Principle #1:
Nothing is ever as bad-or as good-as it first appears.

Principle #2:
Most adversities conceal and provide new, better
opportunities, and a temporary vacuum is not necessarily
a bad thing.

Principle #3:
I do not just want to cope with adversity. I want to kick
it in the butt, smack it around, grab it by it's throat and
force it to divulge it's hidden benefits, subjugate it as my
servant, and profit from it enormously.
(I kind of have and attitude about this.)

Mentors Digest ~ Overcoming Obstacles™

Copyright 2013 Mentors International Associates, LLC.

ISBN 978-0-9850148-0-3

Printed in the United States of America

987654321 – 10

Published by Mentors Digest Publishing

This book is available at quantity discounts for bulk purchases and branding by businesses and organizations. For further information, or to learn more about Mentors Harbor™*, mentorsharbor.com, Mentors Magazine*™*, Mentors ~ Village of Abundance Radio*™*, Mentors HarborTV*™*, or Mentors Digest*™ *and other products and services of Mentors International Associates, LLC., contact:*

Mentors International Associates, LLC.
Attention: Dr. Surya Ganduri
P.O. Box 8256
Bartlett, IL 60103-8256
email: surya@mentorsdigest.com

Book Compilation: Linda Forsythe
Cover and Advertisement Design: Allan Davis
Mentors Lighthouse Logo Design: Allan Davis
Graphic Design and Type-setting: Benjamin Hur, Allan Davis
Illustrations: Kim Muslusky
Editor-in-Chief: Patricia Dietz
Assistant Editors: Mike Henry, Jennifer Stoll
Web Master: Benjamin Hur
Public Relations: Susan Gibson, Cynthia Hayes
German Translation: Monique Blokzyl
French Translation: Dr. Joel Bomane
Chinese Translation: Luigi T. Peccenini

The publisher would like to acknowledge the many publishers and individuals who granted us permission to reprint their cited material or have written specifically for this book.

FOREWORD

Obstacles = Opportunity

by Bob Proctor

When a person picks up something to read, generally the first thought that comes to their mind is, "I hope this is a good book." Linda Forsythe has made *sure* this is a good book. In Mentors Digest's ~ *Overcoming Obstacles*, Linda has brought together a number of excellent authors with stories you will like, and will want to refer back to a number of times, because they will offer hope. If you are anything like me or most of the people I know, you are going to welcome the hope that these stories provide, because you are continually running into one challenging obstacle after another. It is stories like these that provide the motivation, inspiration, and education required for us to meet and overcome every challenge.

Let's face it – life happens, and sometimes the obstacles we face are downright scary. On a conscious level, there's one part of our mind that tells us "we're not going to get through this," but deep down on another level, we know we will. Eventually we do, and move on to another bigger and better obstacle. In truth, obstacles are nothing more than illusions, typically self-imposed. Certainly, at the time we face the obstacle, it feels as real as a huge mountain in front of us. When I worked with Lloyd Conant, cofounder of the Nightingale Conant Corporation, Lloyd once told me that the most fortunate person alive is the person with the biggest problem. Because that's the person with the biggest opportunity! Lloyd was right. Life's obstacles are put in our way as opportunities to raise our level of consciousness, and when we do this, we see the beauty that was there all along.

I have known Linda Forsythe for a number of years, and there are many thousands of men and women who owe her a debt of gratitude – including you and me – for bringing us many of the greatest mentors in the world today through cataloging their advice, and then putting it in our hands. This book is an excellent example of the sage advice and practical solutions that can be used by the business leader and homemaker alike. You are especially going to appreciate the "how to" articles from a number of the mentors that you personally recognize. You will also love the heartwarming stories that come from people you may never have heard of, who share how they have overcome enormous challenges. All in all, cover to cover, this book provides an interesting and thought-provoking read. And, you can bet your bottom dollar, before you get to the end, you will find at least one story that was written just for you.

Regardless of what obstacles lie ahead of you, realize that you have the ability to change the way you think about them, and turn fear into faith. When there are no obstacles in your path, there is no growth. When setting a goal, I always tell people to set a goal that both scares and excites them at the same time, because it's not reaching the goal that's the big deal, it's the growth you experience as you overcome the challenges along the way. That's what's really important!

Maxwell Maltz was quoted as saying, "We are built to conquer environment, solve problems, achieve goals, and we find no real satisfaction or happiness in life without obstacles to conquer and goals to achieve." I recall a story about Maltz, who was talking to an individual who was very downhearted because he was bankrupt, ruined, and disgraced. Maltz explained, "My friend, the fact is you're bankrupt. It's only your opinion that you're ruined and disgraced. Hold your head up and keep on moving." I agree wholeheartedly. As you move along in your life's journey, keep this book handy and know that one person working with God is a majority. You have all the power you require sitting within you, eager to come to the surface.

Let me share a quote from a friend, Steve Bow, who served as a mentor to some of the greatest salespeople in the world. He said, *"God's gift to you is more talent and ability than you will ever use in this lifetime. Your gift to God is to develop as much of that talent and ability as you can in this lifetime."*

Take advantage of the obstacles in your life, beginning with the one you have in front of you. Know that when you solve it, you'll be a bigger and better person. Jane Willhite was right: "Givers gain." The next time a friend shares one of their obstacles with you, give them a copy of this book with an inspirational quote from you on the first page.

Bob Proctor,
Best-selling author of, *You Were Born Rich*.

TABLE OF CONTENTS

SECTION III – THE CREATION OF OUR DAILY BREAD ~ OVERCOMING OBSTACLES IN THE WORKPLACE

SECTION IV – ARRIVING IN THE VILLAGE OF ABUNDANCE

SECTION V – MENTORS DIGEST BRINGS TWO OF THE MOST POPULAR EXCLUSIVE INTERVIEWS FEATURED IN PREVIOUS MAGAZINE ISSUES!!!
(All interviews were conducted LIVE, taped, and transcribed to print.)

Featuring Luigi Tiziano Peccenini and Dr. Hari Harilela with Linda Forsythe.

SECTION V – cont.

A TRANSCRIPTION OF A LIVE MENTORS MAGAZINE COVER STORY INTERVIEW OF LUIGI T. PECCENINI (PECCE).

Pecce was born into a modest family in Italy, and grew to set up the "Wall Street Institute," (the most internationally renowned institution for teaching the English Language), forty years ago. Today the organization has over 400 learning centers in 28 countries around the world. Read how this gentleman became an award winning, powerhouse of information that has positively affected many lives around the globe.

A TRANSCRIPTION OF A LIVE MENTORS MAGAZINE COVER STORY INTERVIEW OF DR. HARI HARILELA.

Hari, as he is known, started cutting cloth in the 1930s. He survived World War II, thrived under the British and did even better after Hong Kong's 1997 handover to China. Today, he sits atop an empire with interests in hotels and general trading. He lives with almost 100 members of his family in a luxurious compound that sits alongside Kowloon Tong's Waterloo Road, a unique arrangement that fascinates outsiders, many of whom wonder how the Harilela patriarch can maintain harmony among so many blood relatives and in-laws.

SECTION VI – THE VISION OF A VILLAGE OF ABUNDANCE

INTRODUCTION

The Village...
That Created This Book

by Linda Forsythe

At some point in antiquity, there must have been a Neanderthal who shivered out in the cold while looking on with longing toward the inside of a cave. The cherry glow of a warm fire with an aroma of cooking meat, would have been inviting. Watching from a distance, people are busy conducting various tasks while working together as a tribe. But, the lonely man chooses to remain a solitary figure, while fighting the many obstacles of his life. Overcoming obstacles in such circumstances are difficult.

Throughout history, it has been found that life is much easier, when humanity combines resources to help each other. Obstacles in these situations are then, not quite so formidable.

I found out (personally and up close), what it meant to be like one of our ancestors shivering alone out in the cold around the beginning of 2009. After making some mistakes in business, plus some poor choices about who I created alliances with; the bad economy decided to show up. This happened right when I was alone and the most vulnerable. Mentors Harbor went through spectacular descent as the business rode the proverbial mudslide downhill... along with my home, vehicle and belongings. Again.

What was even more humiliating was that one of the corporations from this business was getting ready to release a new book title to the world. It was called, *Walking With the Wise for Overcoming Obstacles*. That book never made it out of the warehouse. No matter how hard I tried... it was an obstacle that I couldn't seem to get past. Along with everything else, I lost my reputation as someone who didn't deliver.

But, this wasn't the first time I had sat at the bottom in a collapsed muddy mess. Experience had taught me how to pick myself up and dust off. The first step was to gather up the courage to find someone who could use my talents so I could make a living. Maybe find a tribe?

History has shown, unfortunately, that human nature tends to slam the door on weary travelers during times of blight. When everyone is hungry and

11

having difficulty surviving, generosity and charity seem to be in limited supply, as most people go into a "scarcity" mindset. On top of encountering that reality, for two years I struggled to survive while carrying a great deal of guilt on my shoulders. I relived the past over and over while playing out in my mind how situations could have turned out otherwise. I wasn't quite sure what to do because the climate had changed, everything was different, and the terrain inhospitable.

And then one day, I heard a very old classic tale called, "Stone Soup" written during the Dark Ages. There are multiple versions of this story around the world, but all carry the same meaning. Here is one of my favorites:

———————————————

An old man, bent over with age, struggled hard to pull a cart with a few of his belongings and a large iron pot. He was tired, cold, and hadn't eaten for days.

Ahead of him lay a small village. The village was his last hope because he didn't have the strength to travel much further.

Unfortunately, every door he knocked on was slammed in his face when asking for work in exchange for food or a place to stay. Everyone basically said the same thing, "We barely have enough food to feed ourselves. Go away."

It was at this point, that the old man knew it was time to make his "Stone Soup." He pulled his cart out into the middle of the village courtyard and collected wood to make a fire. After the wood was burning brightly, he unloaded his large iron pot and filled it with water after placing it over the flames. He then sat next to the fire warming his hands while waiting for the water to boil. The villagers began watching this curious spectacle happening in their midst and came outside to observe from an easier vantage point.

After the water began to steam, the old man reached into his coat pocket to pull out a small package. He very carefully unwrapped a stone, held it to his heart giving thanks, and then placed it in the water.

Now he sat back with anticipation, licking his lips.

Finally, one of the villagers had seen enough and went up to the man asking him what he was doing.

He smiled at the villager with his toothless grin and said, "I am making my Stone Soup! Many years ago, a wise hermit gave me this stone and told me to save it for a special day when I choose to make the most delicious, filling, thick stew I ever had. Today is the day."

The villager looked somewhat doubtful, but the thought of a magical stone creating delicious stew, was tempting. So he asked the old man, "I have

12

two carrots left to feed my whole family. If I donate my carrots to your soup, will you share it with us?" "Absolutely!" said the old man.

The other villagers standing around listening to this conversation, immediately offered to do the same thing, for each wanted to have some of this special soup. Some had bits of meat; others had vegetables, potatoes or spices. A few offered their services in exchange, such as stoking the fire or stirring the stew. Almost the entire village donated something. A tantalizing aroma filled everyone's nostrils.

After a few hours when the Stone Soup was finished, the entire village ate the most delicious meal it ever had, and no one ever went hungry again because of the magic recipe.

———————————————

The profound wisdom from this old folk tale inspired me deeply. How far had we drifted away as a society from basic principles of survival? After all, this is exactly the reason that tribes or villages were formed in the first place. Everyone knew their neighbor and contributed to the whole in some manner. Remember that old saying, "It takes a village to raise a child"? Our ancestors knew the importance of all this and practiced it daily.

Armed with this old folk tale, I set out to cook my own version of Stone Soup. All I had left was an empty iron pot buried somewhere in the mud, that was left over from my failed business. The iron pot in my case was a media platform for mentors. I had found that a multitude of people were in the same situation that I was. Each was struggling to survive on their own, while fighting off insurmountable obstacles. But, they all had their own story and unique talents that were invaluable to someone else. We organized and united. Everyone contributed a little of what they had to the whole, and as a result, we now all eat well.

We elected to call this group, "The Village of Abundance," a village where no one ever goes hungry that contributes to the "Stone Soup." And, as any good village, we contain a wide variety of villagers with unique talents to share. Many of our mentors have a Doctorate degree in some area, while others have years of experience and success through the school of "hard knocks." We also have Accountants, Attorneys, Marketing Masters, Webmasters, Graphic Designers or Public Relations Specialists. Plus, we have "Moms, Pastors, Teachers, Gifted Writers, or Public Speakers. The list is extensive. And, they are from many places around the globe.

It was important to keep this group small in the beginning as we were building our village from solid concepts and rules of engagement. Part of the blue print was everyone had to be willing to contribute in some manner and work as a team. When we all came together to give something, (no matter how small), then we all received abundantly.

13

That is where this Mentors Digest came from. It came from the collaborative effort of our village. We combined the most celebrated articles written in Mentors E-Magazine and bound them together in a book form here. We felt the subject of "Overcoming Obstacles" was an obvious choice for our first niche and will now do this as an annual celebration in various areas.

As a group of volunteers, we raised MentorsHarbor.com out of the deep mud it was buried in and scrubbed out our "large iron pot." From there, we created other new entities, such as Mentors ~ Village of Abundance Radio Network on Blog Talk Radio. We continue working together on various other projects to build new platforms for our Mentors with TV shows, Blogs, Webinars, and a University. The purpose of all these media platforms is to give voice to the teachers of the world, teachers who will work together to guide and uplift those willing to learn how to live abundantly while working together to help their fellow man. This vision of a village has now grown worldwide and has already spread to a multitude of countries. At present, we are in various parts of Asia, United States, Germany, England, France, Spain, Italy and Australia.

During this journey, I was blessed to meet and get to know Dr. Surya Ganduri. Because of my previous experiences, I had certain trust issues and have been very careful with whom I align myself. Surya has shown himself to be an honest man of integrity. This amazing gentleman embodies everything needed in a business partner, including an attention to detail that borders on being "anal." He showed up at the perfect time! His many years of experience and peaceful demeanor are what the village needed for an Operations Manager.

Our Village of Abundance has joined together and we all have the same goal of uniting the world together with a common vision of peace. We continue looking for others to join the village, where everyone can eat well, have a strong roof over their head and a warm fire in the hearth – a place where obstacles are easily overcome by making our own brand of "Stone Soup."

LETTER FROM THE EDITOR

Do Yourself a Favor...

by Patricia Dietz

Dear Friend,

As Editor of this edition of Mentors Digest's ~ *Overcoming Obstacles*, it was my assignment to read every single word between these two covers. Not only did I enjoy this task immensely, (even though it was my *job* to read these stories), I found that I became personally inspired by each and every article. In fact, I experienced an epiphany of my own, which caused a profound turn-around in my life. That bonus wasn't in the contract!

If you want to have an incredibly rich and inspiring experience, read this book from cover to cover. What you hold in your hands is a vast container of knowledge, wisdom, experiences, and stories of sheer human will, from some of the most dynamic and inspiring people that you just might ever encounter. ALL of them have quite a story to share, and it is our sincere privilege here at Mentors to be the instruments for putting this information together in print, for your valuable reading experience.

Several important themes weave their way throughout the book, as you will discover. They testify to the truth that each of us is in charge of our own lives, that only by changing what we presently do will we change the results we experience, and that we are all worthy of the best that life has to offer, to name only a few. But perhaps the most important theme that may touch your heart and mind is this sage advice: ***never ever give in, and never ever give up, NO MATTER WHAT!*** If I were to sum up what each of the authors in this book might say upon meeting you face-to-face, those words would be: "If I can do it, so can you!"

I suggest you will discover that this "tool" held in your hands will be far more instrumental to your personal growth than you could ever imagine.

Thank you Linda Forsythe, Ben Hur, Surya Ganduri, Allan Davis, Mike Henry, and the entire Mentor's team; it was a pleasure collaborating with all of you. Until our next book....

Patricia Dietz
Editor-in-Chief
Mentors Digest

*W*hoever Walks With The Wise... Will Become Wise.

*W*hoever Walks With Fools... Will Suffer Harm.

~ *Proverbs 13:20*

Inspirational Journeys for Overcoming Obstacles

$\mathcal{W}$hether You Think You Can
or Can't... Either Way You
Are Right.

~ *Henry Ford*

I Don't Know What to Do!

by Linda Forsythe

Definition of an obstacle: *something that impedes progress or achievement.*

Typical emotional response from a perceived obstacle: *frustration, anger, fear, hopelessness, indecision, anxiety, and a plethora of emotions arising from torment.*

Definition of torment: *the infliction of torture, extreme pain, or anguish of body or mind. A source of vexation. Agony.*

Whew! That tells me that there are probably a few tortured minds reading this book. Most don't pick up and read something about how to overcome an obstacle unless they have one to overcome... right?

Uncomfortable situations are bound to come to everyone. If you are experiencing a number of the emotions listed above, it means you are seriously hurting and want the pain to go away. Therefore, let's jump right in and work to eradicate your hurt.

I would like to begin by sharing with you a very difficult obstacle that happened in my life, and ultimately taught me how to change my thinking. A change in thought processes are a very important first step.

Notes arrive in my office frequently, asking what I did in my previous, destitute state of homelessness. It has amazed me how many multitudes of people are close to being in this situation, or are already there. (I thought my problems were so unique!) Then there are those who want to know how to start or build a business, fix/find a relationship, move out of a financial crisis, or overcome a health difficulty. My answer to each of them is the same: change your thinking in the right direction. Doing this – and only this – is where you should begin.

Many years ago, when I lost everything I owned (and I mean EVERYTHING), including having nowhere to go with my young son at my side... I was afraid.

A long-term relationship that I had depended on was over in a very bad way. Suddenly, there was no shelter, no food, no money, no car, no bank account,

19

no furniture, no clothes, and nobody to help either of us that I could find. My 16-year-old daughter Tiffany had dropped out of school a few months before and ran away from home with a boyfriend who was beating her. I hadn't heard anything from her for months and didn't know if she was alive or dead. Of course Tiffany chose that particular time to want to come home. Now there was no home for her to come home to. My fear was paralyzing, and monsters were coming at me from every direction. I absolutely could not move. I knew then what they meant by how some people become catatonic. Homeless and standing on the street, wondering in what direction my next step should be, I was a desperate and lost puddle of goo.

I also remember feeling that I would have given anything to be a small child again – to have someone hold or rock me – a strong loving person whispering in my ear, saying, "It's going to be okay... you are now safe." I wanted someone to lift me up and give me strength. But nothing came. Nothing happened. No one was there. In my case, I had done everything on my own previously, and therefore, was truly on my own when I needed help. I was at the end of my rope in trying to strategize answers or figure out solutions to overwhelming problems. To say I was drained would have been an understatement. I was completely broken down and empty.

I should clarify that nothing happened to help me until I finally experienced enough pain and came to a place of surrender.

For the first time in my life, I fell to my knees in absolute, sincere, broken submission and asked God to take my burdens from me. I couldn't carry them any longer. I was done. I didn't bargain or even ask for help at that moment. I just "Let Go... Let God" and laid my sorrows at His feet. I opened up my arms and imagined that it was Him who held and rocked me in His arms. It was Him protecting me and offering comfort.

Why am I telling you this? Because surrendering my heavy load was my first step in bringing me to a place of peace.

No more fear. No more "What if…." No more torment.

Please know... it was from a place of "peace and submission" that I opened up my mind and was receptive to guidance. It is in this state of mind and being that miracles begin to happen. And miracles DID happen! I could literally feel the crushing load lift off my shoulders. I felt lighter... and safe!!! I became inspired to take a new direction that drew to me an endless supply of help, when in my previous state of fear, all the noise of chaotic thought would drown out any directive guidance.

After releasing the chaos holding me down, the noise in my mind disappeared.

Be aware that *the type* of obstacle standing in the way, and the emotional stamina of the individual, will determine the amount of pain, frustration, or bad feelings produced. Sitting in a traffic jam can cause very different emotions

20

than being homeless or diagnosed with cancer. But ultimately, it is the emotion and potential of cascading negative thoughts that give rise to varying degrees of torment. If our life is in immediate danger, then we are equipped with the autonomic nervous system responses of "fight or flight" to protect us. We take immediate action. The emotions involved given to us are a good gift. But why then do these emotions arrive for other things? For some, being stuck in traffic can cause significant torment, whereas it won't emotionally affect another at all. Why is that?

The answer is "perception."

Utilizing the example of being stuck in traffic... if there is something you can possibly do to get out of the situation, then you can take action to move beyond it. In fact, the "right" answer will come to you much quicker if you don't have chaotic emotions. If there is absolutely nothing you can do at that exact moment, why allow tormenting thoughts to take over anyway? It serves no purpose. This reminds me of what my grandmother used to say if she was in an uncomfortable situation: "Life is like the seasons, and this season, too, shall pass." If there is serious resistance arising from within you, then this is a negative perception. Another word for a negative perception could be "judgment." Negative emotions are then born from judgment. These types of emotions tend to grow and mature toward negative effects.

Let's look at what happens to any seed that is planted. For the sake of argument, let's "choose" to plant the seed of a weed and hope it will produce a tomato plant. You already know what that seed is going to produce if it is cultivated and nourished... don't you? A weed seed cannot produce anything other than what it is... even if you desperately want it to produce something else. A plant that grows, and the fruit produced, will bear witness to the seed that was planted in the first place. You will know any seed by its fruit. An adept gardener knows to uproot the weeds, or they will choke the life out of an entire garden and keep it from producing good fruit. Therefore, stop choosing to plant weeds or the seeds of negative perceptions.

Your "perceptions" can give rise to blessings or torment. Peace within or endless hell. You can choose your perceptions.

Is a "monster" after you?

For the purpose of this first chapter, I am going to substitute out the word "obstacle" with the word "monster." It may help to look at things with a different perspective. Sometimes that is all that is needed in order to problem solve. Here are two questions to consider:

- What is worse... the "monster" or the emotions produced by the thought of it?

- What is the cause of the monster being in front of you in the first place?

That monster (obstacle) came to be in front of you because of how you think. Somehow, you believe that monster is real. The fruit of your "reactions" evolve because of your thoughts. The "reactions" to the perceived monster seem to take on a life of their own, and then the monster grows right in front of you as if on steroids.

What you focus on grows, and in effect, acts to nourish the seed that was planted.

Looking at something as if it is a "monster" causes a type of knee-jerk reaction of emotions that causes a fascinating domino effect. So, how do we kill the proverbial monster or uproot all the bad seeds of thought?

Let's take care of this silly problem once and for all. (My little granddaughter is the one who is the inspiration for this, by the way.) Apparently I have a really scary closet... or so she tells me when she comes to visit. On a regular basis, she will come into my room at night, terrified and screaming that there was a monster in the closet. It has now almost become a routine where I take her hand and walk her toward that scary dark place and turn on the light. When she can see that her nasty monster isn't real, she immediately begins to calm down.

When the light is turned on, the darkness disappears. If the monster wasn't real, there shouldn't be any more reason for torment, should there? Your situation isn't any different. Your monster (obstacle) isn't real.

For me, it took a very long time and an enormous amount of pain before I realized I was expending energy and thoughts toward something that didn't exist.

An obstacle is merely an illusion: a spirit of false perception arising from your own mind. Remove the false belief of the obstacle, and you take the first step toward realizing what you want.

I can hear the objections already. "An obstacle is an illusion? Yeah right! This problem sure looks and feels pretty real to ME, because I certainly can't move past it!"

Don't misunderstand me here. I am not suggesting that you go into a state of denial and ignore a problem. I am, however, suggesting that you CAN change your perception on how to obtain a goal. *Recognizing a mirage for what it is will cause you to look elsewhere for something real* – something that ultimately will serve you better in manifesting what you need. Focusing through the transparency of an illusion will clear the road for an easier journey to your desired destination. It will take away the torment and allow you to think more clearly.

22

So... begin right now to calm your mind. Bring yourself to a place of peace, and be open to loving direction. Keep in mind that the direction or help offered might not be what you thought it would be. It is important that you not dictate. When I say submission, I mean submission! Also, in order to receive miracles and blessings, YOU MUST BE WILLING TO ACCEPT THEM! Be on the lookout for small things offered. Give thanks and receive the gift, (even if it is something as small as advice). Be aware. Search.

When inspired with guidance...

Now, you must pick yourself up and take action. Swift action. You'll know if it is divine revelation. If the guidance is life affirming (either to you or someone else)... get up and just do it! Don't wait. Yes, it is possible for something to be handed to you, but taking action on guidance should be just as much of a miracle to be realized.

After you've worked yourself out of an immediate crisis, a few important questions should arise for your consideration. How do you move forward and close the gate behind? What are you going to do to build a better life? I don't think you want to come back to this horrible, wretched place again... right? Well... to build anything, you must start on a firm foundation. You've started your building process by changing the way you think. You've planted the good seeds. Now, the good seeds must be fed and nurtured to grow. But what about all those weeds? The weeds must be pulled up, one at a time, or they will overrun the good seeds of your garden again. There is still more work to be done for a good foundation.

I suggest you ask yourself a question: look at your surroundings right now... what do you see?

If you have a life in order, plenty of inner strength with clarity of focus, and your surroundings are in balance... THEN you have a firm foundation to build something on. You don't have to have money to be in balance. Balance is a state of mind. The right state of mind will create fertile ground for inspiration and guidance. The fruit produced will bear witness to your state of mind. What fruit have you produced?

If your life is in chaos, your surroundings are a mess (literally and figuratively), your health is substandard, or you have addictions or any of a number of spirit-killing situations... then you need to work on yourself, FIRST. Remember... God is not the author of chaos.

This is also true for those who have asked for advice, paid for programs and/or coaches, and nothing seems to work. If the advice received is good and nothing is working, then something of a higher priority should be attended to. If you are in bad health or physical pain... your body is trying to tell you something. Listen to the alarms going off! Your state of mind has manifested EVERYTHING you are experiencing right now.

Working on yourself first before starting any new venture or relationship is absolutely necessary, because it is YOU holding you back.

Somehow... someway... you got to where you are now because of how you think.

Bring yourself to a place of "peace." Bring yourself to a place of "no thought." Others may call it a place of "presence." *Know* that you will be guided, and the answer will come. Have *faith* that when you have asked and then released all the monsters and emotions... a process has begun to make things right... even if you can't see it. Completely surrender. Peace... be still.

"Now faith is the substance of things hoped for, the evidence of things not seen." – **Hebrews, Chapter 11 verse 1.**

How to Kick Adversity in the Butt

by Dan Kennedy

Personal Note: *Be certain to read my final comment after this article, because these words were written by Dan over 10 years ago. We've re-published it here as an excellent example of guidance worth listening to and following. His wisdom is timeless! ~~~ Linda Forsythe*

I have lived an interesting life so far. And if you ever want to lay a blessing and a curse on someone simultaneously, there it is: may you live an interesting life.

A few brief resume items, prerequisite to my thoughts about dealing with adversity: I had the unique childhood experience of having entrepreneurial parents who were quite successful and very prosperous until my teens, when they were quite unsuccessful and very broke. I saw and experienced shiny new cars every year and old, rotting, broken down, bad cars. A mansion that resembled the one on "Joe Millionaire," and also a house (in a rural area) we couldn't afford heating oil for, forcing us to sleep in clothes and blankets huddled at the dining room fireplace. By the time I was an adult, I'd lived the Totie Fields line: "I've been broke and I've been rich and rich is better." Since mine was backwards, I started my adult life broke. And I stayed broke for quite a while. Later I went both business and personally bankrupt in a messy and humiliating way. Along the way, my earliest business mentor and closest friend made a sequence of very poor decisions that put him in the state penitentiary for five years. In total, I've gone belly-up and bust in three businesses. But I have since developed very successful businesses and significant wealth, and while not yet 50, I have no need to earn even one more dollar to live comfortably the rest of my life. Instead of working, I get to put a lot of time into my racehorses – which do not qualify me for any kind of investing wizard credential. After all, they are an investment that eats while I sleep.

I stuttered nearly uncontrollably for several years, and continued to have a stuttering problem into adulthood. Yet I became a very prominent, popular, professional speaker, including nine years on international tour with many of the best-known business, sales, and motivational speakers of our time – including *Zig Ziglar*, *Jim Rohn*, *Tom Hopkins*, and *Brian Tracy* – as well as a Who's Who list of former U.S. Presidents and world leaders, athletes and coaches, authors, and Hollywood celebrities. I've addressed audiences as large as 35,000 and spoken at specialized-topic "boot camps" costing as much as $10,000 per person to attend.

There was no way I could afford college. There would have been zero assistance from my family. In fact, I needed to immediately start earning enough money to help my parents financially. So I never attended college, let alone received any initials to plunk after my name, MBA or others, yet I have developed a thriving consulting practice almost exclusively working with millionaire and multimillionaire entrepreneurs, with a few Fortune 500s tossed in occasionally. My highest level coaching program, the Kennedy Platinum Inner Circle, includes 18 individuals, each running large information publishing and marketing businesses, combined, generating well over 150 million dollars annually. As of this writing, I am routinely paid $8,300 per day for consulting, and I turn down twice as many engagements as I accept.

I have had no formal training, apprenticeship, mentorship, or even employment in advertising, yet I've become one of the highest paid freelance advertising copywriters in America. (My current fee to write a client's direct-mail campaign, for example, ranges from $28,000 to as much as $70,000 plus a royalty on all the gross revenues that result from its use.)

Actually I have only had one job my entire life. Right out of high school I spent one year as a territory sales rep. Near the end of the year, my sales manager and I both agreed that I needed to be entrepreneurial by virtue of the fact I was unemployable.

On nine different occasions, I have been confronted with severe, epic, giant adversity. Along the way, I have faced a zillion incidents of lesser significance, yet each a mountainous challenge or crisis in its moment. In my earliest years in business I've had bank loans called, been sued, been wrongfully thrown out of a professional association and had to sue to get reinstated, had two cars repossessed in the same year, and occasionally gone hungry. I have had to start all over again from scratch, with no scratch, more than once. I have at certain times noted a remarkable absence of friends and encouragers. (Former President Nixon said "Don't count your friends when you are on top of the world. Count them when the world is on top of you. It is a more accurate count.") Sage observation! I have seriously questioned my own sanity. For some years, I had a serious drinking problem bordering on alcoholism (I am fortunate to have been able to quit cold turkey). Oh yeah, I've had a few other personal problems, too.

I am delighted to tell you, knock on wood, that for more than a decade now I have been sober, successful in my entrepreneurial ventures, sought out in my businesses, celebrated as an author and speaker, accumulated wealth, and accomplished virtually every goal set – on or ahead of schedule. This does not mean, however, that I have lived or live free of adversity. It only means that I've developed some skill in handling it properly.

There is, after all, only one population possibly free of problems. A number of years ago, I was driven to their community to meet them. Their place of residence is a cemetery.

Anyway, I think there are three principles I've lived by that can be helpful whenever confronted with calamities:

Principle #1:
Nothing is ever as bad – or as good – as it first appears.

Principle #2:
Most adversities conceal and provide new, better opportunities, and a temporary vacuum is not necessarily a bad thing.

Principle #3:
I do not just want to cope with adversity. I want to kick it in the butt, smack it around, grab it by its throat and force it to divulge its hidden benefits, subjugate it as my servant, and profit from it enormously. (I kind of have an attitude about this.)

If you examine my life in this context, each disappointment, frustration, failure, and calamity has directly led to and made possible something of greater benefit that would not have occurred otherwise. Just for example, the terrible financial straits of a small custom cassette production company I had wound up becoming CEO of, led me to selling its manufacturing division to a competing firm, owned by Bill Guthy. Out of that came an invitation from Bill to work on Guthy-Renker Corporation's first TV infomercial, *"Think and Grow Rich,"* which in turn led to a 15-year ongoing consulting relationship with Guthy-Renker that was lucrative, in and of itself. It also established me as an expert in infomercials generating more than 100 million dollars in revenue, and as a consultant integrally involved with infomercials generating more than 2 billion dollars combined. All of which probably would never have occurred had I not been CEO of a company sinking like the Titanic, desperate for a cash infusion.

I have diagrammed this for my whole life – each incident that, in its moment, appeared to be tragic – and the opportunity it subsequently provided. The benefits of what appears to be adversity are many and varied. They may be liberation from a situation or relationship that was not best for you and would wind up a prison – better out sooner than later. Another might be a discovery about yourself that empowers you in a new way, or that yields enormous subsequent profit. Another might be a move to a new place, a new business, a new career, better able to get you to your big goals and objectives.

I've experienced all these many times, at relatively trivial as well as serious levels. The demise and bankruptcy of a company I thought might become a giant "spoken word" audio product publisher, liberated me from a path leading to certain unhappiness. Had the company been a success, it would have been a prison. I've come to appreciate my severe anathema to managing people. That thing had 40 employees and would have had hundreds. For many years now, I've been able to operate with one.

My bankruptcy also revolutionized my entire attitude toward money, and soon provided a new kind of confidence. I thought it would be fatal. To my surprise, it was barely a minor inconvenience.

In one year, I had several short stories and two novels rejected by over 40 different publishers. As a result, I turned my attention to non-fiction, where I've enjoyed considerable success, including 9 different books published and sold in bookstores. Two have been on bookstore shelves continuously since 1991. My non-fiction writing has brought me prominence in two different fields, a flow of consulting clients and speaking engagements, and overall, has served my purposes congruently far better than having a novel published would have.

By the 18th year of my speaking career, the travel was literally killing me. I hated it. I was eating poorly, way overweight, stressed out, irritable, and unhappy. I went from a high of 70 engagements a year to about a dozen. In doing so, I walked away from the Success Events tour after 9 consecutive years of appearing on 20 to 25 of these giant, all-day, multi-speaker events. I took a huge income cut, and also cut off a chief means of acquiring new customers for my "inner circle" newsletter, information, and seminar business. There was a huge "money vacuum" created. I have since replaced that revenue with a coaching business, in which most of the service is delivered via telephone from the comfort of my homes, offices, and backyard deck, while the face-to-face meetings occur at my homes, at my convenience, with everyone traveling to me. The vacuum filled up with better business, which is much more conducive to good health, sanity, and my lifestyle preferences.

Detecting this pattern relatively early in the game led to my commitment to a particular process for each and every apparent adversity, which goes something like this:

First, delay response – to allow for analysis – when not in the heat of the adverse moment. Because nothing is ever as bad (or as good) as it first appears, it's important not to judge and react too quickly. This is not to be confused with indecisiveness, procrastination, or avoidance. I've never dodged confronting difficult situations. It is certainly true that problems rarely reach satisfactory resolution on their own. Nor do they tend to improve with age. However, reacting too quickly usually means reacting wrong.

Second, gather as much useful information as possible as quickly as possible, on which to base my reaction to the situation. When confronted with a problem, I go into massive information gathering and assimilation. It's self-

28

serving to say this, since I am in the information business, but it is my observation that most people respond too quickly to new situations based only on whatever information they already possess, and are, in general, surprisingly lazy and cheap about acquiring new information. Tackling a new situation with old information is akin to staffing an Indy 500 pit crew with blacksmiths.

Third, be open to and alert for the new opportunities and benefits that will certainly evolve from the bad situation. Because I know they are there or will develop, I consciously hunt for them and am eager to act on them once identified.

Let me give you an actual example: my diabetes diagnosis. A few years ago, I failed an insurance physical, because I was diagnosed with diabetes. My blood sugar levels were alarmingly high. I went to several different doctors without getting the kind of assistance I wanted, but I was also into my massive information gathering mode. Sorting out this information was extremely frustrating, as there is considerable disagreement and conflict between one expert and another. After nearly two years of experimentation, I arrived at an eating plan that took off about 25 pounds, and a nutritional supplementation regimen that brought the blood sugar numbers down by about 30%. I also kept searching for assistance. I finally found a doctor (in another state), an M.S., who was involved with "integrative medicine" (i.e., natural solutions first, prescription drugs as a last resort). I'm now 45 pounds lighter and have kept the weight off for over a year, have my diabetes thoroughly controlled, qualified for the insurance as "nondiabetic," and do not use any prescription drugs, including insulin. The quality of the information provided to diabetics by the medical establishment is so poor, misleading, impractical, and negative, that I am busily developing my own web sites, newsletter, and information products for diabetics, to teach them to essentially make their disease go away and live insulin pill or injection-free. As of this writing, I can't say for certain whether this will develop into a significant business or not. (You can check my progress if you like at *"www. damnthedoctors.com"*.) But if it does, it will be yet another instance where calamity leads to opportunity. And whether this turns into financial gain or not, it has produced great health benefits. Having been motivated by the diagnosis, I have made myself an alternative health/weight loss expert, taken off 45 pounds, and am keeping it off. I sleep better, have more energy, eat a healthier diet, and overall... I am in the best shape and condition I've been in 20 years.

For many people, a diabetes diagnosis is one of the greatest setbacks of their lives. Many people suffer acute depression, poorly manage their disease, accept bad advice without question or information gathering of their own, and let it virtually ruin their lives. For them, doors are closing. For me, new doors are opening. Would I rather not have it to deal with? Absolutely! But I am thoroughly schooled and conditioned in the productive response to adversity, so for me, it becomes opportunity (whether it likes it or not).

In 2002, my 22-year marriage abruptly and, to me, unexpectedly ended. I consider it the greatest tragedy I have ever experienced. An entire, very clear picture of the rest of my life was erased and replaced with a blank slate. Certain things will progress and are progressing as planned, but others are now unknown. For the first time in many years, I do not know what I want. I am floundering mentally and emotionally. The very thought of dating is ludicrous and unpleasant to me. But I am in my massive information gathering mode, and I am moving from shock and disappointment to optimism, looking for the opportunities that must be coming down the pike. Will this somehow lead to a better life experience for me in the years remaining? When the axe first fell, I'd have said no, of course. But if history repeats itself as historians insist, then my life history guarantees it will.

If there is a certainty about life, it is that a new adversity is lurking just around the next corner, to confront you and challenge you. No amount of wealth, success, or expertise can immunize you from adversity. It bedevils kings and paupers alike. It would be a very good idea to devise your own modus operandi for effectively dealing with it. I hope you do – and may you have an interesting life.

Note from Linda Forsythe ~ The previous article was written by Dan over 10 years ago and published in a previous magazine issue. I personally think this was one of his best pieces, and felt it worth re-printing here. It is interesting to note that Dan Kennedy definitely follows his own advice because he certainly overcame his obstacles... in fact with flying colors! He also re-married his beautiful wife and his health is back on top because of the changes in his life he implemented. Dan is my most favorite mentor living today and I admire him deeply.

About author.

Dan Kennedy is an entrepreneur, author, speaker, consultant, and editor of the monthly "No B.S. Marketing Letter," the most popular paid subscription marketing newsletter in America. His books include "No Rules," "The Ultimate Marketing Plan," "The Ultimate Sales Letter," and, with the late Dr. Maxwell Maltz, "The New Psycho-Cybernetics." He has been a professional speaker for over 25 years, 9 years featuring his appearances on all the Success Events with former U.S. Presidents Reagan, Ford, and Bush; Generals Norman Schwarzkopf and Colin Powell; famous entrepreneurs like Debbi Fields (Mrs. Fields Cookies); sports personalities including Joe Montana, George Foreman, and Olympian Mary Lou Retton; and Zig Ziglar, Brian Tracy, and Tom Hopkins. Although semi-retired, Dan continues to occasionally accept interesting new consulting assignments and clients, and up to a dozen speaking engagements per year. His information is @ www.dankennedy.com.

The Cycle of Completion: Making Way for Success

by Jack Canfield

Do you live in a state of mental and physical clutter? Do you have a bunch of unfinished business lurking around every corner? Incomplete projects, unfinished business, and piles of cluttered messes can weigh you down and take away from the energy you have to move forward toward your goals.

When you don't complete tasks, you can't be fully prepared to move into the present, let alone your new future. When your brain is keeping track of all the unfinished business you still have at hand, you simply can't be effective in embracing new tasks that are in line with your vision.

Old incompletes can show up in your life in lots of different ways... lack of clarity, procrastination, emotional energy blocks, and even illness. Blocked energy is wasted, and a buildup of that energy can really leave you stymied!

Throw out all the clutter and feel how much easier it is to think! Make a list of areas in your life (both personal and professional) where you have incompletes and messes, then develop a plan to deal with them once and for all. Fix and organize the things that annoy you. Take your final steps in bringing closure to outstanding projects. Make that difficult phone call. Delegate timewasting tasks that you've let build up.

When you free yourself from the mental burden of incompletes and messes, you'll be AMAZED at how quickly the things you do want in life arrive.

Another area where you'll find incompletes in your life is in your emotions. Are you holding on to old hurts, resentments, and pain? Just like the physical clutter and incompletes, your energy is being drained by holding on to and reliving past pain and anger.

Remember, you'll attract whatever feelings you're experiencing. So, if you're stuck in revengeful thinking and angered in muck, you can't possibly be directing energy toward a positive future. You need to let go of the past in order to embrace the future. Letting go involves forgiveness and moving on.

By forgiving you aren't releasing the other person from their transgression as much as you're freeing yourself from their transgression. You don't have to condone their behavior, trust them, or even maintain a relationship with them. However, you DO have to free yourself from the anger, from the pain, and from the resentment once and for all!

When learning to forgive, make sure to complete the cycle. Acknowledge your anger, your pain, and your fear. But also own up to any part you've played in allowing it to happen or continue. Make sure to express whatever it was that you wanted from that person, and then see the whole event from the other's point of view. Allow yourself to wonder what that person was going through and what kind of needs he/she was trying to fulfill at the time.

Finally, let go and move on. Every time you go through this process you're learning how to avoid letting it happen again! After you've learned this lesson, you may now want to consider who to allow into or remain in your life. Who you spend a great deal of time with can have a dramatic impact on what you become or even aspire to be. This is most certainly true when you want to overcome an obstacle.

Remember... You Are Who Your Friends Are

It's important to acknowledge the power of positive thinking. This goes not only for yourself, but also for the people you surround yourself with.

Attitudes are catchy. Whether they're positive or negative, they're rubbing off on you. If you're around people who complain, judge, spread negative gossip, blame others, and play victim roles, chances are you do, too. (Ouch!)

Who are you around most? Are they achieving their dreams or complaining about their circumstances? Do they look up to others who are go-getters and high achievers, or do they make fun of them and roll their eyes? How do they treat you?

If you're spending time with people who don't support your dreams and goals, it's seriously time to look at whom you call your friends!

Successful people surround themselves with successful people, plain and simple. They want to be around others who are achieving goals and making things happen. They want to know their secrets and strategies for winning. They're not embarrassed to be hanging out with people who are studying for success and making good money.

You, too, need to surround yourself with positive influences. Join the clubs that other successful people are in, learn what they're learning. It doesn't matter what walk of life you are coming from. Show up and transform yourself into an achiever! Success isn't just for those who have had it easy, who came from supportive homes, or who had expensive educations. There are so many successful people who rose up from very poor conditions and overcame obstacles to achieve the goals they set their sights on.

32

But they didn't get there by hanging out with negative energy-drainers!

Have you been limiting your success by letting yourself be influenced by other people's negative energy? Make a list of all the people you spend time with and make a note of the kind of personality they have. How many negative people are you around every day? How many people on your list are achieving their dreams, supporting yours, and taking responsibility for their lives? You're better off spending time alone than with people who hold themselves back with a victim mentality.

Simply stop spending time with the negative people on your list. Join the clubs that will put you in with a positive circle of friends. Set a new standard for yourself and don't become friends with people who fall below that standard. Invite your old friends to come with you, and you'll know who has potential and who to stop being around entirely.

You have to take responsibility for this area of your life. Look around you at the people you call friends. Does it make you proud? Are you selling yourself short? Or are you on the right track?

Keep successful people around you and you will be successful! Be around people who can accomplish their goals and you will accomplish yours, too! The choice is yours to make.

The Next Step is to Decide What You Want

In order to get what you want, you must first decide what you want. Most people really foul up at this crucial first step because they simply can't see how it's possible to get what they want – so they don't even let themselves want it. Don't sabotage yourself that way!

What scientists now know about how the brain works is that you must **first decide WHAT you want,** before your brain can figure out HOW to get it. Once you lock-in your desires, your mind and the universe can step in.

Are you ready to get started?

Be Willing to Dream BIG Dreams

As soon as you commit to a big dream and really go after it, your subconscious creative mind will come up with big ideas to make it happen. You'll start attracting the people, resources, and opportunities you need into your life to make your dream come true. Big dreams not only inspire you, they compel others to want to play big, too.

Set Goals That Will Stretch You

Another value in giving yourself permission to go after the big dreams is that big dreams require you to grow in order to achieve them. In fact, in the long

33

run, that is the greatest benefit you will receive from pursuing your dreams – not so much the outer trappings of fulfilling the dream (an expensive car, impressive house, loads of money, and philanthropic opportunities), but who you become in the process.

As I've seen many times over, the outer symbols of success can all be easily lost. Houses burn down, companies go bankrupt, relationships end, cars get old, bodies age, and fame wanes, but who you are, what you have learned, and the new skills you have developed never go away. These are the true prizes of success. Motivational philosopher Jim Rohn advises that "You should set a goal big enough that in the process of achieving it, you become someone worth becoming."

Service to Others

Something else you'll discover is that when your dreams include service to others – accomplishing something that contributes to others – it also accelerates the accomplishment of that goal. People want to be part of something that contributes and makes a difference.

Turn Your Dreams into Goals and Objectives

Once you are clear about what you want, you must turn each item into a measurable objective. By measurable, I mean measurable in space and time – how much and by when. For instance, if you were to tell me that you wanted more money, I might pull out a dollar and give it to you, but you would probably protest, saying "No, I meant a lot more money – like $20,000!" Well, how am I supposed to know unless you tell me? Similarly, your boss, your friends, your spouse, your brain – God, the Universe – can't figure out what you want unless you tell them specifically what it is. What do you want – exactly – and when do you want it by?

Write Down Your Goals

Write down your goals in detail, and read your list of goals every day. This will keep your subconscious mind focused on what you want. For an even more powerful approach, close your eyes, focus on each goal, and ask yourself, "What is one thing I could do today to move toward the achievement of this goal?" Write down your answers and take those actions.

I recommend writing down a minimum of 3 goals in each of the following 7 areas:

1. Financial Goals
2. Career/Business Goals
3. Free Time/Family Time
4. Health/Appearance Goals
5. Relationship Goals
6. Personal Growth
7. Making a Difference

To help your reticular activating system begin finding YOUR wants in unexpected places, **take time now to decide what you want** and start writing!

Celebrate Your Victories and Give Thanks

Research has shown over and over again that the more you acknowledge your past successes, the more confident you become in taking on and successfully accomplishing new ones.

As you stay the course and begin to realize your goals, you need to do two very important things:

1. Celebrate your successes.
2. Express your gratitude to everyone who has helped you along the way.

Let's look at a few of the ways you can acknowledge your positive past.

Celebrate Your Victories

In order to justify all your sacrifice and persistence that is required to create the life of your dreams, you have to enroll your family, your friends, your colleagues and co-workers, your employees, your clients, and most importantly yourself, to pay the price.

In order for them to do that, there needs to be payoffs along the way. Every time you reach a milestone on the path to ultimate success, and every time you achieve a major goal, you need to celebrate by doing something fun and nurturing.

Have an Attitude of Gratitude

Take the time to thank everyone who has helped you achieve your goals. Write them a letter, call them, send them an e-mail, or send them a present. It can be something as simple as a hug and a thank you, to something as elaborate as letting someone use your summer vacation home for a week.

The Power of Acknowledgment

When you take the time to thank someone, they feel acknowledged for their contribution and will be more likely to want to help again.

Your Inner Child

A big part of creating more success in life is rewarding yourself when you succeed. So, it's important to reward your inner child as well. Every time you work hard to meet a goal, the part of you that just wants to have fun has to sit still and be good. However, just like any kid, if it knows it will be rewarded later with a treat, it will hang in there with you.

www.mentorsharbor.com

How can you reward your inner child?

- Take a 20-minute walk after an hour or two of concentrated work
- Go for walks in the morning with your spouse, friend, or significant other
- Take 20 minutes to listen to music and daydream
- Take most weekends off totally
- Take several week long vacations throughout the year
- Get regular massages
- Engage in daily meditation, exercise, and yoga
- Take music lessons
- Go to movies, concerts, and plays
- Listen to comedy tapes and watch the Comedy Network
- Listen to motivational audio programs when driving

Thank Your Higher Power

Finally, it is important to thank God, or however you perceive the Higher Power, for all of the abundance that comes into your life. Start with the little stuff – another day of life, healthy children, a sunny day, people who love you, family and friends. Be thankful for the birds, your pets, the clothes you have, and the food you eat.

And be especially thankful for any additional blessings that come into your life. Take time each day to say a prayer of thanks when you first arise, before meals, and again at night before bed.

Having an attitude of gratitude opens up the channels for even more abundance to flow into your life.

The more grateful you are, the more you will attract things to be grateful for.

About author.

Jack Canfield, America's Success Coach, is the founder and co-creator of the Billion-dollar book brand Chicken Soup for the Soul and a leading authority on Peak Performance. If you're ready to jump-start your life, make more money, and have more fun and joy in all that you do, get your FREE success tips from Jack Canfield now at: www.FreeSuccessStrategies.com.

How to Do, Be, and Have Everything You Want

by Ken Varga

I have had an enormous amount of monetary and family success that I've attracted simply by envisioning the ultimate outcome, then performing the action part to make it all happen. You must learn to listen to your inner-self and not listen to the negative dictates of the world around you. Life is bigger than the material picture.

Life is spirit-directed and not physically directed, as it might seem.

There is something much greater than what we can see with our eyes, hear with our ears, touch with our hands, smell with our nose, and taste with our mouth, and that something is what really counts.

We all can direct our lives the way we want it to be.

Whenever I started any one of my 35 companies, I envisioned what the results would be in ten years, and what my exit strategy was going to be. But the important thing I did was to live as if it already had happened.

Let me tell you a short story. As a child I had a serious disability, and I learned how to overcome it. This disease caused my body to shake out of control. There were times I couldn't use my hands to hold a spoon. The doctors said that they could give me various drugs to slow down the shaking, but they also slowed down my mind and my ability to think.

My Mom gave me the drugs for a few days, but she could not stand the vegetable state I lived in. The doctors said that without the drugs, my Mom would have to do everything for me for the rest of my life.

Imagine growing up in the 1940s and being a young handicapped child. Back in those days if there wasn't a school to accommodate the handicapped, you just didn't go to school. Fortunately, I grew up in Jersey City, NJ and the A. Harry Moore School accepted me.

My Mom noticed that I loved music, especially the Accordion. Now, if you have ever looked at accordion players, you know that they use their arms, hands, and fingers, all moving together in time to the beat to make music.

I heard the music I wanted to play in my head. I learned to read the notes. But to transfer that knowledge to the accordion seemed impossible. My shaking arms, hands, and fingers just didn't want to cooperate to make one sound, much less anything that resembled music.

Sometimes it would take me an entire hour to "will" just one finger to stop shaking enough to press a single key. It was a long slow process. I would concentrate on a finger and with my mind I would will it to stop shaking. I would then go to the next finger and so forth, and I would continue to do this with the rest of my upper body. In addition to physically willing my body to obey, I would envision myself actually playing the accordion, and by the time I was nine, I accomplished it.

I was able to picture myself in the future, at the age of fifteen, walking, talking, and horsing around, as all teenage boys do, completely free from the shaking that racked my body. I was able to see myself a few years later as a completely normal person. That's a part of the secret to getting what you want.

Whenever I'm asked how I knew to do this, I always say, "I simply don't know." To this day, I wonder where I learned that the mind could create anything it wishes. Could it have been my guide or guardian angel? I do know that when I was seven years old, and started on my journey, there wasn't anything I could read, or any mentors around to help me find this secret to getting what I wanted. Nevertheless, I learned early on in my childhood that whatever you create in your mind, you could create in the physical world.

The Truth is that we can create anything in life we want, but we have to create it within ourselves first and envision it actually happening, and then doing the steps necessary to physically make it happen. Throughout our lives, we are touched again and again with this simple truth. Unfortunately, for some individuals it never comes to realization, although it is always there within each of us.

Keep the following two thoughts always in your mind.

Throughout your life, many individuals will cross your path. Stay away from those people who will be destructive to your thinking. Surround yourself by those who will be constructive by helping you be, do, and have anything you want. You can accomplish anything as long as you never have one shred of doubt.

I have created a formula for all of you reading this book. It's called the **SMART** formula.

Simple ~ Meaningful ~ As if now ~ Responsible ~ Toward

Simple:

Why Simple? Because you will be more direct and exacting, and there is no room for confusion in your mind when it is stated simply. The Universe will know exactly what you want because you do.

Meaningful:

This is important because even if you set simple, specific, measurable goals, you may not achieve those goals if they do not have a strong meaning to you. I use the word "goals," but in essence it's your thoughts that are the "goals." For example, many people think in a general way that an extra $20,000 a year would be great, but to get its meaning to you ask the following questions to yourself:

In what way would it be meaningful?

Would it mean that you have more money to blow on things you don't want or need anyway, or will it make a significant difference in your total life framework?

- Will an extra $20,000 help you find love?

- Will it make you more spiritual?

- Will it help you quit smoking?

- Will it mend your relationship with your mother?

Many people make a mistake in thinking that making more money is the answer to everything; therefore, they set all their goals toward this end. But they very often fail to get the money they have asked for from the Universe. Why? Because they have failed to completely explain to themselves how that money will be meaningful within the big picture of their lives.

As you can see, while the process of setting goals (i.e., thoughts) is simple in some respects, it does require some careful thinking. And perhaps most importantly, setting goals needs to be done in a way that fits the entire perspective of your life. Without this, your goals may lack meaning. Thoughts and goals that lack meaning are thoughts that tend NOT to materialize in real life.

As if Now:

You should write down your goals and what you want as if you already had them. For example, it is better to write:

"I make $20,000 more per year," rather than, "I will someday make $20,000 more per year."

Writing your goals in the vital and powerful present tense will energize them in a more powerful and immediate way. It will instruct your subconscious mind that this is now reality. When your subconscious mind accepts its new version of reality, it will automatically work at making this so.

Responsibility:

Responsibility means that your goals should not be something that will cause hurt to others or the planet. It is not a good thing to become a millionaire if you do so by destroying several million acres of forest, or by selling drugs to people who are weak and lost.

Goals can be achieved in responsible and irresponsible ways, but ultimately, irresponsible goals have a way of undoing their makers.

Toward:

Plan a time line of accomplishments for many years to come, maybe even ten to twenty years ahead. You must draw up a blueprint to build your life the way you want it.

There are **five** basic factors, **fundamental laws**, which make it possible for human beings to shape and manipulate the very fabric of the Universe itself. Understanding these principles will give you the kind of intellectual grounding you need to become a total success in all that you want.

The First Law: The Universe is Pure Mind.

Real, solid materials exist only as illusions. The entire Universe, at its most fundamental level, is pure intelligence.

The Second Law: Reality is Vibration.

Every speck of matter, every object in the universe, is made of energy that is either vibrating very fast, very slowly, or something in between. People who hold positive and happy thoughts in their minds send that kind of vibration out into the universe, specifically into their immediate environment.

The Third Law: Every Thought is Vibration.

The universe will give you whatever you think about the most and whatever you feel most often. Happiness has a way of producing more happiness. Your vibrations are picked up by the rest of the universe, and you are thus supported or thwarted according to the world you create for yourself.

40

The Fourth Law: The Universe Seeks Balance.

Extreme cold has a tendency to become warmer. Extreme heat has a tendency to become cooler. For every action there is an opposite reaction. No one stays happy all the time. The tendency is to be pulled back toward a state of balance. With practice, you can spend more time in the upswings of life rather than in the downswings.

The Fifth Law: Action Produces Results.

Every action a person does produces a direct result from that action. We are always receiving something in return for every action we take.

You get what you give. This is true whether that action is positive or negative.

I have taught my children these Universal Laws over the years without knowing that they came to me from the Universe. Can you imagine if all parents in the world learned these secrets of how to do, be, and have everything in life they want, and then taught it to their children each day of their children's lives?

What a wonderful Universe it would be!

About author.

Ken Varga has built 35 successful businesses in his business career. One of Ken's off-line businesses had 460,000 ongoing customers. Ken is the author of over 300 information products, and focuses on being a mentor and motivating force for entrepreneurs, executives, and sales professionals. To learn more about Ken and some of the tools you can use to build your dream business, visit: www. kenvarga.com. If you are in insurance sales and want to sell more, visit: www. sellinsurancelikecrazy.com.

The Secret of Changing Our Negative Programming

by Glen Curry

Even though we might not be head-over-heels in love with our lives and may in fact desire to change some things, most people don't know what to do to make the changes that would make a difference. One thing is sure: if we keep thinking what we've always thought, we'll keep getting what we've always got.

Most people don't have a clue how they got what they have in life. They are certain that "life happens to them" because of random coincidences and happenstance. They would never even imagine that they themselves created or attracted the lack, struggle, and unhappiness they are experiencing by misusing and misapplying fixed scientific laws. That's right! Abundance, blessings, and happiness occur where the laws that govern these things are understood and applied. This means that life doesn't happen to you; life happens because of you!

The results you experience in life (good or bad) are determined by your understanding and application of fixed scientific laws. Understand and master these laws and learn to apply them correctly, and you are guaranteed to be happy and prosperous.

Why Is This Happening to Me?

If you have ever asked yourself, "Why me?" or "Why is this happening to me?" you can be sure more bad things are on the way because you don't have a clue why you get what you are getting in life.

Our programming and attitude determines our behavior, circumstances, and results. Much of our attitude and outlook on life was programmed into us when we were children by our parents and authority figures. We actually heard these well-meaning but negative people describe how life works and what life has in store for us, and having no experiences to compare with what they said, we believed them. Then, as crazy as it sounds, we got busy and worked really hard to create their standards and experiences in our life. Millions of people's lives perfectly match the struggles, disappointments and lack that others told them to expect as a normal part of life.

42

Autopia Programming

When I was a kid, I loved going to Disneyland. The ride I really liked was called Autopia. On this ride the child sat in a little car and drove around a course. The child had control of the gas and brake pedal. He or she could also steer the car, to a point. I say "to a point," because although you could turn the steering wheel and the car would turn, it would only turn a foot or so in either direction before hitting a rail between the wheels. If you were to steer too radically, the rail would keep you from crashing into the curb on either side. You may have wanted to turn and jump over the curb and drive your car through the crowd to Adventure Land, but the rail assures the Disney stock holders that you will stay on track without running over any of the paid customers, ending up where you started when the ride was over.

Your programming, which determines your results in life, is very much like Autopia. It guarantees your staying on a pre-determined track, and will absolutely make sure you can't go where you want to go in life. Like Autopia, you may get the feeling you can steer your life anywhere you want, but in reality you will always go around in circles and end up where you started. Until you change your old programming, you will keep producing the same results you've always produced.

Unless you are in the process of thinking differently than you've ever thought before, it is impossible for you to experience your dream. If the way you've always thought could materialize your dream, you would be living your dream right now. You can't keep thinking as you always have and suddenly start producing different results. Your programming is like a track or rail that won't let you break free from its limiting, set direction. If you want something different, you must install a new program.

Accurate Thinking

By now you realize that a person can be "knowledgeable" in the knowledge that is incapable of producing the desired results. For thousands of years, boats were made only out of wood. Men threw rocks in the water and the rocks sank. They threw pieces of metal in the water and they also sank. Then they observed logs and branches floating down the river and concluded that of all the known substances in the world, only wood floats, therefore, only wood could be used to make a successful boat. They carved out logs into canoes and later cut planks and boards and made boats. They had no understanding about the law of displacement of water, and that a steel or concrete boat would actually make a better boat. Most people are stuck in their limiting beliefs, and to hear that there is a better way of thinking sounds as ridiculous to them as it would sound to a primitive man being told that steel can float.

Changing Your Limiting Beliefs

The size of your success, fortune, and happiness can never exceed the size of your beliefs. You must understand how you learn to believe what you believe. A belief is created by habitual thinking. What I mean by that is: thoughts and affirmations that were habitually repeated to you or by you are what formed your beliefs. That which was repeatedly affirmed to us – either by ourselves or by others – became our beliefs, and along with our thoughts, determines what we attract and receive into our lives. In order to create new beliefs that can help us produce the life and lifestyle we desire, we use the same process that created our old beliefs in the first place, which is habitual thinking.

Visualization

Visualization is an act of the will that enables you – through focus and concentration – to create a mental image of yourself that would exemplify everything you want to be. It also enables you to see yourself doing what you want to do and possessing the things you want to have and enjoy. Don't confuse this with daydreaming. Visualization is the ability of the mind to see things in pictures. The goal is to hold a desired thought long enough to produce a vivid picture of it in your mind. You are then to view this picture as reality. Before long, events will transpire that create, in reality, what you visualized.

Visualize the skill level, the characteristics, and the qualities you want to express. Visualize the success, wealth, and accomplishments you want to experience. See yourself with the very best things life has to offer. Soon you will act like and actually possess what you visualize and desire. Remember, the Empire State Building had to be visualized before it could be materialized.

Visualization actually allows you to view and customize your future in advance. If you don't believe this, then look at the opposite side of the coin. Worry, which is negative attraction, causes its victims to actually experience the heartaches and pains they visualize. Hypochondriacs attract and experience the diseases they imagine. The great news is, when you receive the understanding of how this works, you will be in the position to attract the wealth and happiness you can imagine and visualize.

What You See is What You Get

Your visualizations should be so vivid that they feel real and produce the same emotions of confidence, excitement, and happiness that you will feel when what you've visualized actually arrives. Picture what you want so vividly and in such detail that it seems to you that you are reliving, remembering, or experiencing an actual event or result. Raising the quality of your thoughts and pictures in your mind automatically improves the quality of your life. This is a major part of reprogramming your mental computer.

Affirmations

Affirmations are statements of belief and desire spoken out loud or to yourself stating clearly what it is that you want. Affirmations have no connection

44

or relevance to the way things actually are at the moment. Your present circumstances may be quite different than your affirmations. These statements of belief and desire are based only on the way we want things to be, not on the way things currently are.

If you want what's currently happening in your life to continue, then keep thinking about, focusing on, talking, and complaining about your current circumstances. If you want things to change, then you must think, talk, and affirm the conditions you desire. Along with visualization, this also is a major part of your reprogramming process.

The word affirmation means to validate, confirm, or make firm. When we think a thought or speak the same words over and over, we are repeatedly validating or confirming them as the truth. The more we think something or say something, the more we believe it to be true.

What We Affirm, We Make Firm

What you say when you talk to yourself determines the quality of your self-image, self-confidence, and emotional life. No conversation you will ever have is more important than the conversation you have with yourself. Dr. Martin Seligman of the University of Pennsylvania wrote a book entitled *Learned Optimism.* His book was based on 25 years of exhaustive testing and cognitive therapy. His research indicates we speak to others at approximately 140 words per minute, but we speak to ourselves at about 900 words per minute. He also discovered that 70% of what we say to ourselves is negative.

In other words, the vast majority of people are constantly telling themselves what they can't do, can't have, shouldn't try, will never accomplish, what they regret, aren't good at, etc. It is this kind of habitual thinking and self-talk that causes the majority of people to attract in life things they don't want. The words you use to tell yourself what's happening to you and to describe events in your life trigger happiness or unhappiness. Your optimistic or pessimistic attitude about anything is a result of what you say to yourself based on your perception of you and the events you experience. For this reason, your affirmations, both to yourself and out loud, must contain positive and desired descriptions of the YOU that you want to become, and the life and lifestyle you want to live.

Lack only exists because you have chosen or allowed thoughts and words that are not in harmony with what you truly desire.

45

About author.

Glen Curry is the founder of Fine Tuned for Success. He is dedicated to helping those who desire a higher level of success find the motivation and tools they need to win in life. A dynamic public speaker, radio personality, and author, Glen has developed many tools for success. To view or order Glen's life changing materials and tools for victory, success, and prosperity, please visit **www.finetunedforsuccess.com**. Glen can be contacted at **glencurry@finetunedforsuccess.com**.

46

What You Really Have Inside You

by Brian Tracy

Here's a question for you: What are you made of? What are you RE-ALLY made of? When push comes to shove, when the rubber meets the road, when the chips are down, what lies at the very core of your character? You learn what you're really made of only when things go wrong and you are tumbled, end over end, by some adversity or setback that hits you like a Mack truck coming out of an alley. Since your behaviors on the outside are the real indicators of who you are on the inside, only by observing how you behave when things go wrong can you tell what you really have inside you.

Let's make one thing clear at the beginning: Life is a continuous succession of both small and large problems. They never end. No sooner do you get control of one situation when you are hit by another. Life is a process of "two steps forward and one step back." When you become a great success, you simply exchange one type of problem for another. Before, you had small problems with limited consequences. Now you have large problems with enormous consequences. No matter how smart and clever and careful you are, you'll face challenges, difficulties, and sometimes heartbreaking adversities every day, week, and month of your life.

And thank heaven for that! You couldn't possibly have become the person you are today if you had not had to contend with adversity on your way up. Perhaps your chief aim in life is to develop a noble character, to become an excellent human being, and to become everything you are capable of becoming. Only by contending with challenges that seem to be beyond your strength to handle at the moment can you grow more surely toward the stars.

The starting point in dealing with any difficulty is simply to relax. Clear your mind. Get yourself into a state where you're calm and cool, and in full control of your emotions and senses. Back off mentally and become as objective as possible. Step back and look at the problem with a certain amount of detachment, as if it were happening to someone else. When you can analyze your adversities clearly, you sometimes see opportunities to turn them to your best advantage. One of the rules in dealing with adversity in life is that you are only as free as

47

your well-developed alternatives. You are only as free as the options you have. Only when you can switch and do something else can you be flexible in dealing with your current situation. If you have not developed an option or an alternative, you will become anxious and even panicky when you are threatened with a sudden loss or reversal in a particular area of your life.

For example, if you're in business, look into the future and imagine that your biggest customer could go broke or start buying your product or service from someone else. If that were to happen, what would you do? How would you compensate for the loss of business? What could you do right now to ensure that it doesn't happen? How could you increase the quantity or the quality of your service or your product in such a way that your major customer would never think of switching? How could you develop additional customers so that you wouldn't be so dependent upon a single purchaser?

If you are in sales and your goal is to make a certain amount of money so that you can enjoy a certain quality of lifestyle, you have to look down the road in your sales work and ask, "Where will my sales come from? How many prospective customers do I have who can generate the business that I need to make my numbers?" And ask yourself, "What would I do if I lost my best customer? What would I do if I lost my biggest prospect?"

When I was a boy, I read a story that contained one of the most important messages about adversity that I've ever learned in my life. As I recall, in this story a young man went up to Alaska and worked with an old Indian trapper, learning how to lay traps, clean pelts, live in the bush, and take care of himself in the wilderness. At the end of his apprenticeship, the old Indian gave him some advice. He said, "Remember this. Whatever you do when you travel, always use two logs crossing."

He was referring to the best method for crossing the many small rivers and streams that the young man would come upon between the small town where the Indian lived and the distant wilderness where he would be trapping.

The young man went off on his own and trapped throughout the summer, until he had all the furs that he could possibly carry. When the leaves began to turn, he began his long hike back to the small town where he would trade his furs for enough money to live on for the winter and outfit himself again for the spring. He did everything exactly right, as he had been taught, until he came to the last, fast-running stream remaining between him and civilization. In his eagerness to get back to town, he tried to cross it on a single log that stretched from one bank to the other.

Alas! He lost his footing and fell into the stream. He had to throw off his pack to avoid drowning. He lost everything. His whole year was wiped out. He arrived in town, wet, bedraggled, and exhausted. There he met the old Indian, who looked at him, shook his head and said, "You forgot to use two logs crossing."

The moral of this story is clear. To contend with adversity in your life, you have to develop alternatives. You have to expand your range of choices. You can never afford to put all your hopes in a single person or a single possibility. You too, must use two logs crossing. As a consequence of disregarding the Indian's advice, that young man faced some truly dire circumstances. We can avoid tragedy on that scale by following a four-step method for dealing with any adversity. Dale Carnegie wrote about it more than 50 years ago, and it's still one of the most powerful mental tools that anyone can use when confronted with problems or worries of any kind.

1. Define the problem clearly. What exactly is the problem? What exactly are you worrying about? Write out the definition of your problem. Make sure that it's a single problem. If it's more than one problem, write out clear definitions of all the problems that together constitute what you are worrying about right now.

2. Determine the worst possible outcome. Ask, "What's the worst possible thing that can happen in this situation?" Be frank and honest with yourself. You might lose your money, or your relationship, or your customer, or someone or something else that is really important to you. If everything fell apart, what is the worst thing that could occur?

3. Resolve to accept the worst, should it occur. Having identified the worst possible outcome, you now can go through the mental exercise of accepting that it is going to happen, no matter what you do. The remarkable thing is that as soon as you stop resisting the worst possible outcome, you'll relax, your mind will clear, and your ability to deal with the situation will improve dramatically.

4. Begin immediately to improve upon the worst, which you have already accepted is going to happen. Throw all of your mental resources into the battle to minimize the problem or resolve the difficulty. Concentrate on the future. Don't worry about what happened, why it happened, and who was responsible. Think only about the question, "What do I do now?" How can you minimize the consequences? What's the first step you can take? And the second step? And the third step? And so on.

Successful people are not people without problems. They are people who respond quickly and positively to their problems. They think them through in advance; they anticipate them. And when they can't, they use the four-step method to resolve whatever difficulty they face. They define the problem clearly. They define the worst possible thing that could happen as a result of the problem. They resolve to accept the worst, should it occur. And then they concentrate all of their energies on making sure that the very worst doesn't happen.

In dealing with adversity effectively, your ability to ask questions is essential. As long as you are asking questions, you are expanding the range of options and possibilities that are open to you. As long as you are asking questions, you are keeping your mind calm, cool, and objective. You are not allowing yourself to get caught up emotionally, thereby shutting down large parts of your brain and your creative powers.

Many problems and adversities arise because of misunderstandings and incorrect information. One of the smartest things you'll ever do in facing any adversity is to ask yourself, "Who else may have had this problem, and what did he do?" Ask around. Don't be afraid to admit that you're in a bind. If you made a mistake, or dropped the ball and found yourself in a difficult situation, don't be afraid to go to someone and admit that you need help. You'll be amazed at the valuable advice that you can get from someone who has already experienced the difficulty that you're going through.

In dealing with adversity, perhaps the four most important words that you can remember are these: "This, too, shall pass." Whatever it is, however difficult it may appear, say to yourself, "This, too, shall pass."

Remember, too, that you are never sent a difficulty that is too big for you to handle. Whatever problems or adversities you face, you have within you the resources to deal with them. You have the creative ability to find a solution to your problem. You have within you, right now, everything you need to deal with whatever the world can throw at you.

One of your main jobs in life is to become an expert in dealing with adversity, to triumph over difficulty, to rise above the challenges of day-to-day life. Keep your thoughts on where you're going, not on where you've been. Keep your eyes on your goals, and keep your chin tilted upward toward the sunshine. Resolve in advance that you will meet and overcome every difficulty, and then, no matter what happens, don't give up until you do.

Perhaps the most powerful influence on your attitude and personality is what you say to yourself, and believe. It is not what happens to you, but how you respond internally to what happens to you, that determines your thoughts and feelings, and ultimately your actions. By controlling your inner dialogue, or "self-talk," you can begin to assert control over every other dimension of your life.

Your self-talk, the words that you use to describe what is happening to you, and to discuss how you feel about external events, determines the quality and tone of your emotional life. When you see things positively and constructively, and look for the good in each situation and each person, you have a tendency to remain naturally positive and optimistic. Since the quality of your life is determined by how you feel, moment to moment, one of your most important

50

goals should be to use every psychological technique available to keep yourself thinking about what you want and to keep your mind off of what you don't want, or what you fear.

Arnold Toynbee, the historian, developed what he called the "challenge response theory" of history. In studying the rise and fall of 20 major world civilizations, Toynbee concluded that each civilization started out as a small group of people – as a village, as a tribe, or in the case of the Mongol empire, as just three people who had survived the destruction of their small community. Toynbee concluded that each of these small groups faced external challenges, such as hostile tribes. In order to survive, much less thrive, these small groups had to reorganize themselves to deal positively and constructively with these challenges.

By meeting each of these challenges successfully, the village or tribe would grow. Even greater challenges would be triggered as a result. And if this group of people continued to meet each challenge by drawing upon its resources and winning out, it would continue to grow until ultimately it became a nation-state and then a civilization covering a large geographical area.

Toynbee looked at the 21 great civilizations of human history, ending with the American civilization, and concluded that these civilizations began to decline and fall apart when their citizens and leaders lost the will or ability to rise to the inevitable external challenges occasioned by their very size and power.

Toynbee's theory of civilizations can be applicable to our life as well.

You are continually faced with challenges and difficulties, with problems and disappointments, with temporary setbacks and defeats. They are an unavoidable and inevitable part of being human. But, as you draw upon your resources to respond effectively to each challenge, you grow and become a stronger and better person. In fact, without those setbacks, you could not have learned what you needed to know and developed the qualities of your character to where they are today.

Much of your ability to succeed comes from the way you deal with life. One of the characteristics of superior men and women is that they recognize the inevitability of temporary disappointments and defeats, and they accept them as a normal and natural part of life. They do everything possible to avoid problems, but when problems come, superior people learn from them, rise above them, and continue onward in the direction of their dreams.

Dr. Martin Seligman of the University of Pennsylvania has written a fascinating book based on his 25 years of research into this subject. It's titled "Learned Optimism." In this book, Dr. Seligman explains the basic response patterns of both positive and negative people. As a result of his many years of work in cognitive therapy, and the use of exhaustive testing, he finds quite simply that optimistic people tend to interpret events in such a way that they keep their minds positive and their emotions under control.

Optimists develop the habit of talking to themselves in constructive ways. Whenever they experience an adversity, they immediately ascribe it to themselves in such a way that it loses its ability to trigger negative emotions and feelings of helplessness.

Dr. Seligman says that are three basic differences in the reactions of optimists and pessimists. The first difference is that the optimist sees a setback as temporary, while the pessimist sees it as permanent. The optimist sees an unfortunate event, such as an order that falls through or a sales call that fails, as a temporary event, something that is limited in time and that has no real impact on the future. The pessimist, on the other hand, sees negative events as permanent, as part of life and destiny.

For example, let's say that a salesperson makes ten calls on likely prospects, and every one of those calls is unsuccessful. The optimist simply interprets this as a temporary event and a matter of averages or probabilities. The optimist concludes that with every temporary failure he is moving closer to the prospect that will turn into a sale. The optimist dismisses the event and goes on cheerfully to the 11th and 12th prospects.

The pessimist sees the same situation differently. The pessimist has a tendency to conclude that ten unsuccessful sales calls is an indication that the economy is terrible and that there is no market for his product. The pessimist generalizes, and begins to see the situation and his career as hopeless. While the optimist just shrugs it off and gets on with the next call, the pessimist becomes discouraged, and loses heart and enthusiasm for the hard work of prospecting.

The second difference between the optimist and the pessimist is that the optimist sees difficulties as specific, while the pessimist sees them as pervasive. This means that when things go wrong for the optimist, he looks at the event as an isolated incident largely disconnected from other things that are going on in his life.

For example, if something you were counting on failed to materialize, and you interpreted it to yourself as being an unfortunate event but something that happens in the course of life and business, you would be reacting like an optimist. The pessimist, on the other hand, sees disappointments as being pervasive. To him they are indications of a problem or shortcoming that pervades every area of life.

If a pessimist worked hard to put together a business deal and it collapsed, he would tend to assume that the deal did not work out because the product or the company or the economy was in poor shape and the whole business was hopeless. The pessimist would tend to feel helpless, unable to make a difference, and out of control of his destiny.

The third difference between optimists and pessimists is that optimists see events as external, while pessimists interpret events as personal. When things go wrong, the optimist will tend to see the setback as a result of external factors over which one has little control.

If the optimist is cut off in traffic, for example, instead of getting angry or upset, he will simply downgrade the importance of the event by saying something like, "Oh well, I guess that person is just having a bad day."

The pessimist has a tendency to take everything personally. If the pessimist is cut off in traffic, he will react as though the other driver has deliberately acted to upset and frustrate him. The pessimist will become angry and negative and want to strike out and get even. Often, he will honk his horn or yell at the other driver. There is a natural tendency in all of us to react emotionally when our expectations are frustrated in any way. When something we wanted and hoped for fails to materialize, we feel a temporary sense of disappointment and unhappiness. We feel disillusioned. We react as though we have been punched in the "emotional solar plexus."

The optimistic person, however, soon moves beyond this disappointment. He responds quickly to the adverse event and interprets it as being temporary, specific, and external to himself. The optimist takes full control of his inner dialogue and counters the negative feelings by immediately reframing the event so that it appears positive in some way.

Napoleon Hill, prior to writing his best-selling books on success, interviewed 500 of the most successful people in America and concluded that "Contained within a setback or disappointment is the seed of an equal or greater advantage or benefit." This is one of the great secrets of success.

Since your conscious mind can hold only one thought at a time, either positive or negative, if you deliberately choose a positive thought to dwell upon, you keep your mind optimistic and your emotions positive. Since your thoughts and feelings determine your actions, you will tend to be a more constructive person, and you will move much more rapidly toward the goals that you have chosen.

It all comes down to the way you talk to yourself on a regular basis. In our courses of problem solving and decision making, we encourage people to respond to problems by changing their language from negative to positive. Instead of using the word "problem," we encourage people to use the word "situation." You see, a problem is something that you deal with. The event is the same. It's the way you interpret the event to yourself that makes it sound and appear completely different.

Even better than "situation" is the word "challenge." Whenever you have a difficulty, immediately reframe it and choose to view it as a challenge. Rather than saying, "I have a problem," say, "I have an interesting challenge facing me." The word challenge is inherently positive. It is something that you rise to that makes you stronger and better. It is the same situation, only the word that you are using to describe it is different.

The best of all possible words is the word "opportunity." When you are faced with a difficulty of any kind, instead of saying, "I have a problem," you can say, "I am faced with an unexpected opportunity." And if you concentrate your powers on finding out what that opportunity is – even if it is only a valuable lesson – you will certainly find it. As the parable says, "Seek and ye shall find, for all who seek find it."

One of my favorite affirmative statements, which I use to deal with any unexpected difficulty, is this: "Every situation is a positive situation if viewed as an opportunity for growth and self-mastery." Whenever something goes wrong, immediately neutralize its negative power by quickly reciting this statement.

If you are in sales, and your method of prospecting is not generating the results that you desire, you can view it as an opportunity for growth and self-mastery. The adversity you are facing may be meant to indicate to you that there is a better way to approach this task. Perhaps you should be prospecting in a different place or with different people, or using a different script or a different method. Perhaps your difficulty is simply part of the process of developing the persistence and tenacity that you need to become successful in any kind of market. The difference between the winner and the loser is that the winner faces and deals with the adversity constructively, while the loser allows the adversity to overwhelm him.

The hallmark of the fully mature, fully functioning, self-actualizing personality is the ability to be objective and unemotional when caught up in the inevitable storms of daily life. The superior person has the ability to continue talking to himself in a positive and optimistic way, keeping his mind calm, clear, and completely under control. The mature personality is more relaxed, and aware and capable of interpreting events more realistically and less emotionally than is the immature personality. As a result, the mature person exerts a far greater sense of control and influence over his environment, and is far less likely to be angry, upset, or distracted.

The starting point in the process of becoming a highly effective person is to monitor and control your self-talk every minute of the day. Keep your thoughts and your words positive and consistent with your goals, and keep your mind focused on what you want to do and the person you want to be.

54

Here are five ideas you can use to help you to be a more positive and optimistic person:

First, resolve in advance that no matter what happens, you will not allow it to get you down. You will respond in a constructive way. You will take a deep breath, relax and look for whatever good the situation may contain. When you make this decision in advance, you mentally prepare yourself so that you are not knocked off balance when things go wrong, as they inevitably will.

Second, neutralize any negative thoughts or emotions by speaking to yourself positively all the time. Say things like, "I feel healthy! I feel happy! I feel terrific!" As you go about your job, say to yourself, "I like myself, and I love my work!" Say things like, "Today is a great day; it's wonderful to be alive!" According to the law of expression, whatever is expressed is impressed. Whatever you say to yourself or others is impressed deeply into your subconscious mind and is likely to become a permanent part of your personality.

Third, look upon the inevitable setbacks that you face as being temporary, specific, and external. View each negative situation as a single event that is not connected to other potential events and that is caused largely by external factors over which you can have little control. Simply refuse to see the event as being in any way permanent, pervasive, or indicative of personal incompetence or inability.

Fourth, remember that it is impossible to learn and grow and become a successful person without adversity and difficulties. You must contend with and rise above them in order to become a better person. Welcome each difficulty by saying, "That's good!" and then look into the situation to find the good in it.

Finally, keep your thoughts on your goals and dreams, on the person you are working toward becoming. When things go wrong temporarily, respond by saying to yourself, "I believe in the perfect outcome of every situation in my life." Resolve to be cheerful and pleasant, and resist every temptation toward negativity and disappointment. View a disappointment as an opportunity to grow stronger, and talk about it to yourself and others in a positive and optimistic way.

When you practice positive self-talk, keeping your words and mental pictures consistent with your goals and dreams, nothing can stop you from becoming the success you are meant to be.

About author.

Brian Tracy is a leading authority on personal and business success. As Chairman and CEO of www.briantracy.com and "Brian Tracy International," he is the best-selling author of 17 books and over 300 audio and video learning programs. Copyright © 2001 Brian Tracy International. Printed in Mentors Digest's ~ Overcoming Obstacles by permission.

The Magic Power That Makes Dreams Come True: PERSISTENCE!

by Ted Ciuba

I'm on board the *Pacific Queen*, transiting the Panama Canal. I can hear the water dancing through the propeller wheels and hear the engines purr. The fresh breeze tickles the flags on the mast overhead as the tour guide shares exciting pieces of canal history in the background.

Everything about the canal speaks of an impressive project. It's a great metaphor of what it takes for you to achieve riches and what it's like once you do achieve your quest. This canal is a great work of art. It was inspired by people with vision, people with desire, people who had a practical purpose: to get rich.

Times are prosperous now in Panama because of this vision. As an example, the eight-hour transit can cost a cruise ship $200,000. This is a trip you can make in 60 minutes by car. Depending on where you board, the trip goes from the Atlantic Ocean, south to the Pacific, or from the Pacific Ocean, north to the Atlantic. Every day is a million-dollar day in the canal zone.

How does this apply to you? It all started with a dream. Just as you pick your niche according to your natural strengths, interests, and developed expertise, Panama found itself as the only logical place in the Americas that this could happen. It was a dream shared by many, even from the days of the explorers and pirates. In fact, in 1671 British corsair Henry Morgan ransacked the city of Panama on the Pacific Coast after barely surviving the nine-day walk-ordeal through the jungle from the Atlantic coast. Perhaps he had the thought that it would be nice if you could sail straight across, too.

It came down to just a few people with the desire (the Mastermind), the ability to dream (imagination), and the vision to commit (decision) to start the process of making it happen. What the Panamanians didn't have (specialized knowledge in how to build a canal), they called in from elsewhere.

In 1880, a French company began the long arduous work. A person with great credentials headed the project by the name of de Lesseps. He was a builder of the Suez Canal in Egypt. Panama began to see its future in world commerce.

Of course, if you know anything about history, you know that there were some tremendous problems. In fact right now, as I'm writing this, we are alongside

Gatún Lake (Lago Gatún). This is the area where the hordes of workers you've heard about died from malaria and overwork in the intense equatorial jungle heat.

The French company didn't have the heart or the resources to pull off their vision. In fact, what most people don't know is that there were two French companies that gave it a go. The second enterprise failed as well. Not to be deterred, the determined, persistent Panamanians sought another resource and found it in the North Americans. Most of us have learned through history that they were the ones to finally succeed.

Some have speculated that the French didn't have as much at stake. It was only a contract job to the French – private enterprise, budgets, resources, and hassles were involved. The price quickly became higher than the depths of their desire, motivation, and commitment. On the other hand, the U.S. government brought American companies in. This was a brilliant move because in its own hemisphere, just a few hundred miles from its southernmost parts, the canal would mean economic vitality and a quick transit for military vessels. Motivation was high. The job was completed. (The American presence today is not, of course, what it was.)

So how does this apply to *you* getting rich? Let's remember that the Panama Canal was a great work. Malaria was not the only problem they encountered, although you have likely heard more about that than any other adventure. Mud slides were also part of the problem. Dynamite blasting on the sides of mountains in a rain forest was a necessary part of clearing a path, and this can unsettle a mighty big lot of dirt. It took colossal work. They removed 153 million cubic meters of material. In fact, they removed so much material that, if you were to put it on railroad flat cars, it would circle the globe four times. They made the largest man-made lake in the world during this project, and from the dirt they dug up, they made the largest dam in the world. A project of such gargantuan proportions requires huge efforts.

What it was for us was a dream come true, a dream made reality. And just like your dream of getting wealthy, big dreams don't come that easily. Failures placed to test your resolve never let up. They thwart ordinary people with ordinary desires. The Canal was a grand project. They had great desires (like you must have). They were working for a practical application of their desires. They had setbacks. And they had to stay on task when the going was very hard. This whole thing was not for diversion, not a hobby. It was to further commerce.

It took a tremendous amount of specialized knowledge. They have called it one of the greatest engineering projects in the entire world, and rightly so. It is impressive when you see it. It took imagination even to conceive it could be done. Actually, that first spark may have been pretty simple. Vasco Nuñez de Balboa was the first person from the civilized world who ever saw the Pacific when, in 1513, he climbed up the Continental Divide. Perhaps the dream was born in that moment. Perhaps he talked it up with his team and his Queen. Who knows?

Inspiration born in a moment.

Here's what we do know: **In the beginning it was but a dream – a dream some ambitious people took on to manifest.** It took disciplined imagination to begin to do the organized planning that they put in motion, but it wasn't easy. It took sustained imagination to move through all the hardships that arose. Above all, it took persistence to carry it out. Persistence is actually one of the greatest characteristics that you'll be impressed with when you see what's going on. **Persistence is fueled by desire.**

Now, why do we talk about this today? Ever heard of "get rich quick"? It's a pervasive sickness in our society. And I'm not just talking about the American society or the British society. I'm talking about the whole world. It's what everyone wants. It's the lie of "something for nothing." However, that is what people sincerely want. It's not difficult to sell something to someone when they want something strong with illusion. I refer to these types as "sheeple" because they are seduced by the lie of easy, instant riches. Why do you think the quick fix of the lottery and the business opportunity programs with no real hope of success are so popular?

On the other hand, you who have prosperity consciousness can find it very easy to grow rich and increase your abundance, if you do what it takes. You have much more focus and, therefore, more strength. You realize that you must stay at it for as long as it takes. Sure, it may defeat the lesser of wills. **The size of the dream and the value you place on it will determine how much persistence you will have.** Most people can only dedicate five minutes and five bucks at the lottery counter to prosperity. **You have devoted all your life.** Take the lesson of the Panama Canal. The work, the effort, the dream, the organized planning, and the imagination that came together created something that will benefit humankind for generations! In your own life, it takes the same thought processes to actually, really grow rich. Setbacks come in every quest for wealth. It's part of the human condition. **No big dream comes easily. There will always be work to do.**

Nothing great can be accomplished without a great desire. Remember, when you are thinking about your own personal situations, to chuck this idea of get-rich-quick and realize that great works are inspired by great dreams. You need to acquire the resources and the specialized knowledge. You need to have the imagination to put it into action and the persistence to move through all of the setbacks ahead. Do this, and soon you will enjoy the fruitful days of prosperity, just as Panama has for all these years hence.

About author.

Ted Ciuba, *known as The World's TOP Think and Grow Rich Expert, rewrote the book! His updated version is called **The NEW Think and Grow Rich**. He speaks on the topic all over the world, transforming people's lives who are ready for achievement. Find out more by visiting **www.HoloMagic.com**.*

Forget Your Debt and Focus on Wealth

by Loral Langemeier

Does "wealth" sound like a foreign word to you? If you're like most people carrying loads of consumer debt, it is probably a word you don't hear very often. Consumer debt is the greatest barrier to wealth. And when you're buried by thousands of dollars of it, it probably seems impossible to get out. But it's not.

As a master coach and wealth strategist, I have helped hundreds of people become millionaires in three to five years by focusing on building wealth first and eliminating debt second. I've developed what I call the Wealth Cycle™, a cycle of wealth that millionaires use to consistently and exponentially build their wealth.

Good Debt vs. Bad Debt

To step back for a moment, it's important to differentiate between good and bad debt. That's right – not all debt is a barrier to wealth. In fact, some debt actually adds to wealth. Do you think millionaires don't have debt? Of course they do... sometimes millions of dollars of debt. The reason their debt doesn't concern them is because it's what is known as "good debt."

Good debt is any low-interest borrowing you've done to finance a mortgage or student loans, with the interest deductible against your business operations. Good debt is leveraged against assets.

Bad debt is consumer debt. That's debt for consumer items, such as high interest credit card debt that you acquired buying perishable items. This includes car loans and home equity lines of credit. To build true wealth, you need to eliminate bad debt and – if you want to become a millionaire – strategically build good debt.

Build Wealth to Reduce Debt

When you don't have enough money to pay off your debt, it makes sense to make more money, right? Many people will tell you to scrimp, save, and cut back on absolutely everything that makes life fun. They'll tell you to create a very tight budget and then pay off your debt before you can even think about making investments of any type. A budget is like a diet, and we all know that most diets don't work long term.

The Wealth Cycle uses a series of twelve steps where you generate new income from what I call a Cash Machine, take control of your existing assets, and profit from non-traditional investments. A Cash Machine is a legitimate, legally structured business venture that uses your skill sets, is modeled after a similar successful business, is developed in weeks, takes advantage of teamwork, and generates immediate cash to feed your Wealth Cycle.

Millionaires are always investing – that's one of their secrets to making so much money. Investments act as essential fuel for the Wealth Cycle, so they are a good thing. Additionally, if you are in debt, the passive income you'll gain from your investments will allow you to more quickly pay off your debt (and that's not even mentioning the tax write-offs investing provides).

It's okay if you don't know how all this works right now. The main thing to understand is that the key to success in using the Wealth Cycle is knowing which steps to take, and in what order – your sequencing.

Everyone's Sequencing is Unique

I've been coaching and mentoring people in becoming millionaires for years. And I've had several mentors myself. Having a mentor to guide you can help. For some people, the first step is to develop the proper legal entities for their business and investments to maximize tax strategies. For others it may mean first reallocating assets so you can bring in increased monthly income that enables you to start investing. This will in turn bring in passive income which will allow you to more quickly pay off your debt.

To use an example of when entity structuring might be used first, let's say you have a graphic design business but it's not incorporated. This means your debt includes a lot of expenses – cell phone, office supplies, postage, etc. – that you paid for out of your personal account. If you make your design business an entity, let's say a "Subchapter S Corporation," then the portion of your debt that includes those items can now be transferred over as business expenses. Now you can write off that portion of your debt against your income, giving you more money at the end of the year!

The interesting thing about the Wealth Cycle is that you only focus on debt management after you determine the wealth building sequence that's right for you, and establish your Cash Machine.

Building wealth when you have a lot of debt takes courage, discipline, and positive energy. I realize this is a hard pill for most of you to swallow, but I also know that building wealth can help you get out of debt. I've helped hundreds

60

do it. It takes a commitment to learning to earn so that you think and feel about money in a different way. Let go of your old habits that aren't working.

To your wealth!

About author.

*Loral Langemeier is founder and CEO of **Live Out Loud** and has guided thousands across the country along their way to financial freedom. Langemeier is author of the national bestseller **The Millionaire Maker** and two New York Times bestsellers, **The Millionaire Maker's Guide to Wealth Cycle Investing** and **The Millionaire Maker's Guide to Creating a Cash Machine for Life**. In addition to her sold-out Millionaire Maker events, she has appeared frequently on CNN, CNBC and Fox News Channel, and has been featured in USA Today, The Wall Street Journal and The New York Times, and on the web at ABCNews. com, Forbes.com, and BusinessWeek.com. She is also a weekly guest columnist on **Gather.com** and for **TheStreet.com**, an in-depth financial analysis and news website cofounded by CNBC "Mad Money" host, Jim Cramer. She is the creator of **The Millionaire Maker Game**, a board game that teaches people how to build wealth through asset generating ventures. For more information on Loral Langemeier and Live Out Loud, please visit: www.liveoutloud.com.*

Losing All Your Money After Retirement... Moving on to Become the $20 Million Man

by Douglas Goodey

My name is Douglas Goodey, and I'm 80 years old and from the UK. Oh, I'm also a multi-millionaire – a small fact to mention, which might qualify my story to be heard.

Not just once. Twice over. The first time I became a millionaire was before the retirement age of 65. Unfortunately by the age of 65, I lost everything and was left facing bankruptcy with debts totaling over $4 million. In 10 years, from the age of 65 to the age of 75, I went on to earn $20 million and clear all of my debts.

I've heard nightmares about individuals who went bankrupt during their retirement years, and viewed this as the end of their life. They saw no way out and lost all hope. (Some instances actually led to suicide.) Let me tell you now – there IS a way out, no matter how old you are!

My 80 years of experience, of life, of trials, of success... are all yours for the taking if you choose to lend your eyes to these pages and listen with your mind as you read.

I've overcome many obstacles during my lifetime, and sharing with you a short summary of my life story will hopefully inspire you to realize that no matter what challenges life throws at us, it's not the challenges that matter, but our reaction to them and how we find the courage to swim. Sinking is effortless. Swimming takes effort but it leads us to the shore every time. You just need to choose which beach you want to land on.

I want to take you to my childhood so that you know a bit more about me. But first, a word of wisdom from one who's lived life through many challenges:

Learn to be successful at whatever you do, and that will give you more pleasure than anything else this world has to offer. There is nothing that tastes as sweet as the taste of success. Can anyone achieve success? No. Only those that WANT to – and the more they want to, the more they will.

It is not people who are born with a silver spoon in their mouths who are born to be great.

62

It is people who prove themselves through determination and persistence and choose to carve their own place in life that the world will look up to.

Because THEY have got what it takes and created something from nothing.

So... my childhood... I guess it would have been easy to forget had life not been so exciting and challenging.

I was not born into riches. In fact, I was born into poverty. I spent my formative years switching schools 10 times. Often we would be moving our belongings late at night from one house to another. As I got older, I realized that the reason for moving in the middle of the night was that we could not pay that month's rent or were very much in arrears with our landlord. Despite that, I always wanted to excel at school, even though we spent as much time in bomb shelters during the war as we did at school it seemed.

My father never gave up despite the hardships we faced, and I was ever present by his side, learning what it means to have a sense of responsibility and a commitment to working towards a better standard of life.

I watched him, I listened and learned, and I realized one important truth. You can make excuses in life and stay at the mercy of circumstances, or you can take control and decide that you will never be at the mercy of circumstances. Rather, you will carve and shape your own.

I watched as he worked all hours of the day and night, and learned from him the wisdom of saving. When you know how hard you have to work for your money (you appreciate that through saving what you earn) you can start making that very money work even harder for you. But we'll come to that shortly.

Have you ever seen a kitten when it first starts to walk around? I was like a little bright-eyed kitten finding its first ball of string to play with under its parent's watchful eye. Getting tangled... falling over... discovering... exploring... ever with keener skill and precision.

By the age of nine, I was doing odd jobs for people, earning a few pence a week to top up my pocket money, which was two pence a week when my mother could afford it.

My first regular job, when I was nine, was working for a hardware store. This was when we were living in Ilford, just before my sister was born. There was a hardware corner store in Ley Street, quite close to where we lived. It was owned by an elderly man in his fifties, and I had regularly seen him puffing and panting when carrying his wares into the shop each evening. He had them stacked all around his little store to attract attention.

I didn't have much work to do at that time, so I popped in one day, *and conversation went like this...*

"Mister... all the stuff you've put outside today... I saw you bringing it all back into your shop yesterday."

"I know that," he said. "I was there."

"Yes Sir, but I wasn't and I could have been! It would have made things a lot easier for you."

"You're not big enough," he said.

"What size do I have to be?"

"Well bigger than you are now."

"What can I not do at my size?" I enquired.

"Carry that bag of coalite in," he challenged.

I rolled up my sleeves picked up the bag and brought it into the shop.

"No Laddie... I didn't really want it in here, because I have only just put the darn thing out!"

So I picked the bag back up and put it back out again.

"Alright," he mused, *"You're bigger than I thought, come in tomorrow about 5:30 a.m., and we'll see how it goes."*

He bit his lip, looked at me, and bent down to meet my height. *"But I'm only giving you one and sixpence a week – IF you prove to be worth it."*

I was and he did.

Life, I realized, wasn't going to give you things on a plate unless you seized the opportunities that it put before you. And I'd started to have a taste. When you look, it's amazing how quickly you find.

Another example was in Stratford. Stratford was noted at that time for its large market, with scores of stalls selling vegetables, fruit, fish, and other fresh produce.

Bulk packaging in those days was mostly wooden boxes, and I knew that all the waste was cleared up by dustmen early each morning. I figured if I hung around until the stall owners packed away for the day, I should be able to collect a fair amount of timber. I took my fill, and my barrow was packed high! Not only did I have lots of wood from the boxes, but I also had little extras too – fruit and vegetables that the stall owners felt should be thrown away because it was not up to par, but which was still better in quality than any my family or I ever had.

Because I was late getting home, my mother gave me a verbal lashing (as well as one with anything else she could get her hands on) but she eased up when

64

I was eventually able to present to her the – no pun intended – fruits of my day's patience and industrious approach to opportunity.

The wood, I decided, was better than the bundles of firewood that were sold at hardware stores for about tuppence (two pence) a bundle. So I sawed and chopped up the wooden boxes, and took the wood around the streets in my barrow, selling it at tuppence a bucketful.

I would ask people how long they thought it might last them, and told them that I would endeavor to get back to them before they had used it... OR if they preferred, they could take two bucketfuls right now instead of just the one. I have since learned they call that marketing.

There are many similar stories to this, but my future was fashioned in those early years by following the initiatives of my parents, and their attitudes toward work and opportunity.

Why is all of this important? And why do I mention it? Because from an early age I realized that nothing comes from nothing, and great things come from doing something, that leads to something else that leads to....

Such was the case with my father. By working and saving, and even though he had ducked and dived to keep food on the table, when the opportunity presented itself he purchased his first shop. And from selling lemonade ice cubes that became famous throughout many parts of London, to schoolchildren and adults alike, he earned enough money to ensure its success.

That was just the first of a number of shops he would go on to purchase.

I, of course, worked with him in the shops and left school at the age of thirteen. So no, I didn't have a ton of qualifications to count on, but I was learning life, not studying academia.

At age 18 I went into the Army for two years. At age 20, back in civilian life, I was running the very first shop my father had started, while he and other family members ran others. I have to add here that I did this even though Joan, my fiancé at the time and now wife of close to 60 years, was set against the idea of me working in a shop.

I would run the shop during the day and make home deliveries to people in the evening. I found various suppliers and built good standing with them so that I could get products at better than wholesale prices. Naturally I started selling more for less, moving the business from retail to wholesale and supplier of larger quantities to other shop owners throughout the London area.

A year later I was in another business with a partner, but that partnership ended on a disagreement, and was the catalyst to a new and fresh start to my life: working for someone else.

I saw an advertisement in the paper to work for a newspaper publisher selling advertising space. Within 3 months, I had tripled the turnover of the business and was made manager, replacing the man who had hired me and who had been my manager from the time I had started. I would go out to see clients, and I wasn't afraid to ask for their business.

A year or so later the newspaper merged with another competitor, and the size of the business, the circulation, and the advertising opportunities increased with it. So did my commission.

I had learned from an early age that opportunities can only be seized if you are prepared to take them when they present themselves. I was also a regular saver. I didn't squander my money... I worked too hard for it to do that. I saved it and waited for the right time to be able to invest it in something else.

Two years later no opportunity had presented itself, so another employee of the publishing company and I made an offer to the owners of the company. Now let me say this was ALL from money that I had saved while working for those two years.

We made the offer, and they accepted it. I was now a joint owner of the newspaper and the publishing company after having bought out the original owners. Now life was good. And we did extremely well from the publishing company – well enough to live life without financial pressure or worry.

One day I arrived at work in the morning and saw that the building was gutted. A fire had started and burned the building down during the night. A sense of despair grips you when you see your livelihood go up in flames, as it had for me... literally.

The loss assessors came in, and we salvaged what equipment we could. Unfortunately, a newspaper is only good while it is in circulation. It's difficult to drum up the business and start again from scratch.

During the months of finding new premises and restarting the business, the newspaper side died down and my partner continued to run the business more as a commercial printer than as a publisher. My heart was no longer there in the printing side, as it had been in the publishing side, and one evening I saw an advertisement in the paper for a vacancy to work as a loss assessor. I remembered what a wonderful job the loss assessor had done for me when the building had burnt down, so I decided to go for it.

I responded to the ad, and got the job. So I sold my share of the printing firm to my partner and started a new career. I was 38 years old at the time.

The job was purely commission based, but over the next ten years I rose to the top of the ranks in the profession. However, as I didn't want to see myself going in and out of burning buildings at the age of 65, it was time for another move. At the age of 48.

Most people are afraid to give up what they know at that stage, but I knew what I didn't want, and that was a stronger motivator for me.

Once again I started at the bottom rung of the ladder, on commission only, with a financial company called Hambro Life. Within two years I was one of the top performers in the company and among the top performers in the world in financial services. For ten years I stayed at the top of my game, making hundreds of thousands of dollars, year in and year out.

At the age of 58, I left Hambro and started my own venture in the mortgages industry, building up a string of estate agencies in and around London. But changes in the tax laws affecting house buyers and in the estate agency business suddenly hit me and my business hard. Very hard.

So hard in fact, that at the age of 65, when I should have been retiring and enjoying my life's hard work and earnings, I was facing bankruptcy and was $4 million in debt.

I arranged meetings and payback plans with all of my creditors, and asked them to grant me grace to pay them back. Over the next ten years I went on to earn $20 million. But that's another story for another place and another time.

The point is that whatever your obstacles may be and however big they might seem, they are only as insurmountable as you deem them to be. There is almost always a solution, almost always a fix, and almost always a happier story if you just look for it, recognize where it lies, and go out and make it yours.

To that end I wish you all the success you desire and deserve.

About author.

Douglas Goodey is the **$20 Million Man**. He went from poor to rich, and due to a cruel twist of fortunes, lost everything at the age of 65, leaving him facing bankruptcy, with a $4 million debt. Amazingly, over the next ten years, he not only cleared his debts, but earned $20 million in the process!

Quantum Physics of Belief – Living on the Edge of Chaos

by Dr. Surya M. Ganduri

We all live on the edge of chaos every time something changes. It does not matter what the change is or when the change occurred. This change can be personal, professional, financial, emotional, psychological, or something else. It can be external or internal. When change happens, we are forced to move to the edge of chaos to deal with it.

This is particularly true if the situation forcing our change is new to us: divorce, bankruptcy, unanticipated wealth, death of a loved one, business failure, rules change, and failed relationships, to name just a few of the obstacles that we all face in our lives.

Living on the edge of chaos is where all great ideas happen and real change (personal, professional, interpersonal) occurs. This is what we need to learn to deal with and manage so it does not destroy us, force us into making fear-based decisions, or make us complacent.

Living on the edge of chaos forces us to think differently to solve a problem. Living on the edge of chaos forces us to make sometimes painful choices, to solicit new inputs, to think outside of the box, and to take new actions to eliminate the pain this change has caused.

Living on the edge of chaos requires we think about a situation from a more global perspective. It requires we see things as they are, not as we want them to be. It requires we understand the impact of our actions on others. It requires we make an informed, responsible, and deliberate choice.

Living on the edge of chaos, for this change to be effective, requires that we take in information that may not have been important in the past. It requires that we take total ownership of the situation. Because, only in total ownership are we empowered to take the action required. If we do not own something we cannot effectively change it.

Creating order out of chaos requires creating (or recreating) a sense of order that puts you back in control and allows you to be flexible enough to deal

68

with the problems of being human. It does not require you to judge yourself. It does require you to evaluate your actions and how you contributed to the chaos. Be gentle with yourself, but be fair and objective.

How Quantum Physics of Beliefs Fit in with Chaos

A growing body of scientific evidence in the fields of physics, systems theory, chaos theory, biology, and psychology explains how and why our vision (meaning our beliefs and thoughts) directly influences both the physical world and our perception of it.

Science has not definitively identified how vision works, nor has it found the formula for summoning human desire into existence. However, much scientific evidence supports the fact that vision influences both the physical world and our perception of it – even if it doesn't explain exactly how and why vision works.

There are several scientific theories that support and describe the mechanics of vision. These theories provide evidence that we are direct participants in creating reality at a most fundamental level.

1. Quantum physics supports the notion that reality is not fixed or determined, but operates based upon potentials and relationships that we can influence.

2. Sensitivity to initial conditions, a concept within the Chaos theory, supports the idea that a small change to a system, like your vision, can make remarkable and significant changes over time.

3. Systems theory points out the interconnection that exists between you and everything that surrounds you. Your vision is a tool to make you aware of the connections that are most important to bring you what you desire.

This section is not a scholarly compilation of scientific ideas, but I have made every attempt to present the views accurately. The ideas presented here may challenge your worldview of "how things work." Some of these ideas may be difficult to understand or seem far out, but I hope you will take away an increased understanding of how and why vision works. This will give you greater confidence to use vision in your life.

The quantum physics phenomenon of non-locality provides evidence for the interconnected nature of reality. When you create a vision, you become aligned with this instantaneous, non-local connection between where you are and where you want to go.

Let's examine how our intentions interact directly with the physical world.

An experiment that tests for the influence of intention on the physical world uses a Random Event Generator (REG). This computer, in essence, generates an electronic flip of the coin, producing zeros and ones at random. The REG is a way to do a large number of trials efficiently and objectively. If this binary event generator is used over many control trials, it will produce 50 percent zeros and 50 percent ones.

One standard REG experiment is to ask subjects to press a button on the REG that will produce a significant number of information bits – zeros or ones in this case. Before they press the button, the subjects are asked to intend for the machine to produce either more zeros or more ones.

The accumulated results of these experiments done over time suggest that the machine is influenced by the subject's intention: for example, if a subject intends for the machine to generate more ones, that is what the machine will do. If the person intends the machine to produce more zeros, the machine will turn out more zeros. The increased number of one's or zeros that a subject can intend the REG to produce is small, but significant and not due to chance.

The REG experiments offer compelling scientific evidence that you can influence the physical world with your thoughts. Being visionary is a way to focus your thoughts to influence reality toward what you desire.

Chaos theory is an area of science that explains the underlying order in seemingly disordered and random systems. "Sensitivity to initial conditions" is a concept within chaos theory that provides support for how and why our vision influences what may seem like a randomly operating reality.

There are many different systems: the weather, the body of government, the human body, and the whole reality that surrounds us. You are a part of many systems, such as work, family, and your community. Several ideas will be presented here that will help you to be happier and more successful within the systems in which you live. Chaos theory asserts that small changes introduced into a system can cause dramatic effects in the system.

These concepts are powerful because they suggest you can influence a seemingly complex system by introducing a small change to the system. One small change can make remarkable and significant changes over time.

You might feel that your life is on a certain and predictable path. This leads you to believe that you can't change this path and create a different life. However, by creating a vision and consciously making it a part of your reality, you make a change to the systems of which you are a part. Your vision is the small change that begins a cascade of effects. You can use your vision to influence the system you are in – your current reality – in your preferred direction.

The term "holistic" has emerged in the vocabulary of many areas of science. In the scientific view, systems consist of elements that are in mutual interaction. Systems theory provides a framework to understand the concept of "wholeness" and the interrelated quality of reality.

Your vision organizes the complex connections necessary to bring about your desire. A vision increases awareness of the connection between individual parts that you can link together into your desired future. Moreover, a vision does this without your managing or even understanding the complexity that brings about what you desire.

From the systems point of view, we influence and are influenced by reality through a concept referred to as "feedback loops." Creating a vision and referring to it regularly is a feedback loop. When you create a vision that inspires you to take action, your actions have results that give you feedback. You can use this feedback to engage new actions.

We typically refer to feedback as either "negative" or "positive," but positive and negative are labels rather than facts about the feedback itself. If you are not making the progress you want toward your desired vision, evaluate your current situation instead of focusing on feedback as either positive or negative. Become an observer rather than a participant of past and present events. This requires you to step back from the situation and look objectively and freshly at the information that surrounds you. Later, you can input this feedback into your actions by making choices.

It can also be helpful to become an observer when things are working well. This positive feedback gives you information about what actions work. Positive feedback provides encouragement and motivation to continue toward the vision.

The smallest change builds upon itself, moving you closer to the results you want. This is described as: "Whatever movement occurs is amplified, producing more movement in the same direction. A small action snowballs, with more and more and still more of the same, resembling compounding interest." In a reinforcing feedback loop, it is important that you keep in mind your desired future reality so that your efforts continue to compound in the direction of your vision.

While there is movement within a feedback system, there are also delays. A delay is an interruption between actions and results. This is why continually referring to your vision is so important. Your vision is a guiding statement that can keep you on track during the delay between the current and future reality. The vision helps temper you, focusing your thoughts on the long term, so that you don't overreact or underreact to daily events.

By referring regularly to your vision as a guiding statement, you focus and refocus your efforts toward your priorities. When you remind yourself of your vision, it energizes your efforts. You reaffirm why you started the journey in the first place.

Step back from time to time, and observe your journey. As the observer, you will notice feedback that you can input into your journey toward your vision. Referring to the vision, becoming the observer, and using feedback are ways to maintain your momentum toward your desired outcome.

Vision Is the Starting Point of a Feedback Loop

A feedback loop is a cycle of cause and effect relationships. Cause leads to effect, and effect leads to another cause, and so on. Your vision is the starting point of a feedback loop.

There are many examples of feedback loops in our lives. Take the example of a teacher's expectation for students' academic achievement. At the beginning of a term, a teacher may have the expectation (vision) that some students are high achievers and will advance to a greater academic degree than other students. This is the beginning of a feedback loop for those students' academic performance.

Throughout the term, the teacher will consciously or unconsciously refer back to the expectation, "this is a high achiever," when interacting with students. The teacher will initiate actions that may cause students to think and act in ways that reinforce the teacher's original expectation. This will result in more actions by the teacher, causing a feedback loop in the direction of the original expectation. By the end of the term, it is likely that the students who were expected to be high achievers will in fact be more advanced academically than the students whom the teacher did not envision as high achievers.

This example illustrates how an expectation can positively (or negatively depending on your perception) influence the flow of cause and effect events in a feedback loop. Vision sets the flow of actions-results-actions in motion.

Let me narrate a scenario that illustrates the practical uses of feedback loops in overcoming obstacles. Let's say, we (five friends) are on a backcountry ski trip in the Rocky Mountain National Park. The five of us set out on our adventure, intending to climb a mountain and ski down through fresh, unpacked and untracked Colorado powder. We also have other, short-term visions for the day: not getting injured or buried in an avalanche, having fun, exercising, and enjoying each other's company in the outdoors.

Our destination is a 10,000+ foot mountain that would fulfill our desire for great skiing. We start our journey on a designated trail that meanders through the woods. After about a mile, we consult our map and head off the trail toward the mountain that would provide our downhill turns. After 40 minutes of slogging up through the trees, we are not where we wanted to be. We gather to discuss our situation.

When orienteering in the mountains, feedback comes in many forms. We use a map, a compass, an altimeter, and our most recent addition, a handheld GPS receiver. These tools give us feedback about our position in the environment. We also share our own feedback from the environment, such as the weather conditions and topography that we experience along the way, as well as our own physical conditions. Combining all this is important to the process of moving toward our desired destination (vision) when traveling in the backcountry.

In this case, our orienteering feedback tools indicate that we are off course. We are encountering interruptions and delays as we move toward our vision. We express our disappointment, are concerned about putting in extra energy, and fear we might even be lost.

We then exchange feedback with each other. We decide to change our route but continue toward our original destination. We recommit to our vision of reaching the top of the mountain and skiing down it. We continue to get feedback from our new route and remain on course. This feedback reinforces our confidence in our orienteering skills and use of equipment, and motivates us to keep moving toward our vision.

By revisiting the original vision and taking in feedback from the environment and ourselves, we neither underreact nor overreact to such obstacles as getting off course. We are able to adjust our route, refocus our energies, and take action toward our desired outcome.

We reach the summit of the mountain sooner than we have anticipated. We feel exuberant to have overcome obstacles along the way and to have reached our goal. Had we not revisited our vision and used the feedback from the environment and ourselves along the way, we might have really gotten lost and put ourselves in danger – and we might not have reached our exhilarating goal.

Ways to Overcome Obstacles on your Journey

As an everyday visionary, you will always encounter obstacles and delays as you move toward your short- or long-term vision. Observing feedback, inputting new information into your actions, and connecting to your vision will help you flow with setbacks, instead of feeling stuck or frustrated, as you move toward your desired outcome. These are important tools that will help bring your dreams to life.

If you are living on the edge of chaos and want help, call me. I can help because I have been living on the edge now for quite a while. It is not fun but with the right tools, support, and perspective, great things can happen if you have the discipline to let them.

About author.

Dr. Surya M. Ganduri *specializes in strategic and executive leadership development processes that help People Succeed in an Evolving World – he does this thru Self Awareness of intended thought and manifestation from a Quantum Physics of Beliefs approach. Along with his work as Author, Writer, Blogger and popular Internet Radio Talk Show Host, Dr. Surya is in-demand as a public speaker.*

Fill in the Complimentary Business Diagnostic Questionnaire at **www.embcinc. com/businessdiagnostic1.php** *and receive a free health check on your business! Or request (630.445.1321) a complimentary Multi-dimensional Personality Assessment to get yourself a head start with your Self Awareness to balance your life.*

74

Ignite the Entrepreneurial Spirit in Your Children

by Sharon Lechter

Visit a kindergarten class and you see excited children jumping up and down. "Pick me! Pick me!" they yell, eager to learn anything and volunteering for everything. Now fast forward into the future ten years and imagine those same children in a classroom as high school students. The front row seats are empty. The young people not only do NOT volunteer, they won't even make eye contact with the teachers for fear of being called upon. They stare out the window, more interested in what is happening outside than what their teacher has to say.

What happened during those 10 years? Their love of learning, thirst for knowledge, and enthusiasm for life have been challenged and often stifled, or lost entirely.

The fact that you are reading this book proves you are in control, or well on your way to taking control, of your own life and destiny. If you own your own business, you are already in control and in the driver's seat, the CEO of your life. Congratulations on being ahead of the curve... but are your children ahead of the curve? Are you expecting them to learn everything they will need to know in order to succeed in school?

Whether we like it or not, traditional education today is still teaching our children to become good employees – rather than creative entrepreneurs. In fact, creativity is often labeled as rebellion. We should be encouraging our children's natural strengths, and unfortunately, the school system is not equipped, either financially or with proper staffing, to do this for every child. Are you experiencing flashbacks right now... with memories of experiences you had in school? Were you rebellious? Or were you just innovative in the wrong environment? What's the difference?

Employees live for paychecks. Entrepreneurs live for results.
Employees want benefits. Entrepreneurs want opportunities.
Employees watch the clock. Entrepreneurs watch the bottom line.

Ignite your child's entrepreneurial spirit and start today. What you are doing for a living today, whether it be your job or your business, is a perfect platform for educating your children about business and financial independence.

Share, don't tell. There is an important difference between "sharing" and "telling." Can you remember a time when you were trying to tell your child about something, and all you got in return was a blank look of disinterest? Instead of *telling* your child something, try *sharing* a story with the same message, and include how it affected you, your business or your professional life. You may be amazed by the respect you will get from your children when you talk to them as equals.

Ask for their opinion. Once engaged, they will have great new ideas that you haven't even thought about. Their perspective and insights may even give you new opportunities for new markets, distribution or growth. My friend Judy recently told me how her daughter had shared with her friends how much she enjoyed working with her Mom. The next week, six of these girls' Moms called Judy asking about her business, and have since started their own businesses with Judy as their mentor (and with their own daughters!) This all happened because Judy shared her business with her daughter and asked for her opinion.

Involve your children in bill paying. There is nothing like experiential learning. Our children are often with us when we spend our money. However, they are typically not with us when we make our money or when we pay the bills. They don't understand the effort and costs involved in earning the money. Try having your children pay the bills for your home and business, and let them learn first hand about all the costs of running both a home and business. You will be amazed at how quickly they grasp and understand the economics behind your life and your family's life.

Have a debt discussion. We live in a society of instant gratification and our children see and learn from that. They understand "Just Charge It, Mom." They are with you when you use your credit cards, but don't see you paying off the balance at the end of the month. Credit cards are virtually unavoidable, and if your child has not already received an offer in the mail, the day is fast approaching. Have them read an offer that you've received. Go through the main points and ask if they think it is a good deal. Then go through the fine print and see if they have a new opinion on the offer. There are ways to use debt, including credit cards, responsibly. Young entrepreneurs quickly learn this when searching for funding to start their own businesses.

Compensate your children for *results*, not time. Money talks volumes with young people. Compensate your children based on results. This will ignite their entrepreneurial spirit quicker than anything. Do NOT compensate them for just time worked; that creates an employee "live for the paycheck" and entitlement mentality. Judy pays her daughter a percentage of the income she receives from her six friends' mothers' businesses.

Allow your children to be in control of their own money. Review your monthly financials with your children. Let them see the "whole picture." Then, allow them to have their own money. Allow them to "stub their toe" while they are still at home instead of "break their leg" when they go off to college. That means, when they run out of money before they run out of month... allow them to suffer the consequences... don't cave in and give them more money! Last month I had a mom call me after she had given her son our YOUTHpreneur prepaid debit card to tell me, "I couldn't believe it! He always had to have $250 basketball shoes. Last week we were at the store and he needed new shoes. I told him, 'You have your card... go ahead and buy what you want.' Sharon, he actually bought $60 shoes... and was proud of himself for buying value over brand. That would NEVER have happened if it was MY credit card we were using. Not only did he learn about money, his self-confidence skyrocketed in the process!"

Encourage their ideas. Encourage your children to start their own businesses to earn money. You will see their self esteem increase light years with their first sale in their own business. They will realize they can make their own money and not rely on a parent or employer for their livelihood! They will make mistakes and hit obstacles... but with your support they will grow as they overcome them. It is a priceless education that will benefit them for a lifetime!

Be a mentor, not an enabler. It is easy for us as parents to want to "help" our children too much, and in doing so, we may actually hurt their self esteem. Know the difference between a bribe and a reward... and apply it! Remember, a great mentor asks questions... so ask questions of your children instead of lecturing them. Asking questions will ignite your children's creative process and engage them. Have confidence in that they will find their way, and it will allow them to have confidence in themselves. This will allow them to discover their own value and create their own life of success!

Teach your children the importance of giving back. Albert Einstein said it best when he said, "It is high time that the ideal of success should be replaced by the ideal of service." By teaching your children early to be generous, they will become "givers" instead of "takers," and truly make the world a better place for everyone.

Allow your children to BE FAB. Building self esteem is so important for young people. Less than 30 % of girls and 50% of boys agree with the statement, "I am happy the way I am." Our entrepreneurship training includes teaching the young people presentation skills. Using the acronym BE FAB (Back strait, Eye contact, Firm handshake, Ask questions and Allow answers, and Be bold), we encourage young people to find power and confidence in situations where it might normally be difficult. At a Boys and Girls Clubs of Metropolitan Phoenix awards event for the Youth of the Year, one of the participants of the YOUTHpreneur program was quite nervous about speaking in front of a crowd with hundreds of people, including celebrities. A friend of hers (another YOUTHpreneur participant) told her, "Just remember to BE FAB and you'll do great!" She practiced BE FAB and she was fabulous!

77

I created our products, ThriveTime for Teens and the YOUTHpreneur BIZKit out of my own frustration with the lack of hands-on experiential financial education tools for teaching young people about starting a business and getting on the path to being their own boss. According to a 2005 CNN/USA Today Gallup survey, over 70% of respondents age 18-29 said they'd rather start their own business than work for someone else.

There are many tools available to help you set your young people up for success – starting when they are quite young! There is no lack of curriculum. But there is a lack of experiential curriculum that truly engages your children in the learning process... which is what turns the love for learning back on. It is the gift of your time that will truly make the difference. We have seen that parents who invest just a couple of hours a week over a six week period can change their children's attitude about money, and their self esteem skyrockets in the process!

Only *you* can make sure your children have the financial education they need, not only to survive, but to thrive in the world they face.

About author.

*Sharon Lechter has been a pioneer in developing new technologies, programs and products to bring education into children's lives in ways that are innovative, challenging and fun, and remains committed to education – particularly financial literacy. Co-author of the bestselling book, **Think and Grow Rich-Three Feet from Gold** with the Napoleon Hill Foundation, **Rich Dad Poor Dad** and 14 other books in the Rich Dad series, Sharon's most recent book project is, **Outwitting the Devil** by Napoleon Hill - annotated and updated by Lechter for the modern reader.*

*She is the Founder and CEO of Pay Your Family First, a company dedicated to empowering children with innovative, thoughtful and easy-to-understand programs and products, such as the award winning ThriveTime for Teens board game and YOUTHpreneur entrepreneurial BIZkit. For more information about how you can ignite your child's entrepreneurial spirit, visit: **www.sharonlechter.com**.*

Health, Happiness, and Wealth

by Mark Iriks

You could not have picked a better time than now to read this article. No matter who you are, no matter how healthy, happy or wealthy you are, I have caught you at the very time that you are ready to substantially improve every aspect of your life, and yes I mean *right now*!

Before you continue to read this article, take the time to indicate, on the following "Life Goal Scale," exactly where you would like to be.

HEALTH

{---------------1-----------------2----------------3-----------------4-----------------5--------------}

1) POOR HEALTH 2) BELOW AVERAGE 3) AVERAGE 4) ABOVE AVERAGE 5) ABUNDANTLY HEALTHY

HAPPINESS

{---------------1-----------------2----------------3-----------------4-----------------5--------------}

1) LONELY/DEPRESSED 2) BELOW AVERAGE 3) AVERAGE 4) ABOVE AVERAGE 5) ABUNDANTLY HAPPY

WEALTH

{---------------1-----------------2----------------3-----------------4-----------------5--------------}

1) POOR/PENNILESS 2) BELOW AVERAGE 3) AVERAGE 4) ABOVE AVERAGE 5) ABUNDANTLY WEALTHY

If you have chosen anywhere below "above average" in any of the areas, then you don't need my help, because you already know much more about "under achieving" than I do. In fact, I frankly don't remember what it's like, so I cannot possibly teach you how to achieve your life goal.

If you genuinely would like to have an abundance of health, happiness and wealth, this article can help you.

I was not born into privilege except the privilege of being part of a large and loving family. My upbringing taught me a lot about character and morals, but certainly not about health and wealth. So, what then are my credentials?

On the 19th of January, 1994, at the age of 34, I had a major heart attack. On that day, who I was, was the residual value of everything that I had eaten, smoked, drank... plus the sum total of all of my thoughts and beliefs up until then. Fortunately, I felt that my thoughts were positive – that was instilled in me by my upbringing – but the rest of my existence was pretty well in line with the knowledge level that I possessed, and the behavioral traits that I had been engaging in.

One thing I know is that none of us consciously and deliberately go out of our way to be poor, unhealthy, or unhappy; we live our life the only way we know how to. I knew how to be happy – it was part of my nature. Likewise, I have friends and acquaintances who are financially wealthy, yet extremely unhealthy, and others who are wealthy and healthy, yet depressed. They, like me, are focused on what gives them the most pleasure or what avoids the most pain. In my case, I clearly knew little about how to be healthy or wealthy. I had just had a heart attack, and my only financial asset was $4000 equity in a block of land. And to complete the picture, my Doctor told me I had about 10 years to live, and could not go back to doing whatever I was doing for a living.

Please don't feel sorry for me. Today is the 28th of August, 2012. I am 52 years old and extremely fit, and healthy by any standard. I am in the top 1% of richest people in the world, and I am very happy! And, I maintain very strong personal and business relationships with the people in my amazing world.

A revelation...

On the 19th of May, 2012, I had a revelation. My son Scott and I had just finished a business mastery course, and were flying by helicopter from Namalie (Anthony Robbins' Private Retreat in Fiji), to reach the first of our connecting flights back home. Scott is not only my son, but also my best friend and business partner. During that flight, I turned to him with tears in my eyes and said, "Mate, we are as weak as piss! We think we are so successful, we actually think that we've made it. But with the God-given ability we have, we are capable of achieving significantly *more* in our lives."

Because I had come so far since my heart attack, I saw how I had convinced myself that I had "made it." But deep inside, I knew how pathetic my effort had really been. Yes, I was doing well by any measure, but it was pathetic by *my* measure. I was above average healthy, happy and wealthy, but what a selfish place to be. I was selfish to me and the world.

The purpose for my life...

I now know that the purpose for my life is to take action to ensure that I remain fit and healthy, build awesome, sustainable and worthwhile relationships,

80

and create an abundance of wealth to create as much good for as many people as I possibly can.

I said at the beginning of this article that I am not capable of teaching you how to be below average. I am certain I can teach anyone how to be above average, because I have already achieved above average, and I have to say: it's not what it's cracked up to be. What I want to do is invite you to join me on a *continual* journey of growth in health, in relationships, and in wealth.

It's easy. You need to start with your "why," the very reason you want everything. It may be to ensure that your loved ones have an abundant life through you being the example that leads them. It may be because you want to leave the world a better place for you having been in it. Whatever your "why," if it is a strong, purpose-driven and committed "why," you will find the *how* to achieve it, simply because you are compelled from within to do so.

My "why" is so compelling to me that I discovered my first *how* to do it – what action to take – within hours of discovering my new "why." On that flight in Fiji, I went into a literacy rampage, writing for hours! During my next few connecting flights, I fully scoped out where I need to be and how to get there.

Scott and I have committed to maintaining our strict training regime, to doing everything to continue to improve and grow our relationships with our respective partners, family and friends, and to a financial goal of $100 million net worth by 2024.

HOW?

It really is easy.

Don't just believe; *know* that you are entitled to and capable of having an abundance of health, happiness, and wealth, and then simply take action to gift yourself with it.

You may need to be educated in one or more areas. In my case I knew how to be happy, so that was a good start. But I had to learn how to be healthier, and learn how to get wealthier.

Anyone who believes they cannot achieve an abundance of health, happiness and wealth is 100% correct. If you don't believe that you deserve it or are capable of achieving it, you are correct; you will get the exact outcome you believe and commit to.

Here is the simple start to the rest of your abundant life.

HEALTH

Do some research. Firstly, find out what perfect health means to you. Understand what it looks like and how it would feel. Then, find people who enjoy

81

that level of health and copy them. Yes, simply copy their eating habits, copy their exercise habits, and copy their de-stressing techniques. You can start out slowly, however, it is best to take massive action. Either way, *take action!* Remember, 20 days of a new process creates a new habit.

HAPPINESS

Do some research. Firstly, find out what being happy means to you and understand what it would feel like. Find people who enjoy that level of happiness, and copy them. Yes, simply copy their positive nature towards others, copy the way they add value to other people's lives, and copy what they do to ensure that their health contributes to their happy disposition.

WEALTH

Do some research. Firstly, find out what being wealthy means to you. Decide how much is wealthy, to you. Find the people that enjoy that level of wealth. Yes, simply discover what they did to achieve that level. Discover that assisting others to get wealthier might be your best wealth creation strategy. Please do not do as many do and hang on to the focus of not being poor. Take a risk and focus on being wealthy! Earn more, spend less, invest more... take a *forward* movement.

So where will you find these people? They may be people you know, or there may be outcomes you want that you can search for on the Internet. Mainly, just understand that to achieve a different outcome for any part of your life, you will need to do something different. We are all born with no knowledge, but the vast majority of us are capable of learning exactly what other people know, of taking that action they took, and of achieving the results that they achieved. I'm simply saying do the things you have learned that have given other people the outcomes that you want.

Let me give you a practical example of how you would do this. Recently, I was watching the competitors during the Olympics, and as part of my continual search for growth and development, I decided I wanted to go to a new level in my health and fitness. So, I had a look at the various athletes to see which body shape I would like. It was not hard to see that most marathon runners have similar physiques, most weight lifters have similar physiques, and most gymnasts have similar physiques. Personally, I like the physique of the sprinters, so I Googled their training regimes. As a result, now I do a lot less distance running, I do about the same weight training that I have been for a number of years, and I do sprint training at least twice a week. I don't imagine that I will end up looking like Usain Bolt, or ever running as fast as him, but my physique will unquestionably look less like a marathon runner and more like a sprinter within a few months. With proper knowledge, a disciplined massive action plan, and the belief that I can achieve it, I will. And I can guarantee that I will.

Please accept, believe and know that you are entitled to, you deserve, and you are capable of having an abundance of health, happiness and wealth!

So do yourself a favor. Go back to the Life Goal Scale at the beginning of this article, and whatever you marked down for yourself, now mark down where you want your most significant other to be, and where you think they would like to be. Mark down where you want your children to be, and if you don't have children, where you would want them to be if/when you do. Understand that they have a significantly greater chance if you show them how to get there. Become the example for your loved ones and your peers to follow.

When you take informed and educated action to improve your health, your happiness, or your wealth, they can only improve. You are worth the effort.

About author.

Mark Vincent Iriks is the founder (1992), Managing Director, and major Shareholder of Easifleet www.easifleet.com.au, a leading fleet management and leasing company in Australia. Mark also has a strong commercial and residential property portfolio. Mark's background includes his candidature for both State and Federal politics, as well as serving as a Local Government Councillor. Mark's passion is continuous improvement. He believes that no matter what level of ability, drive or commitment we were innately gifted with, we are all capable of achieving much more, and that the constant pursuit of growth is what makes us happy.

Crossing the Rubicon While *"Zigzagging"

by Dr. Joel Bomane

"The voyage of the best ship is a zigzag line of a hundred tacks."
- **Ralph Waldo Emerson**

At age 9, while lying in my hospital bed – all things being equal – I should have been six feet under (more than once). The truth is that my finest moments were the ones when I felt deeply in pain, unhappy or unfulfilled: *"zigzagging."

It was in such moments that I started searching at a very young age for different ways, or truer answers. I learned that when things are very serious in our lives, such as a deep crisis demanding our immediate action, there is a built-in computer in our head-body instantly *"zigzagging" – correcting itself to keep us alive.

At age 17 I left home, no thinking it over and coming to a decision, but through *action* that was immediate! If we are tremendously alert, watchful, and sensitive, we will realize that Life itself is a crisis to which we respond according to our conditioning, tendencies or inclinations. When in fact, most of the time, the voyage demands a totally non-conditioned action, or *"zigzagging."

*"Zigzagging": *"Two roads diverged in a wood, and I – I took the one less traveled by. And that has made all the difference."* - **Robert Frost**

Ignition: Who Is Your Hero?

"I believe every human has a finite number of heartbeats. I don't intend to waste any of mine." A *"zigzagging" quote by **Neil Armstrong.**

Maybe Neil Armstrong, Commander of Apollo 11, whose pulse was measured at 150 beats per minute as he guided the lunar lander to the moon's surface at 20:17:39 UTC on July 20, 1969, is your hero?

Or Usain Bolt, the Jamaican sprinter widely regarded as the fastest person ever, who suffers from Scoliosis (an abnormal curvature of the spine),

84

causing lower back pain and fatigue with prolonged sitting or standing, and who has difficulty breathing?

Or maybe you want to emulate the success of London 2012 Summer Olympics' hero Michael Phelps, the most decorated Olympian in history, with his amazing *"zigzagging" training diet of 12,000+ calories per day?

My dad is my hero.

The phone rang at 4:00 AM that morning with some dreadful news, 8000 kilometers (approximately 5,000 miles) away from the lovely French Island of Guadeloupe. Dad had just passed away a couple of days before his birthday in January, 1999. He was 73. I was immediately overshadowed with sorrow as a long drawn-out primal scream came up from the depth of my being. I felt empty and dead inside. Though dad suffered many years with illnesses, and never complained about the pain or the discomfort, I did not expect him to die so soon.

The following weeks I crossed my *Rubicon* when I realized there is every kind of sorrow that mankind can possibly experience. This sorrow is there, persistently, continuously, hidden deep down in the recesses of our hearts, which has never been opened and looked at, an unconscious sorrow that has never solved the agony, the despair, the ambition of our species. And we have run away from it through various forms, through hopes, through all kinds of intellectual, verbal theories or ideas. We have never directly come in to a crisis with it and faced it with *"zigzagging."

Stephen R. Covey, a wonderful dad, recognized as one of *Time* magazine's 25 most influential Americans and who dedicated his life to demonstrating how every person can truly control their destiny, understood *"zigzagging" perfectly. *"Zigzagging" is about a **Life of Service and Joy.** You see, Stephen R. Covey frequently played practical jokes on his friends, and let his kids build peanut butter and jelly sandwiches on his bald head. I hope children for generations to come will *"zigzag" a lifetime in Stephen Covey's shoes.

My dad is my hero. What I learned from him is simple: never ever give up, and most importantly, give "unconditional love."

*"Zigzagging" Voyage

In my early 20's I started scouting new trails. I left France alone, with virtually no money in my pockets, to study in the USA. My *"zigzagging" way of life also brought me to serve the poor with Mother Teresa Missionaries of Charity in Kolkata. Upon my return, I made this comment: "Going to India to learn their way of survival wouldn't be a bad idea for many Americans, given the increased poverty and homelessness in North America.... Indians know how to survive. Their life is full of hope in spite of suffering." *The Atlantic Union Gleaner*, MA, USA, 1992.

My *"Zigzagging" Voyage allowed me to learn *"zigzagging" first hand as I met Holocaust rescuer and war hero John Weidner (who received Medal of Freedom, member of the Order of the British Empire, Dutch Medal of Resistance, Croix de guerre and Medaille de la Resistance, Legion d'honneur) who was honored as Righteous Gentile. I also had the privilege of meeting both American astronaut James Irwin (Lunar Module pilot for Apollo 15) and Dr. Benjamin Carson who, at age 36, was the first surgeon to successfully separate Siamese twins – the Binder twins. (Dr. Carson was awarded the Presidential Medal of Freedom, the highest civilian award in the United States.)

This voyage, which became a formative experience in my life, opened my mind to the "Global Village" in which we live. And I was then sure of this: you could be poor and happy while overcoming your obstacles and your demons, and you could also be rich and still be very unhappy.

I had *"zigzagging" questions haunting me during my voyage: why the highest longevity record in the world wasn't found in areas that were technology meccas? But instead found in Cachemire, or far away in Afghanistan, India, China, Peru, or an Ogimi village in Japan... and why the US population benefiting from state-of-the-art medical care had a shorter life span than Europeans?

Enduring Legacy: Crying wolf the *"Zigzagging" Urgency

"What I see are the current devastation, the frightening disappearances of living species, be they plants or animals. Because of its current density, the human species is living in a type of internally poisonous regime."
- **Claude Levi-Strauss**

Why the *"Zigzagging" Urgency to change our ways as individuals and as a species? Although any such number is somewhat subjective, from 160 to 200 million people died in wars during the 20th century. All Earth Citizens can witness now, lenders and markets going even after democracies. As we look at planet Earth we realize that 3 factors helped to enslave us for ages.

You enslave individuals and nations through 3 weapons:
1. Hunger
2. Debt
3. Energy Shortage

*"Zigzagging" Urgency demands we swim against the tide, and that these Global issues be addressed since they are affecting all the citizens of our Global Village.

To neutralize these 3 weapons and free themselves, a new generation of *"zigzagging" Earth Citizens need to:
1. Empower a Global Rule of Law
2. Restore the Habeas Corpus (USA)
3. Embrace the Golden Rule
4. Respect the Universal Declaration of Human Rights (1948)

86

Modern society has left the lessons of the forest far behind. In its search for technological advancement, it is sowing seeds of destruction, seeds which can destroy the beauty and harmony of our world for a long time to come. The *"zigzagging" lessons of the *Bhagavad Gita* and *The Tao Te Ching,* along with many others, contain important seeds of truth for humanity.

Taking the road "less traveled by" once again, made it possible for me to come in close contact with Global Issues. I have tried in a modest way to give a voice to the indigenous peoples, and since 2009 I have been working on translating some of the works of Dr. Jacques Attali for Lexpress and Attali.com. (Jacques Attali of France, was Special Adviser to the President of the Republic from 1981 to 1991, and President of Planet Finance, which advises and finances the development of the microfinance in 80 countries.)

As I reflect upon the multiple *"zigzagging" turns I went through in my life, I can't help but embrace John Harricharan's wisdom found in these words: **"When You Can Walk on Water, Take the Boat."**

*"Zigzagging" means to *be bold* and to *challenge yourself: to work your own miracles*. It is a needed reminder of the inner power we all possess as we struggle with life's challenges.

"Two roads diverged in a wood, and I – I took the one less traveled by. And that has made all the difference."
- Robert Frost

Resources:
The Power Pause - John Harricharan
Surviving the Crises - Jacques Attali, President of Planet Finance

About author.

Dr. Joel Bomane *was born in the French West Indies and left home at age 17. He traveled extensively and later trained as a pastor and physician, serving at Mother Teresa's Missionaries of Charity...USA – INDIA, coming personally into close contact with death and suffering for many years. He has had the privilege of meeting Doctor and Professor "Henri Perrimond" from La Timone Hospital - Pediatric Hematology Unit, in France. Joel is now tackling global issues, being a forceful advocate for peace-building and human dignity with Universal Values. Ever since his enlightened meeting in the early 90's with famed neurosurgeon Dr. Benjamin Carson (who was the first to separate a pair of Siamese twins), Joel has been exploring with passion, "The Role of the Brain in Human History." Empathy is NOT a Business Plan: **www.joelbomane.com.**

*B*ut Wisdom is Shown to be Truth by What Results From It.

~ Matthew 11:19

True Stories & Lessons from Those Who Overcame Calamity

From Heartbreak to Heartbreak – A Survivor's Story

by Helen Maria

How do you explain to a five-year-old that Daddy won't be coming home tonight to take the family to his school's open house because Daddy is once again too preoccupied getting drunk with his friends?

I knew when my husband did not show up in time to take us to the open house that his drinking and drug use had once again gotten in the way of his family obligations. Our son had been very excited about going to open house that Thursday night, but as soon as my husband finished eating dinner he was adamant that he needed to go see his friend, reassuring our son that he would be back in time to take us to the open house.

My heart sank when I realized that my husband lied again. Sighing to myself I knew another promise had been broken, and this time it not only affected me, but our son suffered the consequences as well. It hurt deeply to watch our little boy crying, continually asking for daddy. But daddy never showed.

Out of pride I did not want anyone knowing about my husband's drinking or his drug habits – especially the children – so I usually stayed home alone with my children, seldom going out to socialize. By praying for him and keeping his substance abuse a secret from everyone, I believed I was being a faithful, God-fearing woman. Over time I had made countless excuses for his behavior because I wanted to believe he would change one day. Thankfully for the children's sake, at least my husband would leave the house to do his partying. At first he left only on the weekends to go to the local tavern or to his friend's house, but it soon became a nightly ritual.

My husband was an angry drunk. The more he drank the more belligerent he became. Not wanting the children to be disturbed by any outbursts of rage when he returned late at night from his partying, I always stayed up until he got home in case he needed my help. My hope was that by being the perfect, submissive, helpful wife, we could eventually live the family life I had always

90

dreamed of having. Every day I hoped and prayed he would quit drinking and partying, and stay home with his family.

Long before the disappointing episode with the open house I had promised myself to seek professional help regarding my husband's alcohol problems. Once he discovered my intentions he assured me that he did not have a drinking problem and was going to prove it by not drinking every day. I believed him and was grateful at the thought of no more drunken escapades. I was encouraged that our problems could be resolved without outside help so I decided not to seek counseling.

My newfound hope turned once again into disillusionment when, sadly, my husband began substituting "crank" for alcohol. Crank kept him alert, energized, and motivated. He would be awake for several days at a time, working on projects around the house, followed by weekend-long sleep-fests. He began losing weight, and I was shocked to see him slowly killing himself. When he brought home a gun and explained it was for our safety, I knew we were in deep trouble then; the problem had escalated to a more serious level. Tormented, I feared that he was now dealing drugs.

Fearing my husband was possibly a gun-toting drug dealer made me feel so frightened for him and for our children that I could hardly sleep at night. And there was little I could do to ease my weary mind. Projects around the house began increasing in number, and one project was left unfinished to start another. Our basement was becoming cluttered from his midnight runs at rummaging through dumpsters in the backs of stores, and our backyard began looking like a wrecked car lot.

What was really hurtful was that my husband seemed oblivious to the needs of his family. Each payday before he left to go partying, I had to literally beg for money so I could buy food for the house and pay our bills. The reality of his substance abuse became overwhelming! I did not know how much longer I could continue hiding his activities or explaining away his mood swings unless I started lying for him, which is the one thing I promised myself I would never do. No longer able to manage the situation alone, I finally went to see a Christian Counselor for help.

The Counselor explained, "The mere fact he quit drinking to use drugs shows he is chemically dependent. He merely changed his drug of choice. You are living with an alcoholic/addict, and if he does not get help or seek medical treatment, your life will only get worse." I could not explain to the Counselor why I was willing to tolerate my husband's demeaning behavior, other than I loved him. My belief system had not allowed me to get a divorce, yet this disease was destroying my life! I knew it was time to confront my husband, but I had no clue how I was going to convince him that he had a substance abuse problem and needed help. I cried all the way home from the Counselor's office wondering how I was going to survive this overwhelming disease.

One morning as my husband and I ate breakfast together before he left for work, I somehow found the courage to open a dialogue with him about his addiction. When I reminded him that he had missed our son's open house, to my surprise my husband's face immediately grew somber and he replied, "I'm sorry, I forgot all about it." I knew in my heart this was the right moment to discuss not only our son's disappointment, but whether or not my husband could control his drug use.

Drained physically and emotionally, I felt I had nothing to lose. I found myself speaking factually about the effects of alcoholism on a person's life, explaining to him what I had learned at my Counseling session. I suggested that maybe it was no longer recreational using and perhaps his had become an addiction. Knowing the importance of not appearing condescending, I chose my words carefully. I even suggested he consider going into a treatment program to help him gain control of his addiction and change his lifestyle.

After my husband left for work, I sat amazed thinking about our conversation. I realized the trip to the Counselor gave me courage and the knowledge about addiction that I had just shared with my husband, and it was the first time we were able to discuss his substance abuse without arguing. Later that evening when he came home from work, he spent the rest of the evening with my son, laughing, playing games, and watching television.

The next day my husband did something that completely took me aback! He came home early from work after explaining to his supervisor that he was checking himself into the hospital to take care of his drinking problem. On Monday morning, March 14, 1987, of his own will, my husband entered into a 30-day Alcohol Drug Treatment Program for his chemical dependencies.

I felt both relieved and proud at the same time. Naively I thought that all our problems would be solved, but alcoholism is a family disease affecting every member in the family either directly or indirectly, and I was informed by the program director that I was also going to need treatment. It never occurred to me that I was also part of the problem. While my husband was consumed with alcohol and drugs, I was consumed with his behavior... I was just as addicted to my husband's love and acceptance as he was to his alcohol and drug use. What an eye-opener! This knowledge caused my self-righteous world to crumble.

I became part of the out-patient program and soon, everything I knew or thought I knew was being questioned or challenged. I did not know what to think or how to feel. Years of suppressed feelings began emerging along with unresolved childhood issues over my father's drinking. I learned that I was considered an enabler; I had become a willing participant by pretending alcoholism did not exist in our home. I had grown up with alcoholism in my parent's home and was continuing to keep the disease alive and breathing in my own home now. How would my children ever be able to overcome this generational monster if I refused to face the fact that I had been in denial of it my entire life?

My desire to be a responsible loving parent was the motivation I needed to change my life around. Whether or not my husband stopped drinking or using drugs I learned was his responsibility. My challenge became, how can I be a good parent? Through God's help, I discovered that I had the power to change my behavior, that I was responsible for my own actions, and if I wanted to be a responsible parent I had to learn how to care for myself. Once I knew how to care for myself, then I could properly care for my children. My husband was an adult capable of making his own decisions, and I no longer felt responsible for his behavior.

In the out-patient program, I was introduced to the Twelve Steps of Alcoholics Anonymous (AA) program. A 12-step program is designed to get one's focus onto a Power greater than oneself in order to restore sanity and to equip oneself with the knowledge of God's will for life. Our journey together had lots of bumps, curves, and some dead ends, but my husband and I handled each one by applying principles we learned in the 12-Step program. Even though my husband eventually lost his job during this sobering process, we relocated the family to another state in order to start a new life soberly, vigorously, and with passion!

Proudly we realized the American dream! We were self-employed (we had started two home-based businesses), had three beautiful children, lived in our new house by the lake, and loved and cared for each other very much.

But then tragedy struck.

On May 4, 1997, my husband was killed in a tragic automobile accident. He had fallen asleep at the wheel while driving home late one night from a job assignment and his truck went off the road, down a ravine, and into a tree. He died in the life flight helicopter on the way to the hospital.

I was devastated! My heart cried out for my children and for the loss of their daddy! Losing my husband would have been unbearable except for this comfort: I found the inspiration I needed to continue with my life in Step 11 of AA which states, "Sought through prayer and meditation to improve our conscious contact with God, as we understood Him, praying only for knowledge of His will for us and the power to carry that out."

Today, I am enjoying what I call the abundant life, doing everything I love! I believe I have developed my life into a message of good news for all generations because of my triumphs over alcoholism, drugs, co-dependency, abuse, mental illness, divorce, single parenting, and the death of loved ones. I believe everyone can rise above any difficult circumstance and live their dreams!

About author.

Helen Maria teaches in Learning Centers and Private Schools as well as ministering to children of all nationalities in Children's Church. She has been invited to speak an encouraging word to Women's Support Groups, Church Life Groups, Networking Seminars, Inspirational Conferences, and over the World Wide Web on Streaming Faith. She is currently serving as the Children's Pastor at The Wisdom Center in Fort Worth, Texas. Read more inspirational messages at **www.HelenMaria.com**.

The Unfolding Journey of Living Free of Addiction

by Mark Semple

I never really thought that I had a drinking problem. I simply loved to do it. My family drank. Everyone I met drank. Drinking was simply a normal, natural part of everyday life. It was drinking to excess or at inopportune times that wasn't.

I had a great upbringing – a loving family with devoted parents who spent as much time as possible doing meaningful things with us. My father was in the military, so his life was not really his own. And the nomadic lifestyle did introduce us kids to certain pleasures at an early age: like drinking.

I started drinking heavily in my teens. I loved the feeling alcohol provided – the glow, the can-do-anything energy. I was relatively shy and self-conscious when I was younger. Alcohol released me from that.

My life continued as a fun-filled haze when I entered the work force. Again, I found myself surrounded by people who drank to excess. Thus, there were no consequences experienced from my drinking.

My other love was riding my motorcycle at excessive speeds on twisty English country roads. One night, I made the near-fatal mistake of combining alcohol and riding, and woke up in the hospital with a shattered leg and stitches in my head. The next few days were a blur. I developed blood clots in my lungs and was on the edge of death. My mother was by my side for 48 hours straight, and I was oblivious to it.

The following six months were pure hell! In a full leg cast and on blood-thinning medications, I was not permitted to drink. However, I could think of nothing else but getting back on a motorcycle and drinking again.

Pure insanity.

I jumped on an opportunity to come to the United States when I was 22 years old. It was pure heaven for me. Having moved my entire life, coming to a new country solo was no big deal, especially as alcohol would enable me to quell any feelings of loneliness or homesickness.

Once again, I found myself in an environment of people who drank to excess, and my drinking continued unabated. Life felt really good at the time – lots of fun, no responsibilities – just one big party.

I got married to a lady who served at the bar I frequented, and we "settled down" together (*with alcohol being our constant companion*).

Starting to drink more at home, I stopped frequenting the bars, but life became a drag. There just wasn't any fun or excitement anymore. I started drinking even more to escape the feelings of boredom and my mundane life.

My relationship with my wife and son deteriorated, and the home space became a negative, toxic place to live inside. Of course, it had nothing to do with my drinking….

I continued on this downward spiral until my second son was born in 1991. At that moment, I realized that something had to change. His birth quite literally saved my life.

My journey in recovery and sobriety had begun.

I commenced seeing a family counselor to determine what my family's problems were and how we could get them straightened out. He had the audacity to suggest that I may be the problem!!!

Being committed to my family, I was willing to explore any possibility, and listened to what he had to say. I wasn't willing at that time to admit I was an alcoholic, albeit I did acknowledge that I drank heavily and often. I did not consider it to be a problem, though. Drinking was the only thing I did for *me* – the only real friend and love I knew. Why should I give that up?

Because it was killing me and destroying everything I held dear.

After a few more counseling sessions, I agreed to explore other avenues of dealing with alcohol. After a brief period of time, I could not deny it anymore… I was an alcoholic.

One simple fact was apparent to me: if I wanted to have a meaningful, productive, fulfilling life, I had to stop drinking. This absolutely terrified me at the time. I simply could not perceive life without alcohol.

Again, I was willing and stepped out onto the ledge.

It hit me hard. I felt as though I had jumped out of a moving car and found myself dealing with instant anxiety and depression.

When someone starts drinking heavily, their emotional development becomes inhibited. There I was at age 30, with the emotional maturity of a

96

teenager. I was totally unprepared to deal with life awake, as I had never had to before, and thus never learned how. I had to sober up, grow up, and step up to be the son, brother, father, husband, and employee I desired to be.

Initially it wasn't easy. I was quite upset that I could not drink. I stopped watching sports because it became apparent that I really didn't like them. I watched them because they were synonymous with drinking. Likewise, my social circle disappeared.

It became apparent to me that this journey was not so much about stopping drinking as it was about *living sober*. If I was going to be alone and miserable, what would be the point of denying myself alcohol? Many people return to the hell of drinking because they do not learn how to live a fulfilling life. They clean up the wreckage of the past, keep the demon of their addiction at bay, yet do not replace it with something truly fulfilling. Eventually, life just feels bland or boring.

As addicts/alcoholics are instant-gratification people, they know the instant solution, which to the casual observer, is sheer insanity. Why would anyone want to go back after they put so much effort into escaping?

Addiction is a disease. A very patient disease that you cannot be cured of. If you succumb, you will find yourself back where you left off in a very short period of time. It is that powerful.

Imagine life to be a piece of farmland. While drinking or using, the land gets neglected, littered with debris and rocks, and covered with weeds. As you embrace a sober life, you begin to clear that land. The junk is removed, the weeds are dug up, and the soil is turned.

Thus, you have a beautiful, fertile piece of land where once you had a wasteland. The opportunity now is to plant something worthwhile on it. If you do not, that soil is going to produce something – and it probably won't be beneficial. As time passes, it falls into disarray again, which rapidly creates an emotional space that requires instant solace.

Thus, living sober is about establishing and maintaining a space that is emotionally fulfilling and sustaining. Life is always going to be life. There will still be accidents, job losses, death, divorce, war, etc. – none of which we have any control over. We do have control over the extent to which such events affect us and how our journey continues to unfold.

It is somewhat akin to physical fitness. The more you care for your body on a regular basis, the better chance you will have of staying healthy or of returning to a healthy state faster if you became sick.

Waiting until you are sick or have a heart attack is way too late to start thinking about a fitness regimen. At that point, all your resources are devoted to surviving and just getting better.

97

Establishing and maintaining a better space for yourself is your greatest asset in maintaining sobriety. When you are peaceful and content, you won't feel the need for a quick fix. When you are living a life of faith and trust, fear and other negative emotions simply cannot exist in your space, and thus, will have no power over you.

Note that, for an addict/alcoholic, using a substance is always going to be in the back of their mind. It is simply a part of their wiring. Notice when a digital clock loses power then comes back on; it will flash 12:00 until reset. That is the default setting. *Using* is the default setting for those with the addiction persuasion.

Your opportunity in this instance is to ensure that your "power supply" is like the backup battery. When your resolve is tested, you have sufficient reserves to support you and maintain your preferred space, and not resort to your default setting.

Perspective is a crucial asset to maintaining this space. While early on I was bitter because I couldn't drink, the energy was totally different when I CHOSE not to drink and entered a space of not wanting to drink. When an addict/alcoholic puts a substance in their body, they are unable to control it.

Knowing this is a great asset. Yes, alcohol is my weakness. But today, knowing my weakness is my greatest strength.

Although I initially felt that I was losing something and that I had to give up drinking, it pales in significance when I consider what I have gained by choosing to live sober.

I have the love of my children today, whereas my older son used to despise me and look forward to my absence. My mother knew me as the man she raised me to be before she passed, and not the drunken boy she saw me as, all too often. My youngest son has never seen me take a drink and sees how life can be fulfilling and exciting without alcohol.

And, I have a life! I embrace each day as the gift it truly is, and look forward to the uncertain future with excitement and hope.

All because I choose to live sober, one day at a time.

About author.

*What is that next step to move you forward on your journey? If nothing changes, nothing will change. How much longer do you want to continue living as you are? The right coach supports you in finding clarity and purpose, and walks alongside you in meaningful changes in your life. Email: **Coach@successfultogethercoaching. com** to get started on living your best life.*

Ten Steps Into Light: Surviving Childhood Abuse

by Julette Millien

Growing up in Trinidad, I knew a little girl who went from healed and whole, to broken and pained.

She was pretty, very smart, and full of ambition and imagination of the "better" life. Life in Trinidad was at first all fun and innocence. Then, it changed drastically: she was introduced to the grown up world of sexuality, erotic feelings, and all that comes along with moving too fast along the timeline of life.

Her name was Judy and she so enjoyed a good game of hopscotch! She also enjoyed reading and pretending to be a teacher by spreading books out on her mother's bed and giving them each a name (of her friends at school). She pretended to teach them all that she knew. Judy loved pleasing her Mom and felt horrible when she caused any disruptions in the peace, so she went out of her way to be good, smart and helpful.

When she was about seven, this responsibility of "keeping things peaceful" became the source of her own internal chaos. You see, it was then that a favorite uncle started to abuse her.

The beginning was simple, easy and even fun. He would sit in the family's living room and begin to make suggestive (and secretive) eye and mouth gestures. Judy had no clue why this "flattering" attention needed to be hidden from others, and it seemed especially hidden from her uncle's wife. In her little-girl's head, she surmised that it had something to do with her aunt's sometimes real (and sometimes fake) intolerance for his playful ways.

She could only giggle – quietly – when he would look at her, and move his eyes down her still innocent body.

The first time she followed him to her "classroom" – her mother's bed where she played school – she realized this "relationship" with her fun uncle was now her big dark secret.

For Judy, the weight of that secret was matched only by the excitement of receiving such affirming attention. She didn't understand it but there was a seed

99

of uncertainty growing in her emotions. An absent father and siblings created uncertainty and a constant need for attention, affirmation and acknowledgement. *Was she lovable enough so others wouldn't leave? Was she pretty enough to have friends? Was she good enough to have a regular home with a regular family?*

The excitement was also sexual. Feelings not understood were beginning to grow; sensations were new and enticing. Her "fun" uncle seemed to understand and was willing to provide a place to feel them "safely."

When the secret became a burden, and the guilt began to eat away at her very Catholic conscience, Judy started to dread being around "fun" uncle. Some coaxing and forcing was now needed, but sadly, the "good" feelings betrayed her. Still feeling that sensation when violated was as confusing as confusing gets. The "good" (or natural) mixed with the bad, resulted in only more bad.

Her sense of being dirtied, bad, different and inadequate was confirmed by other experiences where the parents of school friends didn't see her as good enough for their girls. Having sexual experiences under her belt, she felt quite grown and worldly, so when presented with an opportunity to show her friends how grown she was, she demonstrated how drinking rum was "no big deal." Yes, at age 8 she showed her little friends how to put a bottle to their head and take a taste! Their parents didn't take too kindly to this and dismissed little precocious and slightly buzzed Judy from their home *and* from their daughters' lives. It was a sad walk home, Judy tells me. She felt as big as the 8 ounce rum bottle she had just showed off with.

This experience was confirmation that she was basically no good. That feeling went deep into her soul and manifested in all sorts of ways. When you feel/believe you are no good, you pull people to you who will treat you in such a way as to confirm this belief.

Little Judy made a horrendous mistake, one which increased the pain, guilt and shame that had taken root in her soul. She did not tell her mother, or anyone, for that matter. No one was allowed to know this big dark secret. She felt responsible for what was done to her and was not sure how anyone, particularly her mother, would respond to the news – would she be believed, comforted or disciplined?

There was no way of knowing, so she was silent.

Even doing fun things like being taught to swim, became an opportunity to be touched. She felt as if a big red sign was on her pretty dark curls saying, "Here, I'm no longer innocent, fondle me!"

Sadly and not surprisingly, Judy went on to be violated by other uncles, a friend's grandfather, and also by a boy who she thought was a caring friend – in this case, experiencing full blown date rape at 16.

100

If only she had come to me. I would have hugged her and comforted her and assured her of God's love for her. If only she had reached out to me, her wiser inner guide. But she didn't. She was very clever about keeping her secret from everyone, including herself.

I became aware of her pain when I was 26. It was then I reached out to my little girl within and grieved the loss of our childhood.

Becoming aware and knowledgeable by reading everything available on childhood sexual abuse added to my tool kit of strategies for being able to handle the consequences of this all too common violation. One in four girls are violated in the U.S., often by someone they know. It is estimated that over 40 million Americans experienced sexual abuse in childhood.

It was soothing to my soul to learn that what I was experiencing were "normal" reactions and coping mechanisms for a wounded child on her path to womanhood: broken relationships, challenges with intimacy, emotional dependency, fear of abandonment and betrayal, trigger-sharp sensitivity, low self-esteem, guilt and shame, thinking I caused these attacks on my innocence by being basically a bad seed, emotional numbness and disconnect, a yearning for perfection and an unforgiving heart.

In addition to my belief in a forgiving God who loved me as I was, an excellent therapist, Dr. Valerie Bryant in Brooklyn, NY, helped me turn my living hell into something bearable.

I became aware that my emotional/spiritual/psychological growth was essentially stunted. While I grew physically, my emotions, psyche and spiritual world were stuck in time. I was a hurt little girl, confused and riddled with shame, trying to make it in a grown up world

And I did!

Any exposure to inappropriate sexual experience IS abuse, so if you are a survivor of abuse – if there was ANY violation of your childhood innocence of a sexual nature, which can be physical, verbal, visual or auditory – and you are reading this, BELIEVE me when I tell you that YOU CAN OVERCOME! If you have any amount of hesitation about your ability to overcome this challenge, believe me that you CAN overcome it!

My journey to being healed and whole began at age 16, on my way back home from the mall, as I read the first pages of *The Art of Loving*, by Eric Fromm. I decided then that I wanted to love and be loved in a deep and healthy way. I longed for peace and joy, and I knew enough to know I could only have love, peace and joy by being healed and whole.

My journey was a long and difficult one, due in part to my own decisions and mindset. I didn't seek therapy until my first marriage was on the decline (in my early 40's). Neither did I share the burden with my mother, nor did I truly give it to God. I also denied the facts of my childhood by burying them way below the water line of my consciousness. This all helped to keep me in the dark.

Here are the 10 steps I took to wellness and light as I realized God's promise for my life:

1. I **gave it to God through prayer, scripture and meditation** (I SURRENDERED!) and allowed my spirit to lead my thoughts and emotions; I made a commitment to my healing.

2. I **grew my capacity to love**… by loving people.

3. I **wrote it all out,** keeping a journal and writing letters to my abusers.

4. I **learned about my syndrome.** Readings in psychology and self-development provided valuable insights. Knowing why I was the way I was empowered me to press on through the challenging times.

5. I faced the truth and **allowed myself to feel the pain** – raw and real.

6. I accepted that to receive the peace, joy, love, grace and prosperity I sought, **I had to first sow it... I had to *give it* and *be it* in order to receive it.** (Essentially, I behaved as though I was healed before I was.)

7. I was **physically active and healthy** – with daily workouts, healthy habits, etc.

8. I came to **know my passion/purpose** and chose to live a life of **service and kindness.**

9. I realized my painful youth was a way for me to bless others, by **telling the story.**

10. I **decided to forgive** all my violators, and I began praying for their well-being.

    It was clear that holding on to anger, guilt or shame was blocking my blessings. I had to forgive all, including myself. **I forgave myself** for blaming myself and carrying all that unnecessary guilt and shame for so long.

On advice from my wise therapist, I had a little chat with my little girl and asked her to take her rightful place in my life – in my heart. I hugged her deep and long and allowed her to go. I did tell her though that if she ever felt the need to be stroked or comforted, I would be here for her.

How can you start/continue your healing today?

102

About author.

Julette Millien *is passionate about making our world a better place TODAY, and about working with people who share this passion. She believes "We get better so we can do better and serve more." A survivor of childhood sexual abuse, she broke through the chains of lack and limitation to live a life of love, prosperity and service. Connect with her at* ***www.JuletteMillien.com****, or* ***Facebook.com/ JuletteMillien****.*

This Is Not The Life I Ordered

by Erica Davis

I was born to be an athlete! My mom says I came kicking and practically running out of the womb. I was born in Red Bluff, California and grew up in Lodi, California. I am the middle child in between two athletic brothers. They taught me how to be tough, competitive and positive. My entire family has a love for sports. I have been a tomboy since I got my running legs and started as early as the fourth grade with my first 5K running race. I have participated in sports of all kinds: flag football (49 touchdowns in one year), volleyball, basketball, and softball (to name a few), often being named as MVP. Most recently, I participated in my 1st celebrity golf tournament.

After earning my degree in Exercise Science and teaching credentials from Pacific Union College, I went on to teach high school PE, health, and basketball in Hawaii. That's where I got the itch for triathlons. My first tri was in October 2005 where I took 6th in my division. Being the competitor that I am, my sights were set on one day competing in the Hawaii Ironman (2.4 mile swim, 112 mile bike, 26.2 mile run). It was during that time that I was accepted into the Masters Program at Sacramento State University in Kinesiology for Strength and Conditioning. I had my course in life all mapped out, but my sports training and education were about to be put to the test beyond what I could have ever imagined.

Later in 2005, on December 27th, I woke up with the worst backache I had ever had. Being tough-minded, I brushed it off as soreness from the previous day's work out. Three days later, the pain turned into tingling that spread down throughout my legs. That's when I knew something was wrong. After six hours in the ER, they sent me home with a prescription for muscle spasms. By late evening I couldn't support my weight on my legs and had to crawl back to my bedroom. On December 31st, I mustered up enough strength to walk to the couch from the stairs while holding on to walls and door frames. That was the last unsupported day I walked! As I was being transported by ambulance to UC Davis, we were in route as the clock struck midnight. I asked the driver to turn on the sirens to help me ring in my new life! I didn't know what was in store for me next, but I did know that as life was throwing me a curve ball, it wasn't a pitch that I was going to miss.

I was misdiagnosed with Transverse Myelitis, although it's actually called Cavernous Hemangioma, an abnormal cluster of blood vessels which is

104

not that uncommon and rarely has such devastating results. However, in my case (only one in five million), this cluster of vessels ruptured, and a microscopic droplet of blood made its way into my spinal column causing inflammation nine inches up and down my spinal cord. The pressure on my spine from the swelling damaged the nerves, paralyzing me from below the chest down.

Now, it would be understandable if I had felt resentful about the misdiagnosis when I first went to the ER. Or that I was one of the rare statistics that this happened to. But that just wasn't in my character or spirit. My family's focus has always been centered on faith, family and sports. The realization of having my life as an athlete (which defined me) being taken away from me was inconceivable and all consuming! My reaction to the injury exposed me to a soulful part of my being which I had never known. I grew up in a faith based home, learning to be tough and positive… I don't like the word *can't!* But now the rubber was meeting the road. In this case, it was my wheelchair and the road. I could take the high road or one that would lead nowhere.

A few weeks after returning home, my parents introduced me to a man who was an avid handcyclist. He gently rekindled my passion for exercise and athletics, but in a new way. For the first time since the one in five million diagnoses, I was back in the game. The sun on my face, the wind at my back, and I was smiling ear to ear. Enthusiasm had met faith and determination. Handcycling became the first of more than 20 adapted sports that I would explore, some of which I have pursued in the competitive arena and continue to do so.

I have four jobs now. Training, recovery, inspire/mentor, and making a difference. It's my job to be out there showing EVERYONE, both able-bodied and the injured, that anything you want to do you CAN do! So when I was approached by the Challenged Athletes Foundation to be the first woman to wheel/push to the summit of Mt. Kilimanjaro in Africa (the largest free standing mountain in the world), I didn't hesitate in saying, YES!

Soon after I finished with the cycling season in the fall of 2009, I put my bike away and focused my entire existence on making history by doing what most would only see as unimaginable: climbing Mt. Kilimanjaro.

You ask why would I do this? My answer is, why not! All I can say is that something like this brings out more in you than what you thought was ever possible. The expedition team arrived in Tanzania, Africa, after dark on January 24, 2010. Excitement was in the air and I could hardly wait until daybreak to get the first real glimpse of Mt. Kilimanjaro. Sometime around 5:30 p.m. on January 31, 2010, I, Erica Davis, made history as the first paraplegic woman to summit Mt. Kilimanjaro, along with my fellow challenged athlete, Tara Butcher. My team carried me out of my chair to the point of summit to take pictures near the celebrated summit sign. Even though it was sub-zero temperature, warmth filled me as the realization of what we had accomplished surged through our tired and freezing bodies. Yes, I say "we" because in life you need a team.

It was awe-inspiring! Being a Christian and looking around at the beauty God had created, here at the roof of Africa.... So what day stands out for you in your life? Maybe the brightest journey is yet to be, and maybe you are in the middle of it and don't know it. Whatever it is, seize the day! Don't let ANYTHING derail your life's purpose. For me, I know I will always be an athlete. I will always attempt to inspire, and wherever I go and whatever I do, it will be to make a difference for at least one person. But hey, I made it to the top of Kili. I made history. And I CAN do anything! Between you and me, I always knew I would make it to summit!

In 2010 I received the "Paul Mitchell Spirit Award" and competed in several marathons and triathlons. I've taken up wheelchair dancing, and for charity, have repelled off the top of the tallest west coast waterfront building, which is the Hyatt Manchester Regency in San Diego. My friend and publicist extraordinaire Susan Gibson chuckles when she says "I'm the REAL Push Girl."

This Fall I head to New Zealand as the national champion representing the U.S. at the World Championships for Paratriathlon – the highest level for paratriathletes. Then, it's on to NYC for the marathon representing Achilles International. Life IS the adventure. You just have to show up! For me it's in a chair, but that does not define **who** I am, **where** I go, and **what** I do.

You know, my mom cried the first year and a half after my injury. But she stopped the day she heard me speak, and shared that if I could turn back time and live my life as if my injury hadn't happened, I would choose the chair. It has taken me on a path to meet people, experience life, and challenge myself in ways I would never have known. The best is yet to be because I have plans as tall as Mt. Kilimanjaro!

About author.

Erica's journey to Kili was turned in to an award winning documentary, "Through The Roof," by Captured Life Productions. Proceeds benefit the Challenged Athletes Foundation. Erica Davis is a 30 year old woman living in San Diego, CA and is a sought after international speaker, contributing author, and one amazing woman making a difference wherever she goes. Erica has graced the cover of publications as far away as India and Africa, is Paul Mitchell's sponsored female challenged athlete, and is featured on 24 Hour Fitness Club signage. Erica still has the goal of the Hawaii Ironman and also has her sights set on the 2016 Paralympics. Go to www.gowitherica.com to learn more about what she is up to next, become her cheerleader, and help her make a difference around the world with her upcoming reality show.

The Incredible Strength of Family Glue

by Adria Manary

When tragedy strikes at home, the family glue thickens. The only thing that matters is helping each other get through the situation. The things that seemed so important prior to the crisis suddenly have little to no meaning at all.

I am grateful to say that my childhood was very much like the old show, *Leave It to Beaver*, and my small family stayed very close throughout my young adult years. I had all four of my grandparents until I was 30, and I talked to my mom almost every day. However, like the saying goes, the taller you are, the harder you fall, I feel the same holds true that the more you are loved and supported, the harder it is when the primary source of both is gone.

After losing both of my parents the same year to the cruel and merciless disease of cancer, and both of my grandmothers passing away shortly thereafter, I was so emotionally drained I didn't feel like myself anymore. I didn't function as I used to, and felt that my children had lost me almost as much as I had lost my own mom. It seemed there would be no end to the grief that overwhelmed me when we received yet another dreaded phone call upon returning home from the fourth family funeral in two years. It was my husband's doctor. The test results were in and our fears had materialized. He too, had cancer.

I will never forget the look on his face when he hung up the phone, for it was so unselfish. He knew what I had gone through and dreaded being the one to add more pain. Although he was dealing with the shock of his own prognosis, when he took me in his arms it was to comfort me. It was yet another example of his unwavering care and concern for me and our children, and it was in that moment that the rest of the world fell away, and our own family glue not only thickened, but was cemented.

During the next month we researched every possible treatment and chose the one we felt was best for his situation. However, the only place that offered it was all the way across the country. Against most of the advice I received from others, I chose to pack up the whole family and move to an apartment near the hospital for the three months he would be in treatment. We actually rented two apartments so that I could homeschool my eldest son upstairs as well as have a place for all three of them to play when daddy needed to rest.

After enduring and completing the three months of treatments, our dear cousins offered us their home in Southern California to recuperate for a month before returning home. They had been very supportive throughout Joel's treatments, and were headed to Paris for the summer. They knew us well, and felt that the safety and solitude of their home was just what we needed. They were right. The decision to stay that extra month was a very good one for all of us, especially for me. It gave me some time before returning home to the commotion we would be facing, to start the healing process from the overwhelming grief I had dealt with for so long.

There were many special moments during our California adventure, but one in particular stands out in my mind, mostly because I cannot explain it... at least not in earthly terms. During the last week of our stay it was clear to me where we needed to visit before we left, which was Disneyland of course! The happiest place on earth. The place where dreams come true. The childlike delight that comes over you the moment you step through the gates of Disneyland covered us all like a blanket when we arrived. The chill of pain and uncertainty that had lingered in our bones for months was finally warmed and almost forgotten... at least for the next 12 hours. None of us wanted to leave, so we decided to bring a bit of the "magic" home with us. The kids picked out a Disney movie that they could all agree on, and we added it to our bag of souvenirs.

As we settled in that evening, our three little "Mouseketeers" laid on the floor on blankets in front of the TV. I sat on the floor behind them with my feet under the coffee table and my mind somewhere else entirely. The fear of what our future held had come back with a vengeance.

I smiled every time one of the kids looked back at me, but I was crying on the inside. I began thinking about my mom, and how much I missed her... especially now. I longed for her loving shoulder to cry on, her gentle guidance, and the special way she could make even the darkest day a little brighter.

My daughter brought me back from my angst when she got up rather abruptly and walked back to me almost in a daze. I thought she had fallen asleep. What happened next, however, made me feel like I was the one who was dreaming. Since I was sitting on the floor, her eyes met mine directly as she stood next to me. She didn't say a word at first, and then she cupped my face into her tiny little hands, like I had done with her hundreds of times. I always thought she had my mom's brown eyes, but looking into them this time, it felt like my mom was actually the one looking back at me! It is still hard to explain, but not nearly as strange as what my daughter whispered to me in that moment.

108

"Don't worry mommy," she said. "Your mommy is still with you."

I couldn't believe my ears, but her words brought instant relief, and a sense of calm that I had not felt in two years. As she walked back over to the television and lay down next to her brothers, my mind was whirling. There was no doubt that my three-year-old daughter had delivered a message from my mom, the grandmother she was named after, so I tried to let the miracle of the moment sink deeply into my heart. I tried not to question how this could possibly have happened. I guess the family glue that I have been referring to also keeps us attached to our loved ones in heaven.

The point of this story is that a strange and wonderful thing happened during one of the worst possible times of our lives. It turned out to be four of the most meaningful and memorable months that we have ever had as a family, because only two things mattered: healing my husband and enjoying every moment together. The moral of the story is that it is okay to let the world go at times. It will certainly be there when you return, and it is sometimes necessary to heal completely before reentering the chaos of life.

© Adria Manary, 2013

About author.

Adria Manary has a unique blend of talents, and has held quite a few impressive titles… but her favorite and most important title will always be, "MOM"! As the mother of four incredible children and two amusing dogs, her home life is delightful and was the original inspiration for her bestselling book, "Mommy Magic – Creative Activities and Inspiring Stories to Deepen the Bond with Your Child." Recently released in its third edition, "Mommy Magic" is the flagship book in her new series, "The Magic of Life." With degrees in Psychology and Communications, Adria is also a sought after professional speaker who blends researched facts with inspiring stories about the very real magic of love… in the reality series we call life!

She is the author of four books, a contributing author to five more, and the singer/songwriter of her family music CD, "Precious Souls." During her career, two highlights for her were winning the Gold Award from the New York TV and Film Festival, and raising over a million dollars as the Director of Development for the New York Special Olympics.

*Adria has appeared on national television, including Lifetime Television and as a parenting expert on MSNBC, and been featured on dozens of local TV and radio shows such as Good Morning Oregon and Fox Morning News. She has also been featured in many newspapers and magazines. She may be reached at: **adria@ mommymagic.com**.*

109

Kick Cancer In The Can Because You Can!

Bad Dreams: A Dream or a Reality?

by Dr. Marilyn Joyce

Have you ever awakened from a really bad dream that seemed so real that it sent you into a spin about how you were going to deal with the nightmarish circumstances you *thought* you were confronting? And then the phone rang, or your child came into your bedroom to ask for something, and you realized, "Oh my God, I'm okay. It was just a dream. Whew!" And you made a huge sigh of relief, and then got on with your day?

We've all been there at some point, right? But what if you never wake up from that bad dream? What if, in fact, it turns out to be real? What if you just get deeper and deeper into the nightmare, and there seems to be no possible way out of it? And what if you actually get to the point of not being able to differentiate between the waking and the sleeping nightmare? It all just becomes one living hell!

Well, that describes exactly what the second half of the 1980's was like for me. Bad dreams and nightmares became a constant part of my sleeping life at that time, and there was no reprieve when I awoke and started each new day. It all became one ongoing living nightmare!

From the "Dream" Life...

On the surface I appeared to have the dream life: a business that was experiencing exponential growth, a beautiful home, the luxury car of my dreams, a healthy retirement account, global travel on a whim, eating in the finest restaurants everyday, you name it... I had arrived!

... To Bad Dreams Becoming Endless Nightmares!

And then one shocking and unexpected experience after another occurred. Sadly, my dearest friend and namesake, Marilyn, committed suicide the night before her proverbial (financial) ship sailed in. A few weeks later I was driving myself and two close friends to an important business meeting when at an intersection, a Cadillac ran the red light and rammed right into the middle of

110

my car! Miraculously no one was hurt, but the worst of it was that my two "close friends" filed a lawsuit against me for damages. (By the way, they lost!) These are only two serious occurrences of what was an endless barrage of crazy things that happened over that period of time.

Survivor And Thriver – Begins Shocking Journey

Being a survivor who always goes on to thrive, I wasn't going to let this series of bad dreams that were playing out in my waking – and sleeping – life, dampen or destroy my spirit. I picked myself up, dusted myself off, and began starting all over again! Life goes on – you can't wallow in your problems. You just have to keep pressing forward, and adjusting your course accordingly, finding solutions. Well, that was until the fateful day in September of 1985 when... I stared into the mirror early one morning and was horrified to see a big ugly shiny black spot under my right eye. How could this be happening just before a very important speaking event of mine? This "thing" had to be removed immediately!

Within hours I was seeing a dermatologist, who referred me to a skin cancer specialist. It was melanoma! No words can describe my shock and surprise. Whenever we are confronted with the big "C" word, it engenders fear and a sense of victimhood, a kind of "why me?" attitude.

Temporary Relief...

Fortunately we got this handled during the early stage of onset, so relief set in. However, it was a brief reprieve from the escalating nightmare. Less than 2 weeks later I was rushed into the hospital and diagnosed with stage 4 uterine cancer. I was only 35 years old! This was a form of cancer I had worked with often, and it was deadly. AND it was an older woman's illness. I found myself seething with resentment, frustration, anger, even hostility, and definitely denial.

But I Had Done All the Right Things, Or Had I?

In my mind I had been doing everything right. I had consumed a vegan diet for 14 years prior to this diagnosis. Yoga was the foundation of my day-to-day life. I walked miles everyday. And I released job stress by whimsical traveling and spontaneous "anything fun" activities.

From Doctor to Doctor – No Hope – Or Was There?

However, the nightmare thickened. I found myself going from doctor to doctor – both in my dreams at night, and during my waking hours. It became difficult to separate the nights from the days, and the dreams from reality. Especially when I was going through those horrendous chemotherapy treatments, I felt like I was suddenly removed from any reality I had ever known. And in fact, I was!

Over the following five years of going in and out of remission, an overwhelming sense of defeat set in. The nightmare became increasingly intense, and my hope for any form of life after cancer became just a dream of hope that had no chance in the face of this powerful and relentless nightmare. In my quest to find "the" answer that would end this nightmare, no stone was left unturned. Yet, just when hope was ever so briefly experienced in the form of a remission, it was just as quickly dashed into oblivion by another recurrence. And the nightmare again resumed its ever escalating and all-encompassing position in my life…

Until That Miracle Weekend That Changed Everything!

And I don't use the word "miracle" lightly. The fact is, *I should have been dead!* But I was not. In spite of all the odds against my survival, I was still here. But barely here: I was 88 pounds, in a wheelchair, and unable to eat any solid foods or drink any liquids. I could only suck on ice cubes and ice chips. And then my young hero entered…. At a home show, Jim the Vita-Mix man introduced me to ice chips with real living food blended into the chips. I went from plain water ice chips to real fruit infused ice chips.

Then that same weekend, Dr. Bernie Siegel introduced me to the Gratitude journal, and I was about to learn a truly profound lesson.

You know the expression, "*It's darkest just before the dawn*"? Well, that was exactly where I was. I was at the "darkest" possible place – and this miracle weekend was about to be my "dawn," my escape from the darkness of the continual nightmare I had been living, day and night, for 5 years. (The details of this journey are written in my book, *INSTANT E.N.E.R.G.Y.™: The 5 Keys to Unlimited Energy and Vitality!* So I won't spend a lot of time explaining it all here.)

From Terminal to Eternal

This miracle weekend of mine encompassed five very important lessons for overcoming any obstacle in life.

Lesson #1 – Quitters Never Win, Winners Never Quit:
How we relate to our experiences in life is more important than the experience. If we give up and quit, we lose. As a 98-year old woman (a 35 year cancer survivor at that point!) said to me in the Soviet Union in 1987, "It ain't over 'till it's over!" She told me in no uncertain terms to "stop pissing and moaning" about my life, and get on with it. Life is for the living, not the complainers and blamers! Midway through my cancer journey, this was a lot to swallow. But I got it. And I never gave up the fight, as daunting as it seemed at times. More than 23 years later, I can tell you that it was the best decision I have ever made.

Lesson #2 – Thoughts and Actions Shape Our Destiny:
We create our own reality by the thoughts we think and the actions we take, based on those thoughts. Here's a question I ask my patients: "Am I moving towards health, or am I moving away from illness?" Really think about this. (By

the way, this question can be used for anything in life.) If you're moving *away* from something, you're carrying/dragging that baggage behind you. If you're moving *towards* something, it's much lighter and much more positive. You're so focused on that forward positive "healthy" movement, that there is no time or attention wasted on the heavy negative stuff of the "moving away from" condition.

Lesson #3 – Gratitude Attitude Expands Possibilities:

Dr. Siegel challenged me on that fateful day in 1989 to get a journal and begin writing 5 *"gratitudes"* a day – 5 things I'm grateful for. The doc's caveat: if you can't think of 5 things to be grateful for, write the same thing 5 times! So the first day I wrote the same thing 5 times. But on day 30, I wrote 137 *gratitudes,* and they were all different! What we focus on expands – in every area of our lives, including what we have to be grateful for. That was 1989. It is now 2012! What do you think? Did it work?

Lesson #4 – Gotta Have Whole Food for A Whole (Healthy) Life:

Whole natural raw food, in whatever form, i.e. fresh raw veggies and fruits, sprouted legumes and grains, and raw, unsalted nuts and seeds. These foods contain essential life force, along with thousands of vital enzymes (catalysts for every metabolic function in the body), micro-nutrients (vitamins, minerals, antioxidants, phytochemicals, bioflavonoids, fiber), and macro-nutrients (proteins, carbohydrates and fats), that enhance your body's potential for living no matter how far down that rabbit hole of poor health or illness you may be. If you can't eat solid foods, or drink liquids, try ice chips with real food blended into them. You've got to start somewhere – and if it's ice cubes or ice chips, make them count for something.

Lesson #5 – Daily Hugs, Kisses and Love:

When was the last time you told someone you love, that you truly love her or him? This goes back to the "what you focus on expands" concept. Give love freely. Perform random acts of kindness. And just love unconditionally. Then watch the good start to happen!

I came from a very dysfunctional home, as many of us have, where we NEVER hugged, kissed, held hands, or said the "LOVE" word. So when each of my children reached their 25th birthday, I asked them what they loved about me, and what they disliked or even hated about me. You know what they said? You never hugged us, kissed us or told us that you loved us! Whew! I was blown away. Those conversations changed my life! I make it a rule today to tell at least 5 people everyday that I love them. I do it via phone, email, text, in person, whatever form shows up. And when I'm with people (I am known as a hugger) you can bet I hug everyone and everything in sight. No people, no problem! There are lots of trees and animals out there that need a hug!

Simply put, overcoming obstacles is about getting out of our own darned way! We can all find ways to be stuck in the obstacles of our lives as victims, or

113

we can change our perspective, our patterns of behavior, and our decisions about who and what is important to us, and become the victor in our lives! So, start with the above 5 strategies. And enjoy the ride of your life!

Oh, by the way... the nightmares ended soon after my "miracle" weekend, and they have never returned. Well, other than the occasional dream that's not a real ton of fun. And who doesn't have those from time to time? That's called LIFE! Or maybe, sleeping....

Sweet Dreams!

About author.

Dr. Marilyn Joyce, RD, T*he Vitality Doctor*™, Internationally acclaimed speaker, writer, best selling author, media personality, and 5-time cancer survivor, the former director of nutrition for "The Cancer Treatment Centers of America," will help you create **INSTANT *E.N.E.R.G.Y.*™** and outstanding health, in your life right now, using *5 simple, time-tested keys* that have already transformed thousands of lives from *life-less* to *life-full*!

For almost 40 years, Dr. Joyce has touched hundreds of thousands of lives globally as an inspirational & motivational speaker. She has been featured on such diverse shows as Leeza, Montel Williams, Maury Povich, Jenny Jones, Doctor to Doctor and Essentials on PBS, as well as hundreds of other media appearances, including radio and print. Her newest book, **INSTANT *E.N.E.R.G.Y.*™** is the *ultimate guide* to whole person health (Mind-Body-Spirit).

Visit her websites at: ***KickCancerInTheCan.com*** and ***TransformStressNow.com***. Email her at: ***info@MarilynJoyce.com***, or call her toll-free at **800-352-3443**. Begin today to create your own vital, energetic, healthy, happy life!

The Rollercoaster Ride of My Life... Chronic Illness and Its Lessons

by Camryn Oliver Lemmon

As an adopted child from birth, I didn't know the background of my birth parents. We were well-off, well-known, and I wanted for no material possessions. I credit mother for teaching me the skills to entertain judges, senators, and anyone of importance. My parents also made sure our family went to Sunday school and church every week, instilling a faith in God and knowledge of Jesus.

After completing my high school credits a year early, I left home, married, and began a life as a wife and soon-to-be mother. I registered at FSU (Florida State University) and began my college education. Over the next 20 years I worked hard to be a good wife and mom, and I made sure we always lived in good neighborhoods with the best school system. My son and daughter were given the best and taught the truth about life. I also instilled in them confidence to accomplish great things. They also learned to have faith in God.

My first marriage ended after 4 years when I found welts on my 3-year-old son's back that his dad had given him with a belt. I left my husband *that day.* He could hurt me, but NOT my children!

Single parenting wasn't easy. I worked a 9-to-5 job and took work home to do at night after my son Keith went to sleep. I also joined a cosmetic sales company to earn extra money. Soon, I joined a wonderful church. I remember one service with a band and a slideshow, and the overwhelming sense of love and calmness that enveloped me. This feeling I cannot accurately describe. Many would call it being "born again" in Christ. While attending that church, I went through the stages of "a new Christian" after being told previously in my life that I was *not* a Christian (which had a profound effect on me at the time). Soon, I became comfortable with my spirituality and learned to live my faith rather than constantly preach it. I loved learning about religions, and I became open to learning again. While not changing my own beliefs in the process, I nevertheless gained respect again for most all religions.

After six years as a single mom, I met my second husband, John. We met at a New Year's Eve party at midnight. We were married eight months later. He encouraged me to become the true entrepreneur I was at heart. My businesses and work became my main identity. I was well-known and well-liked. At one point, my father thought that I might like my adoption file. The file had stayed in storage until I was 31, at which time I pulled it out and began the process of finding my birth mom. When I did find her it was one of those "God Moments." We had a wonderful meeting. She informed me that my younger sister had died at age 22, and that her son had been diagnosed with cancer relating to Agent Orange. He had little time left to live.

During those years, I was happy as long as I was working. While I took having *my second* child in stride, John was enamored with his *first child*, a baby girl we named Kate, born in December, 1983. But leading up to the mid 90's, John and I separated several times, and each time I discovered that I was always happier when on my own. I still loved John, but he became more like a dear friend or brother. He no longer wanted to be a husband. (Oddly, we have always been there for one another in good times and bad.) Today I live in his home in Alabama, something I never dreamed in a million years would happen! He taught me to have unconditional love for everyone in my family simply by learning to love people exactly the way they are.

In 1994 my life had changed direction. I was a single mom again. I had a dream position with a corporation that I enjoyed and respected. During political season, I worked as a consultant for a political consulting firm (since 1984). I was a public speaker, writer, and also consulted with small businesses when I found time. This dream life was soon to end.

On October 11, 1996 I was diagnosed with Lupus. "Lupus" is Latin for "wolf" and it is an incurable disease which can cover many forms of disturbances in the immune system, central nervous system and is present as a connective tissue disorder. Lupus, in any one of three types, can attack in a blink of an eye. It is a debilitating, life interrupting, and a depressing disease. Mine is systemic.

My doctors said that due to the organs involved and the seizures I was having, I might live ten more years. From that I thought the worst. I *knew* that my body was already shutting down, so I began treatment for each of the particular problems, knowing I would never see age 50!

The day I was diagnosed, I went home, got into bed, and made peace with dying. I believe in heaven and hell and I knew I would soon be with my Heavenly Father. It wasn't for me to understand *why* this happened.

Sixteen years later my life is a different story. Today, I anxiously think about what to do next. Age 50 was my expiration date! Today I am 57. Most everyone wants their life to mean something, to leave a legacy. I've written a "timeline" to put things in perspective. I pray for guidance. The timeline outlines my key life changes: 3 marriages, divorces, 2 children, 1 miscarriage, 2 separate rapes, numerous surgeries, 4 pairs of parents, all dying from one form of cancer or another, the deaths of friends and a younger cousin, then dealing with Hospice, and then cardiologists, rheumatologists, neurologists, and internists – all with

116

diagnoses regarding my Lupus – finding my birth mother, and on and on the rollercoaster of my life up to, and since 1996.

I had been getting better until last year when my health began to plummet again. With symptoms of seizure disorder returning, this "timeline" document and the "memory books" I've made for my grandchildren have helped me remember parts of my past that were buried in my subconscious, and more importantly, lessons I've learned along the way. I realized why I became ill: I did it to myself by choosing a stressful life… by not taking good care of myself, therefore, my body reacted.

In hindsight, the last 10 years have been the most stressful and the most demeaning. The way in which I dealt with situations over that time has brought me to this point. And yet, I must say that during this stressful time, I have found new joy in being a grandmother to 6 incredible children, bringing much light to the dark times. Even though I haven't been taking getting older well, since God isn't letting me off this 57-year long "D Ticket ride" in life, I'd better find a good way to make the rest of my life work. I desire to regain control of my health. Is it possible? Of course it is. On my knees I continually pray to God for guidance.

To solve a problem, you have to go back in time and examine how you came from there to here. I remember the promise that God does not give us more than we can deal with.

In making my plan for the future, where should I begin? Should I start at my birth, first recollection of abuse, my teenage years, my first marriage, second, or third? What about the time I testified against my adopted Mother for the fraud she committed against my Dad regarding property they jointly owned, or when I was diagnosed with Lupus and my world came to a crashing end? Learn from the past. *I start at the here and now.* What did I most enjoy in my career, and how can I apply my life lessons to helping others and doing what I love? That's the starting point.

One thing I know: my faith is strong. I'm alive and ticking at 57 and have no expiration date stamped on my forehead. My daughter now has 3 beautiful children, 2 boys and 1 baby girl. The saying "Bloom Where you are Planted" is what I'm doing. My first priority is taking care of and raising these children with Katie and her husband.

But, I also need to focus on my new career. The most joy over my career has been from writing for clients, public speaking, and consulting on special projects. God's plan has been for me to be a spokesperson for Lupus, a friend to the newly diagnosed, scared patients, and to be a full time, loving caregiver and Grandmother to my family.

Spirituality comes from within. Faith is unseen. We believe, despite the fact we can't see it. As I look back throughout the history of my life, there have been many miracles, angels, and "God" moments that make me reassured that all is right with me, and that my faith is firmly planted.

117

I don't believe my God gave me a disability; it is how I go forward each day that counts. Comforting newly diagnosed patients is something I do everywhere I go. God has a plan for me, but it's up to me to *work* His plan. He has always supplied all of my needs, so why would I doubt Him now?

Today, I have a full, active, stable life, absent any risks. It is just the kind of life I never dreamed I would have, and in fact, do. My joy comes from my children and my faith.

About author.

*Camryn Oliver Lemmon is a media, public relations, and business consultant, public speaker, and writer. Camryn has developed and managed several successful small businesses in California and Florida since 1972. Based in Birmingham, Alabama, she has extensive training and experience with all stages of business growth, focusing her public relations and marketing communications services aimed at professional service firms and small to mid-size companies. Camryn is an active member of the Northwest Florida Chapter of the Lupus Foundation of America. She can be contacted at: **Camrynoliver@aol.com** and be found on many social networking sites.*

Obstacles 2 Opportunities

by Jordana Carroll, M.S.

*M*y *Voice and My Words are my ULTIMATE POWER*, has been my mantra and trademark for over the past two decades. My life is by all accounts, enviable. I have worked with some of the most well respected authors and inspiring world class speakers on the planet as a master vocal coach, as well as teaching the art of softening accents in the international business world. In my own way, I feel like I have left a bit of my own mastery in every page and presentation. Touching the world via my clientele has allowed me to live in my professional bliss.

As the saying goes, "life can change on a dime." In my case, it was a severe auto accident, not a shiny coin that changed the landscape of my future. My life was altered drastically in an instant when an elderly man ran three stop signs down a steep hill in San Diego, CA and hit me with such force, I felt as though I was knocked into next week! He ran into my driver's door as I was making a sharp left turn up a hill. Thankfully, I turned quickly and avoided it being a fatal collision, as I was later told.

Hmmm... FATAL...

At the time, I thought *that* would have been the blessing, not living. I had a motivational speaking/coaching practice, and now I was having trouble putting words and thoughts together, not to mention having to deal with the problems of the overall physical recovery process. All was affected as I could not remember how to sequence words, memorize my openings, or recall final quotations. When I was speaking, some words would simply just not appear to flow. For this "word smith," the only path that I welcomed in that moment of confusing despair was to spin myself into a very deep depression, and on my terms became a bit of a recluse.

My immediate world went into chaos. I didn't realize how bad it had gotten until one day while attending a conference, I couldn't remember my friend's name or her telephone number. I do remember going back to my hotel room, sitting down in the ladies room and simply allowing myself to weep uncontrollably in a puddle of pain and fear. What was this entertaining, talkative, ball of fire of a young woman going to do, or better yet **BE** for the rest of her life?

Then I remembered from my early college years of Speech Pathology about the results that could be gained from *repetitive sequencing* and stimulating my damaged brain with such an activity. I began to create jewelry with colored gems as I stayed in with my neighbor who blew magnificent glass beads one at a time. In the first few years, a fellow artist viewed my work and suggested I take my collection to be seen at the Spanish Village Art Center at Balboa Park in San Diego, CA. I ended up as an artist there for 12 years. Every weekend I met and created jewelry for people from all over the globe.

Isn't it just amazing how serendipitous life can be!

What can I say? When you crack your head open, some good and some not so good shows up. In my case, I was becoming world known, but for a new skill. Ironically, it was my educational training to become a vocal coach and speech pathologist that ended up helping me heal my brain. Isn't it just amazing how serendipitous life can be! One of my friends said it was a "God-thing" happening in my life. All I knew was that this was a blessing, and for the first time in a long time, I saw light at the end of the tunnel that had been so dulled for so long.

Since that fateful day, I have experienced growth in all phases of my life. I have become a certified yoga instructor to heal my body and serve others, earned a Master's of Science degree in Human Services, and have had the honor of teaching at several colleges over the years. While I'm still known in professional coaching circles as the woman who states, "My Voice and My Words are my UTIMATE POWER," I now know that my intention behind those words and that tone in my voice are the true sweet spot in my mastery, especially my inner dialogue, that self-chatter we all know. I now choose to be very kind to myself in all things, and I live with a profound knowing that no matter what life serves up, it's up to us to decide how we react to it and what we create out of any situation.

At 63 years young, this journey has allowed me to celebrate the good fortune to verbally dance with many on my roller coaster journey. Progressing onward, I have encountered many swift turns, colorful BOULDERS, emotional obstacles, and some downright "goofy" OOpsises! I prefer to view all of these life lessons as opportunities of healing, trend setting, and major paths to achievement in my Master's Degree in Life of Crone-age. OMG, did *this* WIW (Wise Intelligent Woman) just identify herself as being a CRONE?

I can now say that I wear the badge of courage, wisdom, knowledge, and PASSION that accompanies this distinction, and I'm so thankful that the dark side of depression was just part of the overall journey, and not the end. Yes, I even learned from that experience. I learned to let friends in and serve me, and to allow myself not to be the world's version of "perfect," but just to BE *my* version of PERFECT BLISS.

I am a happier and more present version of me.

While I will never be the same person I was prior to the accident, I think I am a happier and more present version of me. I have re-entered the coaching

120

world to open arms and with a deeper knowing that helps my ability to serve clients in a much more meaningful way. I am grateful to have had the privilege of being in conversation with thousands of women, families, youth and men from all continents who have shared some of their life stories with me on how they have dealt with some strange and obstacle-infused deck of cards thrust upon them. Some of these dear souls have been leaving their beloved country of birth in order to save their lives and the lives of their children, as are my sisters from Somalia, or others from Cuba.... Some of them are leaving because of emotional or physical accidents that changed how they thought or moved or did not gracefully move around their community after catastrophic encounters brought upon them by violent acts.

Do I miss acting in theatrical productions after 45 plus years? Absolutely! But I figured My Higher Power had other lessons for me to embrace and to share. Overcoming Obstacles is necessary if we are to allow ourselves to SOAR WITH THE EAGLES! Super flyers, outstanding athletes, Olympians, best-selling authors, along with Walt Disney, Steven Jobs, Erma Bombeck, Gilda Radner, Golda Meir, Nora Ephron and others like them in the world allowed themselves the LUXURY of failure. If you allow yourself to fail, then you will KNOW what it is to be truly successful.

I am putting out the call to all WIW (Wise Intelligent Women) to look at your stories and share them. Get out of your mud, throw out what is no longer serving you, climb aboard the WIW plane, and soar with me. Sisters, we are here to learn, laugh, live and share our stories as we flow with PASSION, PURPOSE, and PIZZAZZ.

Ultimately I am here to create my path, and possibly create a clearing for other Wise Intelligent Women to take responsibility for looking at obstacles, turning points, opportunities, and to truly view the passionate movie of life, for as I've heard it expressed, "It is not a dress rehearsal!"

About author.

*Jordana Carroll, M.S., sparks authors, CEOs, other professionals, and non-native American speakers to communicate with purpose, clarity, and enthusiasm. Jordana's past speech therapy training, teaching, counseling, and community involvement – in conjunction with her theatrical background – turns ordinary seminars into those packed with power, excitement, and a high level of participation! Look for the soon to be released **Wise Intelligent Woman** out in the fall of 2012, and also her new book: **Don't Kiss Me Like I Am a Pastrami Sandwich,** for tentative release in early 2013.*

To learn more about Ms. Carroll, please visit: www.JordanaCarroll.com.

The Creation of "Beauty"...
Begins Within You

by KC Kang

As a young child, there was a feeling within that something was fundamentally wrong with me. I was born in Japan as a Korean descendant. This can be a type of natural handicap in Japanese society. It caused me to be discriminated against as a result of historical consequences, (without it being my own personal fault). These ethnic ingredients set me up as a young child to be looked down upon, socially.

But to add to these ingredients, I was also born as a sister of a mentally challenged brother, who had been bullied by his peers for many years. This also caused me to be made fun of... just because I was his sister. Having to deal with social judgments was tough enough for my sensitive heart while growing up.

However, one other major difficult experience was encountered in my life at that time. I had developed a severe skin disease called Eczema, or Atopic Dermatitis. As a treatment for this disorder, I grew up having to use multiple medications, which eventually caused me to become a steroid addict, leaving me with "burned looking skin." Because of the steroids, a full series of allergic reactions were added to it. This situation led me to wrongfully believe that I was not only a lesser citizen... but also a lesser human.

Born as a woman in Japan, my cultural beliefs (as well as the social expectations) were that in order to be accepted by others and do well in the society, I had to have a beautiful appearance. In many Asian countries where males dominate most activities (up to the 1970's and 80's), it was culturally critical back then to be born "a pretty woman" in order to get ahead in life. The ultimate purpose was to be chosen by a rich or highly recognized man. One who could provide a decent life-style for the woman he married.

In order for me to prove that I was "acceptable" in my society, one of my dreams as a teenager was to become a fashion model. I felt that this would help me win over my inner battle of inferior vs. superior citizen. Even though I had this dream, I felt defeated with the fact that I had this skin disease which nobody knew I had (as I covered it up with a steroid cream which worked like a magic

122

wand). Up until my late teenage years, the magical cream was working very well, making me look completely normal, albeit with rather pale skin. Yet, I knew that if I didn't use the cream for few days, my skin would start to erupt with rashes all over my face and body. (Some severe cases of eczema can even create significant hair loss and damaged eyesight, due to the side effect of long term usage of certain medications.)

One day, I finally made it as a model on the front page of the teenage magazine in Japan. Although part of me was proud of myself and felt I had won... the other part of me also felt fake and afraid that someday, somebody would discover the real truth about how ugly a woman I would be without my medication.

As I suffered from severe Eczema, the chemical dependency with the medications was becoming too difficult to turn around. In my early twenties, my skin problems continued to progress, and it came to the point where the strongest medication no longer worked effectively. By then, my skin was thinning as a side effect, and started to show some veins through the skin on my face. Also, other parts of my skin that I had intensely scratched due to the itchiness from allergic reactions were forming dark scars (almost as if I had a severe sun burn). The medications were no longer working to completely diminish my rashes. My dermatologist told me that I would never be able to heal, and there was no cure for my condition. I would be like this for the rest of my life. Emotionally, I felt threatened that nobody would love me if I truly revealed my physical self.

It was almost as though I had a Cinderella complex. I was told and also believed that I was ugly and unworthy, even though I had a taste of what being a beautiful princess felt like. I had limited time before my medication would stop working completely. Never would I be able to become a princess for the long term, feeling beautiful and worthy of love. It felt as though I had to run back to the carriage by the stroke of midnight, before I would turn back into the ugly peasant again.

Unlike Cinderella, who was finally favored and rescued by the rich and respected prince (due to her beauty) and who lived happily ever after... I was told by the doctor that there was no hope or cure for me.

After I went through my divorce, my skin disease became aggressively evident due to the stress. One day I decided to take a risk and stop using the medication to see what would happen to my body, since the medication was no longer working effectively on my skin anyway. At that point, I began my long journey of healing. During two years of intense therapy and a detoxification process, I went from conditions of fever to insomnia, night sweats to infection, and very painful cycles of skin regeneration. My skin had many open cuts and scratches, but there was no chemical in my body to stop the inflammation. All this had occurred as a result of the long term dependency of the hormone medication I had used to heal the inflammations. Because of this, my body had stopped producing hormones on its own.

There were many mornings that I would wake up, and my pajamas would be sticking to my skin because of dried blood and fluids. It was extremely painful to take off my pajamas as it would peel off my skin which had regenerated over the night. During this difficult time, I began to seek answers and tried everything that was available as a remedy for my condition. This included certain types of bathing and sauna, exercise and meditations, acupuncture and Chinese herbs, different types of oils and creams, supplements and food regime, counseling and hypnotherapy, and even energy healings.

I had asked myself many questions during these humbling experiences. Why is this happening to me? What have I been doing wrong? What do I need to do in order to heal? Why do I have to overcome this experience in the first place? What is the purpose of it all?

I spent most of my days in a bath tub with natural "hot springs" water. This was most pain relieving, relaxing and detoxifying to my body. I used my time to read many books, trying to find answers to my many questions. The books ranged from spirituality, philosophy, medical, natural healing to psychology and more. As a result, I discovered a new vision of holistic thinking during my healing process.

I tried almost all the possible remedies and therapies available during my difficult time. I prepared an organic food regime, practiced yoga, read many spiritual books, obtained counseling and hypnotherapy, drank Chinese herbs and much more. The powerful understanding that I ultimately reached... was that none of these individual things worked to cure my condition by themselves. Yet, by doing all these "combined" practices everyday and in all possible areas of my life, it brought about a balance of mind, body and spirit. Eventually this created the healing within myself and improved my condition. It was all about creating balance, and trusting my own ability to heal.

This entire experience also gave me the significant realization in my life about unconditional love. Something I experienced for the very first time from a surprising source.

At the worst time during therapy, I looked like a burned victim. My skin all over my body cracked and bled. Some parts became like the skin of an elephant. People on the street would stare at me when I went for a walk outside. Friends and family started to look at me differently, and gave me words of sympathy or pity. This actually hurt more, rather than encourage me. Some even expressed concern, wondering if I were contagious (which I was not).

During this time, my son was only 2 years old. He would wake up in the morning and call for mommy as usual, begging me for a hug. He was the only one who did not change his reaction to how I looked. I was nothing but his "beautiful mommy" in his eyes. I realized that as a little child, he did not have any judgment

124

about anything and taught me that I was truly worthy to him, no matter what I looked like. He demonstrated unconditional love towards me. I cannot tell you enough about how much I appreciated the experience of having someone totally love me regardless of my external appearance.

I can honestly say this was the hardest time in my life, but it turned out to be my greatest teacher and guide. It has caused me to fulfill my life's purpose, which was to accept and love myself, while at the same time, facilitate holistic ways of healing and bringing out authentic beauty in others. I now live life completely free of any medication or sign of disease. We all have an amazing ability to heal ourselves!

An "authentic beauty" is the holistic view of beauty. It is not about focusing on what is beautiful externally or internally. It is all about embracing who we are and appreciating who we are.

Some people spend much energy and time trying to fix something externally, in order to reach the proverbial "ideal appearance" so they will be acceptable – not only socially, but also to their own judgments and expectations. On the other hand, others say, "It is not about what is on the outside, but about true inner beauty," yet they never appreciate what they already have with their physical body. They miss the opportunity to make the best out of what they do have. This true authenticity comes when we appreciate ALL that we are given, and how we uniquely express ourselves in body, mind and spirit.

In order to be beautiful, we need to feel beautiful. Even if you have the best make-up artist do an intense make over, or spend days in a spa taking care of your skin, hair and nails... if you do not truly see your own beauty within and on the outside, it is still difficult to maintain the feeling of beauty and self-worth. It is not just about external fixation, but our internal mindset that will create our emotional state. This all has a crucial affect on the expression of our authentic beauty.

Through this experience I was able to transform my perception of the world. I was able to come out of my place of judgment (which was depending on external perceptions), yet able to rely more on my own inner reality to create the life I desired. I learned and cultivated the unconditional love within myself that my son taught me during my hardest time... which is to truly love and appreciate myself regardless. Once I did that, I could do the same for others.

Life can become so rewarding, once we all connect to our authentic beauty within.

About author.

KC Kang owns several successful companies internationally. She devotes her life to inspire others and work as a cultural bridge between East and West. In addition to being an entrepreneur, KC is a Holistic Health Practitioner, Clinical Hypnotherapist, and she also works as a Japanese/English translator for self-development seminars. Please visit **www.kckang.com** *for more information.*

Don't Survive – THRIVE!

by Marshall Sylver

L ast night at midnight I was sitting on the balcony of the beach house, watching the waves. The temperature was perfect, a totally quiet night except for the hypnotic, rhythmic crashing of the waves. (Heck, yes, I love this stuff!) I had just gotten off the phone with my production manager for the live show we are putting into Harrah's, and was taking a few moments before I needed to get in bed and get some sleep. As I sat there feeling very grateful as always, I saw the moon was reflecting on the water in such a way that the distant reflections on the furthest waves were more like little explosions of light. A fireworks show just for me! I must be hypnotized. It got me thinking about things, such as why was I so special that God would put on this show just for me? An even bigger question was, how did I get here and how can I continue to inspire others to do the same?

Five years ago I was going through a divorce from a marriage that lasted 11 months (the divorce proceedings took four years – don't ask), and put me over seven figures in debt. The church that I was attending ended up being a cult whose only agenda was to take total control of the minds of the congregants and milk them for all their money. (You can imagine how that went over when I exposed them!) I was being falsely accused by a government agency of a wrongdoing that would ultimately take me four years and hundreds of thousands of dollars to successfully prove my innocence. I had just found out that in the midst of all my challenges that my best friend had embezzled almost a million dollars from me.

As a man who has spent his entire life in the public eye performing and teaching, this was an extremely tough time. In the past, when I needed an ego boost or validation that all the challenge was worth it, the reinforcement would come in the form of a chance meeting with a seminar attendee or someone who had seen the show. Their exclamations of how I had changed their lives or that mine was the best show they had ever seen kept me focused on *getting living* rather than *getting dying*. During this troubled time, the government saw fit, since they had no authentic case, to attempt to put me out of business by piling on negative publicity. Since 95% of the world is led around by their noses by the other 5%, I would encounter people from time to time who, rather than compliment me, would believe what they saw or heard in the press and throw an insult my way. As a man whose whole life had been in the service of others, this was the toughest

127

blow. I began to question what the reason for all this was – what was the meaning for me? I teach that all things happen for a purpose, and they serve us, but I was having a very tough time believing my own lessons. My brain was clichéd to death with "What doesn't kill you will make you stronger" and "Fall down nine times stand up ten." I went through a month in which I would be disappointed in the morning that I woke up and hadn't died in my sleep.

During that time, purely as a survival mechanism, I put together my own list of mantras or thoughts that helped me to function. If you are dealing with challenges, and we all certainly will at some time, I believe these will help you.

1. This too, shall pass. It's a fact. Maybe slower than you want it to, and yet it will pass. You may die before it does, and yet it will pass. Remembering that all things are temporary will not only give you greater strength to handle the tough times, it will give you a greater appreciation of the good times since you won't be as likely to take them for granted.

2. Life will teach us lessons and the lessons will get harder until we have learned them. We will know we have learned our lessons when we finally change our habits. Everything that is happening in our lives is neutral. The meaning we attach to those experiences is our choice. When the government was attacking me and trying to put me out of business since they had totally fabricated the entire matter, I had to make a choice. Would I take the easy route and just quit, or would I take all of their attacks and create better programs to better take care of my students? Obviously I chose to take better care of my students and kept bringing more and more value to my programs. The ultimate outcome of being attacked by the government for over four years is that my programs are better, my students are having more success than ever, and my company is more prosperous than ever… all because I chose to look for the lessons.

3. The truth always reveals itself. For a while I was in so much emotional pain from being falsely accused on so many fronts that I felt a great need to defend myself. It took great energy to try to convince others of what I knew to be the truth. Finally I just surrendered and realized that the evidence is always in the fruit. The government's attack wasn't working because we have incredible life-changing seminars. Even though I was going through a divorce and my ex was lying to the courts, saying what a horrible person I was, there was no shortage of women that wanted to go out with me since I wasn't the person she was fabricating. Even if your life is temporarily challenged, are you still getting by? Are you doing better than surviving? Are you even thriving a little? If so, let the evidence be your argument and stop defending yourself, since the people that are attacking don't listen anyway.

4. The ankle weights will make you stronger when you take them off. I am typing this on my private jet on my way to Washington D.C. to do a program with my great friend Robert Allen. I left the aforementioned beach mansion this morning after having a perfect latte with my cat, Gandolf. I will profit hundreds of thousands of dollars for a few hours of my time, and I love every moment to the degree that I would do it even if I wasn't getting paid. All of the efforts I made

128

during the hardest time, just to get by, massively bless me now that the burdens are gone. I learned to work under the toughest of stress to the point that what other people think of as stress doesn't even phase me. I have a new radio show, a live Vegas show, three new books, and three new seminar programs – all coming out simultaneously – and I am not feeling any additional stress at all. With the hell I went through this is heaven!

5. Take care of downtime planning to prepare for uptime opportunity. I had many wonderful things go away during my challenged time. I had strategic partners who knew and loved me but who, for their own protection, couldn't be closely associated with me while I was being attacked. I understood and never held it against them. I had two television contracts signed and complete that fell apart because my matters were drawn out for so long – one for a daily television talk show, one for a weekly comedy series. It was sad to have things I had worked on for decades come so close and then be destroyed because I was being falsely portrayed and accused. Instead of letting it crush me, I kept working on my seminars, television shows, and books when the opportunities were shutting down, knowing that they would one day reappear as long as I was true to myself. We are once again very close to having the two television shows be a reality and bigger than they would have been before.

6. Exercise and diet. Such a simple thing and we all know it works. I had an expression, "Run or die." While the depression was setting in, I didn't feel like working out. The less I worked out the worse I felt. Finally I decided that the only thing that I had control of in the moment were my thoughts and actions, and I decided I needed to at least stay healthy. It wasn't easy and yet it was the trigger that got the other stuff rolling. My increased discipline and self-esteem kept me going when my bank account opportunities and relationships weren't. Feeling frustrated? Go for a run or at least a brisk walk.

7. Get sick and tired of being sick and tired. People reach a point of readiness for change when they reach their own personal bottom. For some that is a specific body weight, bank account level, or health or relaxation level. They get so fat, broke, worn out, or stressed that they say, "ENOUGH!" For others, they never get sick of it – they just become accustomed and decide that it's tolerable. They decide that it's their lot in life to have to live the way they are, so they never take charge of anything

8. Fix it or accept it. Some things are in your power, some things aren't. Have the sense to know the difference. If you are complaining and challenged by something that you can do something about, stop talking and get busy. I know that it can be overwhelming to look at tough times in their entirety and not feel the overload syndrome kick in. Some is always better than none. I have never had a workout that I wished I hadn't. I have never woken up and said, "Gee, I wish I had gotten really drunk last night!" One day of good choices is better than none. When I was going through times that felt like everything was going wrong, I often said to myself, "One fire at a time." When fire fighters go to put out a blaze, they focus on one fire at a time so they are not running back and forth, and being ineffective.

They make sure the fire at hand is completely handled and not about to start again before they focus on the next one. For the things that you cannot change in the moment, surrender and accept it, for now. When you believe you have exhausted all ideas, energies, and resources in solving a challenge and it still exists, surrender and find it perfect. What other choice do you have?

9. Avoid pity parties and the people that let you hold them. They say that misery loves company, and I would agree. I also know that what we focus on expands, and the more we can avoid talking about the challenges and talk about solutions, the faster we will see a light at the end of the tunnel. Grieving is natural, being stuck is deadly. If you need to get it out, find one or two people only, not everyone you meet. Better still, go to a professional: a shrink, a pastor, a bartender (just kidding, the bartender is too expensive). Find a higher and better reason that you need to get over it, and get on with it. For me it is often other people's wellbeing that reminds me that I am required to be better.

10. Fantasize about a better time. Write it down. Make the fantasy rich in details and sensory stimulation. The more you write the better, because it crystallizes the fantasy and allows your subconscious to get to work and make it a reality. Keep expanding on the fantasy until it becomes a mini novel. It is your life; you are the writer, director, and star. You are writing the story of your life as you live. What if you were writing the future script instead of the eulogy? This private jet, my home on the beach, my Rolls Royce, and all the business successes I am currently enjoying were all fantasies that I imagined every day while I was in my most painful of times. All are here now because I decided I was not going to survive – I was going to thrive! Now where is that beautiful girl I was fantasizing about? ;)

One Final Thought: get out of your head and get into your life. Remember: living in the past is depression; living in the future is anxiety. You cannot change the experiences of the past. You *can* change their meaning. What you want to have happen in your future either will or it won't. Worry doesn't affect the outcome. Stay focused on the present moment, live in satori, and realize that you are a gift to the universe and that there are still great works in you.

About author.

*Marshall Sylver is a world-renown hypnotist and master of interpersonal communication. He is a respected business consultant sought by Fortune 500 companies and also the creator of the number one personal development program worldwide. Today, Sylver is recognized as the #1 leading experts in subconscious reprogramming & the master of persuasion and influence. For more information on Marshall Sylver, please visit his website: **www.sylver.com.***

Life's Trials

by Jeff Crandall

Just like a real family, I thought to myself as I listened to my mother and new stepfather discussing what to do for the evening one Friday night. My mother had sacrificed much as she had worked her way up from being employed as a clerk, to a senior accountant for the State of Michigan. I had sacrificed much, too, being an only child to a very busy mother. My real father left us well before I had any memories of him. My mother would repeatedly tell me that he was no good and that I was better off without him. "He's just a drunk and a womanizer," she would say. (Later, in my young teenage life she would repeatedly tell me that I was just like him, and that I would never amount to anything.)

In many superficial ways, I had the ideal life: a nice home with two parents. Then one day, I was listening to my mom and stepdad arguing *again,* and I remember crying to myself, not sure of what I was feeling. Soon afterward, I came home from school and the majority of his belongings were gone. I would never see my stepfather again. He disappeared nearly as mysteriously as he had appeared. Shortly thereafter, my mother sat me down for *the* talk – the only real conversation I ever remember having with her. "Son, things are going to be tough for a while around here. I have decided to go back to college and get my degree. You will need to take care of yourself." I was 12.

Being the functional alcoholic and workaholic that she was, she disappeared from my life as well. Being an only child, I felt alone. I became resentful, depressed, and lost my self-esteem. Life became about surviving day by day, and at times, minute by minute. Smoking cigarettes led to smoking pot, drinking, and eventually experimentation with other drugs when the opportunities presented themselves – created by sneaking out of the house at night, first on the weekends, then practically every night. Getting drunk or high was a way to stop feeling alone, sad, hopeless, and stuck. It worked well… for a while.

I began running with the wrong people and eventually got caught stealing. I ended up in a children's home, which likely saved me from myself at the age of 15. I saw it as the escape I needed, and I parlayed it into an opportunity to get out of my miserable home and miserable school (educational system). I completed my last two years of school in one, and graduated early – much to the amazement of the mainstream students, jocks, and cool people.

131

One Christmas day a couple of years later, I found myself pumping gas for minimum wage. It was freezing in the iced rain, and everybody stopping for gas expressed pity as I sent them on their way to their loved ones. I would have no Christmas or loved ones. It was then that I decided to "go for it!" by joining the Navy and marrying the girl that had been begging me to marry her for months.

I needed to get out of this low-wage, no opportunity state and make something of myself, and I wasn't doing it alone. Connie (my soon-to-be wife) supported me in anything I chose, and her family was loving and supportive. It was the family I never had. Off I went to boot camp, eventually settling in at a Navy base in Key West, Florida. Connie joined up with me, bringing our newborn (Amy) and her first-born (Eric), who was 3 years old at the time. I found myself working two other jobs to make ends meet, often coming home and finding my wife drunk and depressed. The relationship spiraled down, and we divorced.

I carried on much the same until I was 30: partying, numbing it all out, and working hard, hoping that someday I would arrive somewhere. I guess my mom was right about me. No amount of booze, drugs, or women could take away my pain or loneliness.

At 51, my mother died of a heart attack. I flew home to Michigan to deal with it. It was my first real experience with death, and being the only child, I was responsible for all of the arrangements. After the funeral, I began prepping my childhood home for sale. It was a neglected mess – walls coated with smoked-stained depression and loneliness. It took weeks, with my old alcoholic friends helping, to put the place back in shape enough to sell. The last thing we took from the property was a pickup truck full of empty, crushed beer cans we had accumulated while working on the property: a testament to what my life had become.

Once home, I found myself paralyzed with unexpressed emotions and sadness, not only for my mother, but for what my life had become as well. Finally, going to my court-ordered AA meetings due to my second DUI, took on a new meaning. I stood up and declared, "I am an alcoholic." I went home and searched through the yellow pages looking for rehabilitation centers. "I can't do this thing myself," I thought. I entered a 30-day program on my 30th birthday, declaring, "I am going to break the chain in our family."

After getting sober, I cried myself to sleep for six months, processing old emotions that I had never let myself feel. I learned self-hypnosis and calmed myself often when I needed to get free from the churning of my runaway mind, which seemed to be out to get me. Once I had worked through the 12 steps and found some freedom and peace for myself, I began working with other alcoholics, helping them to get free as well.

When I was a teenager, I ran across a book on my stepfather's bookcase that he had left behind: ***How to Win Friends and Influence People*** by Dale Carnegie. I read it from cover to cover in one sitting, and from it I learned more about myself and others than from any other experience to date. Most importantly,

132

it gave me a new found hope. My teenage mantra became survive until I was old enough and capable of being responsible for myself. That hope and mantra probably saved my life as a teenager. This book was my first experience with personal growth. Naturally, in my newfound sober state of mind, I also began seeking personal growth activities by attending numerous seminars, reading books and by constantly listening to personal growth audios when in the car.

I finally took on my last addiction: nicotine. By this time I had smoked for 27 years, over a pack a day. Again, I realized that I needed help because all my previous attempts had failed. I searched online and found another 12-step program: "Nicotine Anonymous." I started attending meetings, and within a few months, I was a non-smoker. This was my last addiction – it was one of the hardest things I ever did – but it really shifted my life. I had never been so in control of my life and body. I became so healthy that I ended up running the Los Angeles Marathon!

I continued learning and employing personal growth skills, and was doing well. I had grown a tax and financial planning practice specializing in real estate investors, and had reached the point of having someone running the day-to-day operations and being responsible for the employees. I was out promoting the business by doing public speaking events, writing articles for trade magazines, networking, creating referrals, and rubbing shoulders with the people to know in the real estate industry. I was also doing well with my own real estate ventures.

Suddenly, everything came crashing down on me when I found that a real estate deal I was involved with was being fraudulently represented. Very long story short: the FBI became involved and charged multiple people, including the people investing in the deals… me being one of them. I fought it in court and lost because the FBI testified to the jury that I had confessed to them. I did not, but the prosecution went into my long-gone past to explain to the jury that I was not credible. Ultimately, I spent two years in prison for a felony I did not commit.

While in prison, I created an alcohol and drug rehabilitation program, I created a full music program, I created a personal growth and success principles curriculum, and to my knowledge, these programs are still going today. I also coached and mentored inmates on how to switch their perspectives on doing time to successfully create a life behind bars as well as creating a life when they got out.

I have been out of prison now for over three years after winning my appeal. In prison, I envisioned (declared) the life of my dreams; I am now living that vision despite an unemployable felony record during the "Great Recession." All of my study, belief, and hard work are paying off despite any *"obstacles."*

In summary, I want this to be the message that you are left with: YOU are responsible for your life, and YOU have the power to create anything YOU want. DO THIS: Learn success principles; implement them into your life until they become who you are. Looking at yourself from your successful future, create who you need to be to fulfill that future. Place collages of your future on your

133

walls, your mirrors, your screen-savers… *everywhere*. Take action to fulfill your future, always, every day. Hang out with others who are optimistically creating their future. Find mentors/coaches along the way who have been where you are going. In order to have a successful journey, you only need to envision your results (already achieved) and see what's immediately ahead, then steer to stay on the road. There will be pot holes, detours and bad weather…. That's what makes the trip exciting!

More will be revealed as we track this highway together. I look forward to meeting you when our journeys cross. Until then, happy motoring, keep your car tuned and the wheels in the right direction. I promise you, no matter what obstacles show up on your road; you will overcome them if you know where you are going!

About author.

Jeff Crandall has lived many roles: hopeless, depressed teenager; alcoholic adult; success on the outside with emptiness on the inside; falsely accused and imprisoned inmate; and today, a COO living the fulfilling life of his dreams. If you would like to know more about Jeff and what he is up to, please visit www.smartmentorsystems.com. For more details on his amazing story, look for his upcoming book, "Life's Trials," or purchase his daughter's book, "Growth Hurts – A True Journey of Breaking the Chain and Filling the Void" by Amy Crandall.

How I Overcame My Fear of Happiness

by Dr. Leila Marsha Peterson

Before the photographer takes a picture, they instruct everyone to smile and say "cheese!" But this has nothing to do with being happy.

Laughter contains a certain vibration that can put a smile on your face. However, laughing is a *conditioned* response that I have learned, like most born and raised under Martial Law in the Philippines. I laugh when I am embarrassed, or whenever I make mistakes, but most of all, I laugh when I am scared. With this programming that I was raised under, my mind has been unable to connect laughter with true happiness.

So, recently I became motivated to open boxes of pictures that were waiting to be placed in a picture album. I was searching for reminders of when I was radiant and happy; I could not find any after my daughters were of school age…. In fact, the pictures revealed that I had stopped smiling altogether….

What should I do now to change my present reality, I wondered to myself. Since self-awareness is the first step, I decided to take an inventory of who, what, where, how and why I am.

Here's a snapshot of what I want:

I desire to make more money than bills through online services that I love participating in; buy my parents and my daughters a house each, in one compound where every house is shouting distance from each other; have a place by a lake so my husband can go fishing and golfing; get my grandchildren's college fund ready; maintain excellent physical and spiritual health; travel with like-minded individuals to places like the Rainforest; and start a business for my family in the Philippines.

Now, what is *really* my *ultimate* goal? To be Happy! If all of the "above" are fulfilled, I will be really happy.

Here are some things I did to get the "Leila Marsha Happiness Ball" rolling….

In the center of a white poster board I pasted a yellow post-it note with the words, "Be Happy!" I then scoured magazines and the Internet for pictures to show my subconscious mind on a daily basis what my Ultimate Target List is, and then I placed those pictures with descriptive words beneath them onto my poster board.

I know that the root chakra is the center of manifestation, so I make sure that it is vibrating properly by playing with the Root Chakra Singing Crystal Bowl. This practice has been used by pre-Buddhist monks over 4,000 years ago during their meditations. And since red is the color associated with the root chakra, I bought red underwear for "power." Also, to help decongest the root chakra area, I give myself sitz baths!

I remembered Joe Vitale and his story about *Ho'oponopono*, a practice of forgiveness and reconciliation, so my practice now is to repeat the mantra: "I am sorry. Please forgive me. I love you. Thank you." (These are magical words that help to change any situation, without a long drawn out therapy session.) At the same time I take slow, deep breaths as I lay in the hammock with all my different colored eye glasses. I also place my hand at the back of my neck with the intention of connecting with my reptilian brain, which the scientific world has documented to be the oldest part of our brain. In Reiki, this is how we connect with our ancestors.

Knee troubles began for me when my daughter Christine – who has Down Syndrome – refused to get out of the van because she did not want her brand new sneakers to get dirty from the mud and leftover snow. Suddenly, without warning, she decided to jump straight into my arms, all 210 lbs. of her! I slipped and fell with her right on top of my knees.

I waddled to the doctor's office for x-rays. Blood was extracted out of my knee and he gave me a cortisone shot. The Doctor told us that I had a torn Anterior Cruciate Ligament, and as he explained to me and my husband what surgery needed to be done, I was staring at my x-rays, amazed at how beautiful my knees were. They did not have the osteophytes that is prevalent in people my age (I am 60), that would show the presence of arthritis.

My husband nagged me to have the surgery right away because the Doctor said that if I waited any longer, I would never be able to walk again! But I refused to budge. I believe that our body can heal itself if given the ingredients it needs to be whole again. Research has shown that not all surgeries fix the problem. And in most cases, the pain gets worse! I preferred to take a different route.

I sought care from seven different health care providers. The list included an Orthopedic Surgeon, a Medical Doctor, 2 Chiropractors – with different areas of expertise – an Acupuncturist, and 2 Massage Therapists performing different styles. I was the perfect patient, but even after almost a year, no major improvements could be seen.

136

Then, I found my old, worn out copy of Louise Hay's book: *Heal Your Body*. It was like a jolt of lightning had hit me and I realized that I had to take my power back! According to Louise Hay, my knees represented my inability to be flexible for what I feel my life holds in the future. It is also about me being stubborn and arrogant in thinking that I know it all. In Traditional Chinese Medicine, knee issues represent a disharmony in the kidney, which signifies fear. In the past I have studied all of these connections and have used them to help my patients, but never did it occur to me to apply them to myself!

I cried like I have never cried before, with sounds coming out of me that still haunt me to this day.

With this knowledge in hand, and by the Grace of God, I am walking now. It is still difficult for me to use walking as my regular form of exercise, so I bought a rebounder (mini-trampoline), and I bounce and stretch frequently throughout the day. I also make time to do feet exercises as I go up and down stairs.

Another thing that I do is spend time "dancing" to different rhythms as I give myself permission to release stuck energies inside of me.

Deepak Chopra M.D., in his book entitled *Grow Younger, Live Longer*, stated that "You Can Reverse Your Biological Age By Lovingly Nurturing Your Body Through Healthy Food." I am all for that, but since I am on the road a lot, I do not have the luxury of organic, healthy home cooked meals. So, I opted to do what works for my patients.

I answered different questionnaires that I usually have my patients fill out to find out where they are regarding their health and emotions. I had my hair and saliva samples sent out to have them checked for chemical imbalances. Then, I put myself on a food based nutrition protocol with extra support for my liver, the organ system that holds anger.

Remember, one man's nutrition is another one's poison; I have to know what is right for ME!

A favorite thing I do to get unstuck and to help my inner child feel loved is to buy some soap bubbles, an ice cream cone, and then head to a local park. There, I blow bubbles and enjoy my ice cream. And yes, I even force myself to laugh out loud! I also put my worries or concerns inside the bubbles and send them to my God.

I discovered where my "money thermostat" is located, and I have been making sure that it is set on "right."

Giving and receiving using the correct hand is something I've known about for ages, and am now using it to my advantage. When I pay someone I use

137

my right hand, and when I receive money I use my left hand – this allows the energy to flow. (With most people, the right side is the giving or the *yang* side of our body while the left side is the receiving or the *yin* side.)

I scrub my lymphatic area with Celtic sea salt, baking soda, and a drop of Ocotea weekly to help move my lymphatic system, which in my mind is the dumping ground of my body for all the emotional stress I put it through.

A practice that works for me is to change my sheets every night, so that I may have fresh dreams! (This practice may be helpful for anyone looking to stop nightmares.) I apply Peace and Calming Essential Oil on my feet, my hands and my ears, and then I continue to give myself reflexology, paying attention to ouch spots. When I encounter one, I then check a chart to see what organ system is out of balance at the moment. These are all part of my winding down routine, to help me re-learn how to get a deep, restorative night's sleep. For anyone with sleep problems, these practices can be a big help.

Slowly, my life seems to be better. My mood has changed. I am a lot nicer again. My finances are changing around. My issues are in "remission."

I recently had my picture taken, and wouldn't you know it? *I was smiling!* Not a big one yet, but I feel I am getting there…. Right now I am at peace with the decisions I have made to improve my health and to learn how to smile again.

Small changes can make a big difference, so, jot down those little things and email me to let me know how you are doing!

About author.

Dr. Leila Marsha Peterson is a Chiropractic Physician working on her Master's in Psychology. She loves brainstorming with individuals on how to break the habit of pasting a smile on their face that is not connected to their heart. She will help you decipher where you have been, what you are going through, and create a goal towards where you want to be, plus a step by step plan on how to finally get "there"! You are a unique individual. Your fingerprints are yours alone. Don't you want to work with someone who sees you that way? Give Dr. Peterson a call at 630-696-3400 for your free, 15 minutes personal goal setting consultation. It is time!

Email: Leila@your-gps-to-a-fulfilled-life.com. Skype: IntuitiveStrategist, Twitter: @deStressDoc, Facebook: www.facebook.com/marshapeterson. Join the conversation at https://www.facebook.com/groups/happyagain.

I Did Not Commit Suicide Because...

by Helice "Sparky" Bridges

I turned 70 years young March 31, 2012. I am a grandma to five adorable grandbabies. I know who I am, why I was born, and the difference I make. Life is a miracle!

Yet, at the age of 37, I had been married for 18 years to a controlling, intimidating and verbally abusive man. I was trapped in hell, invisible, and screaming silently for love. I contemplated suicide on a daily basis.

My parents were caring, encouraging and loving people who always called me their little angel. I was voted *Peppiest* in my school Hall of Fame. The captain of our high school football team was in love with me. So how in the world could I have gotten into such a mess?

It amazes me that out of my despair emerged the unconditionally loving, unstoppable and powerful woman I am today. I have enormous compassion for children and adults who contemplate or even resort to committing suicide. It is for this reason that I invented the "Who I Am Makes A Difference"® Blue Ribbon Acknowledgment Ceremony.

You may think that there is never a good enough reason to commit suicide. I can see that now. But when I was married, I was so damaged inside that my will to live was completely destroyed.

He was a bully. He kept all the money I earned during the first twelve years of our marriage. He told me that I was fat, and that other women were prettier than me. I was subservient, a door mat, and totally invisible. No one had a clue, the pain I was going through; I had nowhere to turn.

To the outside world, we had the American Dream. We were parents of two amazing pre-teen sons. My husband was highly respected as a brilliant and generous businessman. I was recognized as the #1 salesperson in the Western United States for my company. Together we had built a million dollar home overlooking the Pacific Ocean. Three luxury cars lined our driveway.

Yet no amount of material wealth could ease my pain. On Monday, June 18, 1979, I decided to end my life. Tucked in a fetal position, I lay naked on our bed, trembling and sobbing uncontrollably.

I cried out to the heavens, "STOP THE WORLD, I'VE GOT TO GET OFF! I NEED TO FIND A PLACE WHERE PEOPLE LOVE EACH OTHER!"

In that instant I heard a sweet voice deep inside my soul, quietly whisper, "You cannot take your life. You will sing, dance, write, and someday star in a musical on Broadway in New York City."

I suddenly felt alive! It didn't even occur to me that I couldn't sing, dance or write. Somehow I absolutely knew that this was exactly what I would do.

I raced to my husband and shared my dream. He simply rolled his eyes to the ceiling and returned to reading the sports section without ever saying a word. My next door neighbor told me I was crazy, reminded me that I was too old and too short to be a dancer, and that I'd never be a published author. Finally she exclaimed, "You can't even carry a tune!"

Why didn't she encourage and cheer me on like my parents? Angry, I stormed away and auditioned for a musical comedy in downtown San Diego. Young professionals from Las Vegas & Broadway stages were also auditioning. When they sang, everyone burst into applause.

It didn't matter that I couldn't read music or sing... I was so excited! When I screeched out the song, the entire room went silent. Not a soul applauded.

Despite this, I stood proudly, grinning from ear to ear, buttons popping off my blouse and simply asked, "So how was I?" Everyone doubled over with laughter. They couldn't stop laughing. I landed the role, not because I could sing. It was because this was a musical *comedy,* and they thought I was a comedian.

During the next 3 months of rehearsals, I learned how to sing and dance. Everyone supported each other. I was no longer alone.

When our production completed in September 1980, I made 3 important decisions. I retired from real estate, filed for divorce, and walked out of our magnificent ocean view home.

I found a place where people loved one another as volunteer co-chair of The San Diego Hunger Project. In the next year, I spoke to over 50,000 people about ending world hunger. Following my talks, I had intimate conversations with people who told me that they didn't feel their lives mattered. That's when I realized that people were literally starving for love – just like me.

I decided to do something about this problem. So I invented the "Who I Am Makes A Difference"® Blue Ribbon and "10-Step Acknowledgment

Ceremony"™. In a minute or less, this *Pay It Forward* tangible visible tool gave people permission to express their appreciation, respect, and love for another person, and cheer them on for their dreams.

Today more than 30 million people throughout the world have been impacted by this message, saving lives, healing broken relationships, and empowering dreams.

From 1983 – 2012

- I founded *Difference Makers International*, a nonprofit educational organization committed to creating communities where all people would feel appreciated, respected and loved, valued for their unique talents, and empowered to fulfill their dreams.
- I co-wrote the "Who I Am Makes A Difference"® song which was performed on ABC's *2020*. I wrote, produced and starred in "The True Story of the Making of a Blue Ribbon Nation" with a cast of friends and 150 Miss Teen America contestants.
- Our "Who You Are Makes A Difference"® story appeared in the first *Chicken Soup for the Soul* book.
- The "Who You Are Makes A Difference"® story was made into a 6-minute photo movie that received over 3 million hits on YouTube.
- Our youth and adult leadership programs have been proven to eradicate bullying, avert adolescent suicide, and help all children feel loved.

Before my husband passed away, we had healed our relationship. This story appears in the introduction of my book entitled, *Who I Am Makes A Difference®*.

In 2011, we launched our "IGNITE WHAT'S RIGHT"™ global movement – *Giving Youth a Voice to Create Positive Social Change*. Our goal: 300 million people honored with our Blue Ribbon by the year 2020, led by youth with their results shared around the world.

Join me… Catch the Spark… a Blue Ribbon over every heart by the year 2020.

WHO I AM MAKES A DIFFERENCE ®

by: Helice "Sparky" Bridges
Story originally published in *Chicken Soup for the Soul*.

A teacher in New York decided to honor each of her high school seniors for the difference they made in her life. Then she presented each of them with a Blue Ribbon imprinted with gold letters, which read, "Who I Am Makes A Difference."®

Afterwards the teacher gave each of the students three more ribbons to acknowledge others, to see what impact it would have in their community. They were to follow up on the results, see who honored whom and report back to the class the following week.

One of the students honored a junior executive in a nearby company for helping him with his career planning. The student gave him a blue ribbon and put it on his shirt just over his heart. Then the boy gave him two extra ribbons, explained their class project on acknowledgement and enlisted the executive's help.

Later that day the junior executive went in to his boss and told him that he deeply admired him for being a creative genius. The junior executive asked him if he would accept the gift of the blue ribbon and would he give him permission to put it on him. His surprised boss said, "Well, sure."

After placing the ribbon above his boss' heart, he asked him to support the efforts of the class project and pass on the extra ribbon.

That night the grouchy boss went home to his 14-year-old son and sat him down. He said, "The most incredible thing happened to me today. I was in my office and one of the junior executives came in and told me he admired me and gave me this blue ribbon for being a creative genius. Imagine. He thinks I'm a creative genius. Then he put this blue ribbon that says 'Who I Am Makes A Difference'® on my jacket above my heart. Next he gave me an extra ribbon and asked me to find somebody else to honor. As I was driving home tonight, I started thinking about whom I would honor with this ribbon and I thought about you, son. I want to honor you."

"My days are really hectic and when I come home I don't pay a lot of attention to you. Sometimes I scream at you for not getting good enough grades in school or for your bedroom being a mess. But somehow tonight, I just wanted to sit here and, well, just let you know that you do make a difference to me. Besides your mother, you are the most important person in my life. You're a great kid and I love you!"

The startled boy started to sob and sob, and he couldn't stop crying. His whole body shook. He walked over to a drawer, pulled out a gun, stared at his father and, through his tears said, "I was planning on committing suicide tomorrow, Dad, because I didn't think you loved me. Now I don't need to."

© 1993 Helice "Sparky" Bridges

About author.

*Helice "Sparky" Bridges is founder and C.E.O. of Difference Makers International, a nonprofit educational organization 501c3, dedicated to creating a world where all people feel appreciated, respected and loved. Helice is a sought after speaker and trainer throughout the world. To learn more about Helice "Sparky" Bridges, her Foundation, and to order ribbons, go to **www.DifferenceMakersInternational. org**.*

*To help Sparky "Catch the Spark"... a Blue Ribbon over every heart by the year 2020, contract her at **info@BlueRibbons.org**.*

Letting Go

by Sharon McWilliams

Let the littleness go
See only the Grandeur
Live from this Place.
   - **Sharon McWilliams**, *Daddy, I Remember* ©2004

I've been told that what I've learned over these many years has moved me into an honorable place known as the W*ise Woman Elder.* It has taken all my hard knocks and experiences to get me here, and then some. Still, I am learning; and still, I am making mistakes along the way. It goes with the territory – the territory that lies uncharted for all of us – the territory that we stumble through with small steps or just plain free fall right to our knees, then flat onto our faces. "Ouch" again and again and again! How much longer, God? I am beginning to feel worn and fatigued. Wise Woman, you may find that my story has elements of your story. You see, I decided I needed to change my story somewhat, letting go of obstacles of my own unconscious choosing mostly. Changing wasn't easy. I didn't like change. But so be it, and so it is… change.

As a little girl, I used to watch my grandmother Mary Liz buzz through her house with a well-worn apron and bonnet, heel toeing it with all her chores: baking, cooking, cleaning, gardening, milking her cow and plucking a chicken for dinner, while raising children and caring for grandchildren – including me – daily. How did she do it? How did she keep her smile with her laughter so infectious? Loving and giving, a forgiving soul, she was truly a peacemaker of her time, always wanting everyone to get along.

At the same time, Grandma's middle daughter, my mama Ruth, dealt with depression most of her life, and all of my childhood. Since I was the oldest, and a girl, I spent most of my childhood as a "little mother" for my three younger brothers. I did the best I could. I hope they can forgive me for my ignorance. My mama seemed lost with life. She loved being outdoors, dancing and singing, laughing with friends in her early years. She didn't like cooking and all the mundane chores of the housewife, although she did it well. She, like many women

144

of the fifties era after World War II, didn't get to live their dreams. They were living the dreams of their husbands. Mama got by in life, sadly. I so loved her beautiful smile, her kindness and patience, her sweetness and gentleness. I pray I have some of that in me. I miss her. I miss what we didn't have as mother and daughter.

So in my early years, Grandma was my support, my strength, my main role model for a strong woman. Grandma Lizzie seemed to have an innate knowing about life. She seemed to know her role, what was expected her, and how to do it with grace. I loved Grandma's laughter and chutzpah. As her first granddaughter, I followed in those busy footsteps. I juggled my teaching career with the raising of my own babies and teenagers, going back to school, having a home and a marriage – doing all the things I was supposed to, making my list and checking twice – going and doing, going and doing!

In my later years, my sweet mama kept telling me, "Sharon, you must slow down and take a breath." Of course, I chose not to listen. I chose to give and give and give and give, taking no time for myself, just like my grandmother and my mother. I knew what to do. I had learned their roles well, I thought. I could do what they did, and more. I could have my career, too! Yes, I fell into the Super Woman Syndrome story, having no clue.

On my fiftieth birthday, the bottom fell out of my story.

I was hurrying early one morning in December, out the door to school. In an instant, I slipped and fell on black ice! What I thought was just a broken arm that would heal quickly turned into a major disaster for me. My life as I knew it ended. I became homebound for five years. At first, I felt really sorry for myself. Having lost the use of my right arm and hand, my major source of doing, I had to relearn almost everything. All my friends worked. My children were in school. My husband had a new career that involved lots of traveling.

Here I was, poor pitiful me, home for the first winter of my adult life. It was quiet. There was snow. One clear, crisp morning, I walked outside to hear the hush of winter. I could hear me breathing. I was still here.

I could feel whispers of some sort. I could sense Someone or Something working behind the scenes now in my life. It was during that time I began to find myself. I stepped onto a new path, the one that's called "The road less taken." I call it "The journey of letting go."

I began to take the time to study the models of wise women in my life. I realized that I had unknowingly absorbed scarcity thinking, worry, depression, the victimization of the beloved women before me. I had become saturated with my mother's stories, my grandmothers' stories, and even my mother-in-law's stories that were passed onto me.

145

I had to ask myself some hard questions now:

- Who am I now that I am not who I was?
- What am I passing on to my daughters and granddaughters?
- How do I let go of this hurtful stuff?
- How do I rewrite my story, one that honors my ancestors, original family of women, my daughters and my descendants?
- What steps can I take to move me forward while simultaneously letting go of the obstacles that were blatantly showing themselves now?

This silent indoctrination begins early for all of us. As little ones, we are innocent and so loving, soaking up every breath of life as little sponges. It is not unnatural for us to continue the very same roles in our own lives. And, many times those roles may include "little woman" thinking laced with physical, emotional, and even sexual abuse. Many times we are caught in the role of victim, not realizing that we have the power to let that go. Until we become aware that we *can* release obstacles from our stories, until we realize what *has* held us back from our childhood, until we *are* willing to step out of those places, we can end up repeating the past. Even worse, we can pass it on to our own daughters and granddaughters. So I asked myself more questions:

- What do I as a wise woman want to pass on as heritage?
- Do I want a repeat?
- What gifts do I keep?
- What obstacles do I release?

So many questions led me to the philosophy of the poet Ranier Marie Rilke, who so passionately wrote:

> *...have patience with everything unresolved in your heart and to try to love the questions themselves as if they were locked rooms or books written in a very foreign language. Don't search for the answers, which could not be given to you now, because you would not be able to live them. And the point is to live everything. Live the questions now. Perhaps then, someday far in the future, you will gradually, without even noticing it, live your way into the answer.*

It has been many years since that black ice event. I am still living my questions, but with a twist – *out loud!* For the most part I am conscious now and very aware. I still have my moments of difficult lessons and experiences. The difference is I choose to live these moments as opportunities to go deep within myself, co-creating something wonderful to pass on in honor of my family of origin and for my most precious daughters and my granddaughters.

Seven generations forward and seven generations back, so the Bible says. The gift of my "letting go" heals my ancestors as well as releases my descendants from "littleness," according to quantum physics! Mystical, miraculous and

146

magnificent! I am most grateful and honored to do this, to be this. I found pearls in living my questions.

I love my life now with all its meanderings, its ups and downs, over and arounds, tears and laughter... no matter what. I saw "through a glass darkly"; now I see "face to face" the wonder of living my questions in the beauty of letting go. (A little secret: I have found an Answer – She's known as Grace.)

I am a baby boomer woman who is now beginning to understand Mark Twain's wisdom:

> *"Dance like nobody's watching;*
> *love like you've never been hurt.*
> *Sing like nobody's listening;*
> *live like it's heaven on earth."*

I found it the hard way. Yet, I have my new story, where I *am* dancing, singing, loving and living full out. Yes, I have had to work hard to change the dynamics of my story that I may live a joyous, fulfilling life. There may be a rug pulled out from under me again; there may be another moment where I am walking on eggshells. That's life! The difference now – I know I can choose to let go! I smile in this moment with such deep compassion and gratitude.

Those dynamics of my story remain in a continuous loop of change, moving up the spiral of life. When it seems like I am going nowhere, I realize I am in a place of "pause." I take that pause now. When it feels like I am sliding backward, I know I am just building momentum to get to the next level in my life.

Wise Woman, I share this with you that you may reweave your story into the beautiful tapestry of the life you want to pass on. You see, upon reflection, I have discovered that my grandmother's chutzpah has another name. She's known as Courage.

> *Courage*
> *A kind blessing*
> *With quiet eyes of*
> *Strength so*
> *Powerful*
> *It silently and serenely portrays*
> *Honesty as*
> *The simple truth of*
> *Forgiveness*
> *Love*
> *The silent bridge to*
> *Heaven's gate*
> *A little laugh*
> *I had it all the time*
> *Courage*
> ~ sharon mcwilliams © 2004

Know this, Wise Woman: Letting go... *you* can do this.

About author.

Sharon McWilliams *is a speaker, author, singer/songwriter, educator, certified master retreat, life and woman's empowerment coach and Reiki Master-Teacher! A co-creator with wise women, Sharon shares her discoveries with you in her multifaceted experiential retreats and coaching programs. Tune into to her radio show, The Wise WomanSoul Show with Mentors Harbor!*

Visit her Facebook Page: Wise Woman, Take a Breath!
Website: __www.wisewomansoul.com__
Email: __sharon@wisewomansoul.com.__

The Creation of Our Daily Bread ~ Overcoming Obstacles in the Workplace

Follow Your Bliss and the Universe Will Open Doors for You, When There Were Only Walls.

~ *Joseph Campbell*

Money and You...
a Firewall to Protect YOU
in a Financial Crisis

by Dame DC Cordova

I grew up in a wonderful middle class family in Chile, with female role models that taught me to be self-sufficient, successful, and with an entrepreneurial spirit to go for my dreams. My mom was a hottie in the 1950s that owned a beauty salon. She was beautiful, she was loving, she had cash, and she had consciousness... great footsteps to follow.

My mom and my auntie, who was even more entrepreneurial than mamacita, taught me hard work – and leverage – though I didn't learn that term until I met the Mentors that I inherited my work from. I learned to leverage time, resources, networks, money – and through building several organizations – to leverage myself through systems.... What good is financial success if you have no time to enjoy it?

In Spanish we have a saying: Salud, dinero y amor – y tiempo para gozarlo: Health, money and love – and time to enjoy it!

Money has never been a struggle for me in this life. My lessons have centered on my emotional well-being: to stay loving to others in the presence of adversity and stay connected to myself, no matter what is happening around me – including a financial crisis.

My emotional well-being was highly affected when I was very young. I experienced the loss of my first love through a tragic auto accident, and within a few months, the miscarriage of his baby. Not even out of my teens yet, that was a very tough way to come into adulthood.

Though I was very sad inside, I sailed through college; I excelled in being an interpreter in the legal system, and later as an official court reporter. I was making all the money any 20-something could want – and more. Short of minor ups and downs, I sailed through my life in many areas, until the Asian Financial Crisis of '97 – '98. I was married. Living in Singapore and Hawaii. Had a very thriving business with my then-husband, and was continuing the work that

151

I had been doing since 1979 – the Money & You® Program and the Excellerated Business School® for Entrepreneurs.

I didn't think I had any major money issues, until it looked as though a business I had been working wholeheartedly for 18 years called "Money & You®" was in the middle of the worst financial disaster that Asia had ever seen. We traded over a million dollars the year before, and were well on our way to another great year. Then it all stopped. Everyone felt that entrepreneurial education or getting more distinctions around money and "you" were no longer important. People were fighting for their financial lives; it was so intense to experience. The news talked about nothing else. The whole of Asia was brought to its knees, and it was no rock'n roll ride. Most Westerners around the world (except Australians and New Zealanders) had no idea how intense that time was for the Asians – it affected billions of people.

Until then, I always thought that people who would get so traumatized around money (even committing suicide) were selfish, self-centered, and more concerned about themselves than their loved ones. I just couldn't understand why anyone would take such drastic actions around money. Little did I know that it's actually not about the money; it's about all the emotions around the situation: the shame, the guilt, the blame... the constant chatter in your head that, "If I had done this or that, I wouldn't be in this situation."

It was such an intense experience that it cost me my marriage, because we disagreed so wholeheartedly as to how to handle the crisis. He wanted to bankrupt the company and I wanted to salvage it. I went through my nest-egg to attempt to do that. After nearly a year of almost running myself ragged, and the rest of my business in other regions down the drain, I had to stop.

In order to save my sanity, health, and well-being, I decided to stop and take stock of how things were really happening. Through trial and error, I learned to overcome my own mind on how to handle this. This is what I did, and this is what many of the financial gurus – the "masters" of prosperity consciousness – have done in order for them to move themselves out of their "emotional crisis." Believe me, I know, because I've been right there with them as they went through some of these steps. I turned my business around in 18 months. It was a short time considering the circumstances. They, too, turned their lives around, and went on to become "gurus."

Here you are:

Know this is about YOU: It's not about the economy. There are many people making money when others are not.

Don't go into agreement about what is happening around you. Move to another city or country, if needed. You can always go back "home."

152

Handle your emotional well-being. Work on yourself immediately. YOU are the one person who can control your destiny – not the circumstance around you. This is a crucial step. If you cannot get up in the morning and do what it takes to get yourself up and running again, nothing much else will matter.

Now you begin to take care of the cash. You need money coming in.

Determine what you are good at and what will bring you money now – not later – but now! Don't worry about the tasks. Some of us had to roll up our sleeves and do jobs we had paid others to do for many years.

What can you sell? What are your resources? What can you give to someone in a good financial situation in exchange and have them support you?

Create a plan, and then work the plan!

When done with your personal financial crisis, keep your agreements and pay everyone back. If you cannot do that for years, create new agreements as necessary.

Continue to get educated in entrepreneurial activities, which include sales/marketing, people/organizations, money/finances – the key skills for a successful entrepreneur.

You must learn to sell if you don't know how to. Salespeople can get a job anytime – no matter which way the economy goes – anywhere in the world. You can always sell for commissions. If you are building a non-profit organization, you need to learn to sell your idea... your vision.

Focus on income-generating activities. Let go of all those things that waste your time and don't bring in the cash flow that you need.

Tighten up your belt. No new clothes, cars, or any other doodas that are not going to create money for you. You now spend money only on those things that will make you more money.

Continue to clear your blocks to financial well-being on a daily basis for at least an hour. Your financial life depends on it. Do affirmations, keep a journal, and release any negative thoughts about your financial well-being.

Do a good transformational program that will "kick-start" you in making new decisions and creating new references for yourself.

Surround yourself with loving and supportive people – particularly a good mentor – who will tell you the truth and give you good feedback to accelerate your progress towards getting back on your feet.

153

Create a good business team that will support you.

Do something once a day that brings you pleasure. Exercise, ride your bicycle, spend time with your loved ones, watch your favorite program, read a novel.... This is crucial to keep your spirits up.

Don't make yourself wrong – forgive yourself for things that you think you could have done differently. Move on... don't talk about that time of your life.

Keep being involved in income-generating activities and leverage.

Keep taking action. Your life will turn around!

Be generous with the money that you are now making. Donate at least 10% to charitable organizations; this will activate the Law of Tithing.

Be generous with your time. Support others. Donate your time to charitable activities, this will active the Law of Receiving.

So as I continue to grow and prosper, I continue to do many of the steps mentioned. Some have become habits that support my financial and personal well-being.

I don't know any good entrepreneur who hasn't had some very intense learning experiences. All I know is that if I create good firewalls that will keep me in the right track, and keep spending the extra money that I bring into my business on things that will bring me more money, I am in the cycle that creates wealth.

And remember, it's about YOU!

Congratulations for having picked up this publication. You are learning from the best.

May you live long and prosper.

About author.

Dame DC Cordova is the CEO of Excellerated Business Schools®/Money & You® Program. Since 1979, a pioneer of high-speed, experiential entrepreneurship education. Her global organization has more than 70,000 graduates from over 60 countries in the Asia Pacific and North American Regions both in English and Chinese. If you wish to learn more about her programs please visit her website: www.excellerated.com.

Breaking Through...
How to Walk on
Your Own Chosen Path

by Monique Blokzyl

On September 17, 2010, I handed in the keys to my company car, together with the certainty of my monthly salary. I gave up a 15-year employment career in leading marketing and change management positions for some of the biggest corporations worldwide. I left behind my life as I had known it thus far. What would have given me a rush of fear in the past, now gave me a thrill of excitement! For the first time in many years, I knew with absolute certainty that I had finally stepped onto the right path: I was about to build my own business.

For me, it had been a long journey of getting to this turning point in my life. I grew up in Eastern Germany behind the Iron Curtain, in a system where owning a business was a very foreign concept. Companies and resources were state owned. Everyone was state employed. Building my own business was beyond any realistic vision.

My childhood dream of becoming a teacher had been shattered because I did not blend in with the socialist concept of the German Democratic Republic. Someone like me who was active in their church community was not seen as a good fit to educate socialist children. My whole life plan collapsed when I was refused the opportunity to teach. I gave up dreaming early on and stopped asking myself what it was I truly wanted. I did not know what to do with my life. Losing my direction, I stumbled onto a path towards nowhere, studying a subject not chosen out of passion.

Einstein once said, "The intuitive mind is a sacred gift and the rational mind is a faithful servant. We have created a society that honors the servant and has forgotten the gift." And this is how I lived my life. For many years I became a master at ignoring my inner voice, even though I knew to my core that I was on the wrong path. But I kept on, even to the point of signing a contract for a new job while every cell of my being was screaming at me to "Get out of here!"

In spite of promotions and bigger paychecks, much too often I came home from work feeling frustrated. Believing that there was something wrong with me, I beat myself up for not giving my "all" in a job I was not passionate about. Why could I not simply be happy with my career? I had a great salary, a new company car, an impressive corporate title, and great colleagues to work with.... But I knew something was missing.

Feeling unfulfilled, I knew that I was not contributing to anything that was worth spending all this time on. All that really mattered to me occurred after working hours: I had built a public speaking club, I was studying, coaching, and was helping people to build their business. It was in these late hours each day I felt that I was growing and that I made a difference for myself and for others.

One day I received an e-mail that would change everything for me. While in my office I was hit by a friend's message that said my soul mate, Michael, had died two days after brain surgery. My eyes blurred with tears. In a split second, as though I had died myself, I saw a movie with all the beautiful moments we had enjoyed together. I clearly saw Michael in front of me being someone who had turned every day of his life into magical moments. He never rested content for anything less than fantastic! In that moment of memory, I committed myself to following in his footsteps, and never again to settle for anything less than *great* in my life. So, in those days of endless grief, I finally allowed my suppressed inner voice to be heard again.

What do you really want to do with your life? If you only had a short time left on this earth, what would you still want to see or do? What is the legacy you want to leave behind when you have to leave forever?

It was as if my eyes and heart had opened wide, and it dawned on me that as long as I did not have clear answers to these questions, I would be bound forever to my path towards nowhere. Motivated to take action, I started studying how people make sense of their life, and I hired a coach to help me gain more clarity. I realized that the very first step to take towards a life of fulfillment is to:

Listen to our inner voice and let it tell us what we really want.

There are many people who ask me how they can find a dream that drives them, how can they find out what they truly want, what keeps their fire burning....

Keep asking yourself these questions, and take time out regularly to listen to your inner voice for answers. Enjoy quiet moments and let the answers come to you. Some of the biggest discoveries in the world were triggered when scientists were not paying attention. We all know the story of Newton, who, in an idle moment saw an apple fall from a tree, which inspired discovery of the law of gravity.

Take action and observe yourself!

What do you love doing so much that you would do it for free or even pay to do? How ready are you to tell your manager tomorrow that your job is giving you so much pleasure that you will start paying your company instead of them paying you?

156

You might think, *"Yeah, but I am not Rockefeller. I have to earn money. I cannot daydream because I have a family to take care of and bills to be paid."*

I would ask you:

What if you could make much more money than you have today by doing what you love doing most?

A few short months after stepping out of my corporate life, I worked on a consulting project that paid me more in three months than I had earned in six months as head of marketing. In the last two years, I have been building a business together with amazing partners who I was able to meet only after leaving my job. In my first 12 months, I received more insights into more corporate organizations than I probably would have in my entire corporate career, even if I had switched jobs regularly.

Every morning, I jump out of bed full of energy, looking forward to my day ahead! I tremendously enjoy inspiring people by making all the support they need available to find their own dream, and by empowering them to build their own business.

I have the freedom to accept speaking engagements whenever I am invited, which also boosts my energy. In the last two years, I have given speeches and workshops at different conferences all over Europe. Mentoring and coaching is something I adore doing! I love helping people become brilliant on any stage, in front of an audience of 10 or 10,000 people.

The day I learned that I had lost my dear friend, I did not have clear answers to any of the questions I have posed here, but I was able to give my quest a tremendous boost by starting to gather all the puzzle pieces of my life and lay them out in front of me. It had dawned on me that it was entirely up to me to take the first step. I realized that no magic wand would change my life overnight, that no help would come if I did not help myself first.

So, on that memorable September day in 2010, I left the office for the last time with my heart filled with faith and certainty that everything would turn out great! I did not have the faintest idea of how my future would evolve. I did not have a well-defined business plan or a ready-to-go-to client list. At that point, I did not even know much about what it takes to build and run a business… I simply knew that I was finally starting on my right path.

Are you walking on your true path? Are you making decisions based on what you truly want at any moment in your life? Or, are you following a trail that someone else has chosen for you because you do not know what you truly want or how to make your dream a reality?

Many people tell me that they could never take a bold jump like I did. They would rather run things in parallel, to remain employed and to build their business slowly. Taking this stable bridge from one side to the other never worked for me. I craved for years to find the right business idea. And whenever I had a sparkling idea, I got lost in exploring possible business models and creating wonderful plans. But I never really started anything. It was only when the pain inside me became bigger than the comfort of the golden cage that I realized:

You need to bring yourself into a position where you HAVE TO TAKE ACTION.

Many battles in history were won when surrender was not an option. A lot of stories in this book show us that most great mentors laid the cornerstone for their success in moments of absolute adversity or defeat. They were in a position in which not taking action would have killed them or their loved ones. These are the moments when we have no choice but to TAKE A FIRST STEP.

I am not saying you need to bring yourself into danger, to give up your job right away, or to accept self-induced bankruptcy. But you do need to create enough disturbances in your mind and heart so that you have no choice but to take action. One way is to ask troubling questions that don't offer you easy answers:

Are you planning to have your own business up and running in 5 to 10 years because you WANT IT LIKE THIS or because you think "sooner" is not REALISTIC? What if you had only three years left to live?

Or...

What would you want your life to look like while running your own business? How would it look if you were still doing the same old job, 10 years from now?

With that dawning clarity, take action! Take the first step. Procrastination is what kills your dreams. There will always be things and people that need your urgent attention. Are you happy with a mediocre life? Or, do you want more? And who could help you along the way?

One of the most important things I learned on my way is how to:

Build a support network that gives you wings.

Another misconception that held me back for so many years was my belief that I had to do everything on my own. I believed I needed to have all the skills an entrepreneur needs, within myself. I overlooked the simple truth that the world is full of amazing people with special skills ready to step up with you.

What made all the difference for me in the last years were the many people I met who were ready to partner with me, to exchange experiences and services, and who helped me in countless other ways. Today my network is bigger

158

than ever! I have gotten to know people from all over the world. Some of them I have never met in person, yet they have become my strongest supporters.

You might say:

"But I am not a social butterfly. How can I meet potential partners and clients? How can I build my support network?"

Just start speaking about your dream. Join networks where you find people who are doing what you want to do. Build your own support network including at least a coach, a mentor, an accountability partner, and a Mastermind group. The coach will ask you the right questions to gain clarity, and will help you see what you cannot see on your own. Choose your mentor wisely as someone who has already done what you are aiming to achieve. He or she can give you incredible hints on how to do it yourself, and can help cut your way to success much shorter. Your accountability partner will make sure you take action and stay on track on a very regular basis. In a Mastermind group, you provide a trusted platform to give each other inspiration and create new ideas, to support each other through difficult times, and to multiply your access to empowering people and networks.

Since September 2010, there was not one single moment when I considered going back to my old life. Every day I wake up being grateful for the path I have chosen now, despite all the daily struggles that I know exist to make me grow. Any obstacle is an opportunity as long as we have people around us that can help, inspire, and support us. Unlimited support is available to all of us.

You can make anything happen as long as you are listening to your inner voice and are clear about what you truly want. I invite you to take the first step... and another one, until you get where you want to be!

About author.

Visit Monique's website www.moniqueblokzyl.com to take a brief test for FREE to see if you have what it takes to become a successful entrepreneur. In addition, she has a FREE weekly newsletter that will give step by step instructions and tools, to rocket your ideas into enterprise! **Monique Blokzyl** *is the founder of the Business Launch Portal and is dedicated to help aspiring entrepreneurs, turn their business vision into a powerful enterprise. As an international public speaker, trainer and coach, radio host and author, Monique inspires and supports founders in many ways to jump-start their business. (Note: Monique has been chosen by Mentors Magazine to be the CEO of the German version of this publication in her country.)*

A Silver Spoon of My Own

by Burke Franklin

I popped out into this world into an environment of wealth. My grandfather had made a lot of money in the tubing business after World War II. So far so good. But when I looked around, I noticed that not everybody enjoyed my good fortune. Even *I* didn't fully appreciate my good fortune. And, like a typical spoiled brat, I wanted more. On top of that, I was envious of those who had even more than I did!

As you already know, the golden rule is: "Those who have the gold make the rules." I could have whatever it was my grandparents wanted to buy me, and sometimes, that was what I wanted. From early on, my problem was how to make my own money so I could buy whatever it was that I wanted, without begging, explaining, or selling.

Also, one of the questions I pondered was why I was so fortunate and others were not? Yeah, I felt some guilt and embarrassment because people were looking at me, and I couldn't explain it. Was there a way to help others have what I had? Both so I could feel better, as well as have some friends to play with?

Wait a minute...

I couldn't have any friends to play with unless they had more stuff? If I had more stuff then more people would like me? Or was I confusing envy with popularity? There it was.... To my 6-year old mind: Stuff = Popularity & Happiness.

While growing up, I can't tell you how many times I heard, "All you need is a good idea... sell it... and live happily ever after." I guess it's the American Dream. I heard it from my grandfather who founded a tubing distribution company after World War II. His company, TubeSales, became a successful worldwide distributor of industrial tubing.

Dinner table discussions were often about the tubing distribution business. When I was six, my grandfather imparted this wisdom to me: "You'll never make any money working for somebody else." He also advised, "Get a product (or invent one) and sell it." This was the answer I thought I was looking

160

for! I scrounged around the house looking for something to sell. Because my grandmother was on a political election committee, the next day I was in business for the first time, in our driveway, selling *Ronald Reagan for Governor* Buttons for 25 cents each. My mom and grandmother each bought one. Not exactly the success I had dreamed of.

There must be a scheme for me to get rich on my own.

I figured that when I got rich on my own, I would help other people do it, too.

In college I majored in engineering and business, but I was crazy for finding something to do that was real.... I learned about a do-it-yourself used car lot concept, and I built and ran it from my fraternity bedroom. After college, I sold software for analyzing real estate investments. Next I sold electronic components for Texas Instruments, and after that, I sold financial software for mid-sized businesses.

Sales... selling... ugh! Was this what it took to get more *stuff* so people would like me? So, I reversed that – I got a job at the *Sharper Image Catalog* as the electronics buyer.... I knew electronics and I knew which stuff I'd buy. That worked. What a great job that was! Imagine having access to all that stuff! One weekend, another buyer and I were going skiing, so we went to the sample room to grab as much cool stuff as we could. After an hour, we looked at each other and all the stuff, and agreed that it was more trouble than it was worth. We put everything back and went skiing without it! Hmmm, stuff can be a burden.

During this time, I started reading books on business success and taking seminars on personal development. It never ceased to amaze me what changed in my world after I reconciled some immature assumption or idea left-over from my childhood. I learned that most *realities* were merely a point-of-view – often, someone else's. When I changed my point-of-view, things changed. Sometimes everything changed. The telephone would ring from someone I hadn't spoken to in years, or a customer would call in an order, and things like that. This kind of stuff really works. My frustrations and anxieties were *transformed*. I learned to use the BS of my past as fertilizer for my future! And this was the start of my new perspective of *stuff.*

Use the BS of your past as fertilizer for your future!

Back then, I thought I wanted to either get rich on something silly like a Pet Rock, or change the world with something serious like Penicillin, and I'd always wondered what happened to the inventions and other stuff featured in *Popular Science* and *Popular Mechanics*.

Some 22 years ago I learned about business plans. Before that I had heard little of them. I was surprised at how many business owners did not write a business plan at all. The owner/entrepreneur had some ideas in his/her head, and just went forward. If you've ever worked for these people, you've probably also experienced a lot of screaming and frustration.

I discovered that writing a business plan actually enabled others in the business, not only to understand the big picture, but to be pro-active, make better decisions, and work together to forward the action in favor of the big idea. A friend needed help writing his business plan to sell his software to Apple. I worked long and hard to develop what I thought was an elaborate brochure to sell his idea, at all levels of his business. He got the deal and my phone started ringing. A business plan is an unusual document, something most people rarely write, but while they are all very unique, there are specific characteristics that all require. Long story short, I invented a "template" that proved wildly effective.

Perhaps inventors and others could benefit from my business plan template. Perhaps supporting others to introduce their solutions for our world was better leveraging of my skills and a more important contribution for me to make to the world right now. This was cool stuff!

Being wealthy comes from being worthy.

Being worthy comes from progressive realization of a worthy cause. Throughout history, great minds from Aristotle to Newton to Einstein have studied causality. What is the cause that creates the effect? What is your cause? What is your cause that will create your effect? (From Roger Hamilton's book, *Your Life, Your Legacy.*)

Today people buy – not just your product or service – but WHY you developed your product or service. My favorite example is Patagonia. The founder & CEO is an avid outdoorsman, rock-climber, surfer, etc. I like the idea of buying a jacket from a guy who himself hangs on a cliff using his own equipment and keeps improving it for a better experience. He makes useful stuff for him to do what he likes to do – and you can have one, too.

My cause is to help others succeed in delivering their ideas, innovations and inventions to the world, to build their businesses, because that's exactly what we need right now in this time of economic uncertainty. The point of this story is to put *stuff* into perspective. What kinds of stuff are you creating, and why?

At the end of the day, my best product is me. Your best product is you. Your business' best product is a solution to someone's problem. Something that makes someone's pain go away. Something that provides joy to others. That's the stuff they want.

Asked why people buy from me it's because they want to buy from *me*. After all this time, the stuff I was looking for to make me attractive, liked, and happy was in me from the beginning. Today, I am more appreciative and thankful for that. Working on my own stuff provides my best return on investment. Helping you evolve yourself to deliver the stuff we need in our world is what I love to do. And it's working!

162

I wrote my book, *Business Black Belt* to share my favorite business and life lessons. Everything I learned from the workshops I participated in, from the consultants I worked with, from my experiences working for large and small companies, as well as for 20+ years invested in developing business-building software tools, I actually studied and documented what worked and what needed to be done differently. Think of it as a 20-year head start in business and life. It's full of actionable specifics for what you do AFTER you've taken the motivational seminars.

Although your life is your dojo, my niche is in your business being your dojo – where everyday events provide opportunities for growth. Here's where I can help you to be, do, and have what you want.

About author.

Burke Franklin has been a sought after international speaker and keynote for over 20 years. He is the founder and CEO of JIAN (jee'on – a Zen word meaning "the master of every art") Software, a successful Silicon Valley software company renowned for their flagship product: BizPlanBuilder® – the popular software system for producing a comprehensive business plan. BizPlanBuilder® was voted number #1 in its category in PC Magazine, and JIAN's suite of other products has garnered accolades worldwide.

*Burke's highly praised book, **Business Black Belt** teaches more than 70 contemporary real-world lessons, and is rich in hard-won advice for building and running a business today. Visit his websites for more information: **www. Jian.com** and **www.BurkeFranklin.com**.*

163

Creating Diversity in the Workplace for Optimum Results

by Caroline Newman

One of only two black lawyers at a top city law firm in London, I had been with the firm for 4 years, working many hard and long hours as a corporate lawyer. One day as I was walking down the corridor, one of the senior partners strode up to me and uttered these words that would change my life forever. He faced me squarely and told me that *I was a "Black Sheep" who did not belong there!*

My jaw dropped; I could not believe what I was hearing. I felt as though someone had punched me in the stomach. The feeling of being physically sick washed over me as I struggled to maintain my composure. This was a clear case of direct race discrimination, so what was I to do? A huge obstacle had been placed in front of me and I worried that my career as a lawyer was over. I began doubting myself and questioning my own worthiness.

To make sure that I wasn't going crazy, I turned to my peers for their help. They sympathized but could not do much for me. The challenges that lay ahead were mine, and it was up to me to draw on all my reserves and strengths to get through them.

After much soul-searching, I chose not to sue, but decided to use my experience of discrimination to help bring the subject of creating diversity in the workplace to the forefront of the conversation in the legal and other professions.

In the professions such as legal, accountancy and investment banking, there is a "war for talent" going on. Everyone wants to attract, recruit, and retain a "dream team." At the same time, they also want to attract the best clients. The question is how can you attract and keep the right people to deliver the best services to your blue chip clients? Some firms believe they have to lower the quality of their dream teams because they feel obliged to take on this diverse range of people.

Retaining staff and recruiting at mid-career level are becoming increasingly difficult. The pool of high quality talent is not growing and those

164

people who are high quality usually have no illusions about their marketability! Employers are addressing the critical issue of staff retention to maintain growth, innovation, and competitiveness. Legislation is changing, and the issues of diversity are becoming more prominent. Professional organizations worldwide are looking at the means of attracting and keeping a team that provides great service and that ticks all the diversity boxes.

Many of my clients are leading law firms that are currently grappling with these modern day issues. Diversity is a hot potato! It's one of the most important and challenging issues facing both corporations and professional service firms today. Diversity is valuable because the more diverse your team, the broader the expertise and knowledge you have to offer your clients. Diversity brings richness to your professional environment both internally and externally. There are even organizations that use their understanding of many cultures and ethnicity as a selling point for their service. What's in it for you if you adopt diversity and flexible working policies?

Retaining Stars

High performers are not always those who live and breathe their work. Many of them have families and leisure pursuits. This does not mean they are not committed to their employer, it simply means they have a wider perspective on what life is about. If your firm is known for offering a diverse and flexible working environment, that will be a big factor for potential employees to join you, or for current employees to stay rather than move on. Professionals at all levels have more choice; they are moving much more often and are more demanding. Employees from diverse cultural backgrounds want to see diversity policies in action, not just on paper.

So what do they expect?

- A working environment where people are recruited and promoted on merit, not because of age, sex, ethnic roots, or length of service.
- A work/life balance so they can spend time with their families and be less stressed and more productive.
- A more meaningful and responsible job.
- Respect for productivity. Rather than simply long hours, at the end of the day it's results that count.
- Clarity over roles and advancement. They need to be able to see the road ahead.
- Removal of the stigma attached to flexible working hours. As long as the job gets done and the clients are happy, it shouldn't matter what time it gets done, or for that matter, where it gets done.
- Mentoring and career development. It all adds to the feeling of being valued.

- Professional knowledge and soft skills development, along with practical help. Appreciation usually keeps people with you; if they leave they probably would have done so in any case.

- Career breaks and returning employee integration. People need to know they are valued and are not simply a disposable resource.

- Connection with the community or society (corporate social responsibility). You'll be surprised at how much more effort your staff will invest in pro-bono projects if you meet them at least half way.

- Active, effective equality and diversity policies where everyone in the organization walks the talk. This is worth every penny invested in "free" public relations since happy employees tell their friends and acquaintances.

- Respect for individual strengths. Everyone can't do everything! Play to each person's strengths and your team will perform beyond everyone's wildest dreams.

- More visibility earlier, and recognizing contribution and client engagement. These all contribute to job satisfaction which is a big retention magnet.

Attracting Stars

The Law of Attraction states that we are energy. We are all connected. What you give your attention to always expands. What you focus on you will receive. As members of the professions, are you prepared to suspend belief and use the universal tools and resources at your disposal to create the company, the firm, the business, and the workforce you desire?

Whether you are a corporation, a professional practice or an individual, you can embrace the Law of Attraction to attract whatever you want. However, you must decide what that is. What philosophy, belief systems, and values will make your firm an environment that others will desire to work in? All these need to be crystal clear and in specific detail to enable you to focus your attention on attracting those employees and clients who match your philosophy and values.

It may sound unlikely, but it has been proven over and over again that you can literally manifest your dream team and your dream clients. Are you ready to take responsibility for creating your firm the way you want it to be?

Personal Responsibility

We all have the freedom to choose – to make the decisions that will take us in the direction we want to go. We are all accountable for the things we do and don't do. If you choose to focus on discrimination and lack of opportunities, then the universe will ensure that you get more of the same. On the other hand, if you see only abundance and create a world free from oppression, discrimination, and poverty, then that is what you will attract. Decide how you want your personal and working world to be; it starts on the inside.

Using my experiences, I'm able to help others bring about diversity and create dream teams in their organizations. My particular niche is diversity consulting and coaching, especially with law firms and other legal professions. Creating a better understanding between people of different cultures, religions, genders, ages, and beliefs creates a cohesive and highly productive team.

The Route Map to a Diverse Future

Here are some of my tips to bring the best of diversity into our professions.

1. Shift your paradigm in relation to diversity

Change the way you see the world, the universe, and your role in it. Many organizations have already started this shift. Barclays, Starbucks, Dell, and Microsoft are just a few of the international corporations that have changed their thinking about diversity. Create new ways of thinking about people of different cultures, religions, orientations, ethnicities, ages, and genders. Having a diverse working environment is good for business. Different people bring a wealth of experience and expertise to any environment. In a diverse workforce, if your team can learn to become interdependent, it allows each person to play to their strengths.

2. Begin with the end in mind

Start with a clear understanding of your destination. In what direction do you want your organization to move? Focus on the type of environment you want to create. Visualize how you want your environment to be in one, two, three, five, or even ten years.

3. Get commitment from traditionally disadvantaged groups

The individuals from disadvantaged groups in your organization will know whether you are serious or not about diversity. Find ways to involve everyone and use their expertise. Involvement creates commitment or "buy-in."

4. Link your diversity goals to your mission statement

Diversity is essential as part of an organization's mission and goal, and must be included in your mission statement. As part of getting "buy-in," involve all your employees, managers, leaders, and clients in the process. Listen to staff and communicate with respect. This will require a paradigm shift because most of us need to learn how to listen. This is not easy; it requires time and patience, but if you can empathize with people, you'll find the rewards are enormous!

5. Change the way you think about things

Most people have a fear of change – there's a level of discomfort to any change that makes it much easier to carry on doing what has worked for years. Professional firms may need to change the way they have traditionally operated. If diversity is truly embraced, everyone involved will almost certainly need to go through radical change, from the firm to the profession to the community, and even to society. Are you prepared to challenge the status quo?

167

6. Use the synergy principle in mediation

Synergy is what happens when people work together effectively. Synergy is often defined as the whole being equal to more than the sum of the parts. The combined effort and co-operation of a diverse workforce makes for better synergy. Instead of using disciplinary action and grievances, organizations can use the principle of synergy to mediate disputes, particularly those that have discrimination or harassment as a component. Mediating and finding a "win-win" solution is far better than pursuing punishment for the so-called "guilty" parties. Learn how to use synergy instead of punishment.

7. Plant the seeds, and then harvest the crop

If you want your organization to develop a character of maturity, integrity, and an abundance mentality, you need to sow the seeds to get the crop growing. This will require an investment of time and effort. Attitude is everything, but most firms spend far more teaching people only the technical aspects of their job. While you cannot change people's attitude per se, you can create an environment where a positive attitude and a "can do" approach is standard. The seeds must be planted by the leaders or the rest of the organization will only pay lip-service to it. Make sure your organization is populated with healthy seeds that grow into high quality "crops."

8. Changing language is a key to changing the way things are framed

Be *for* diversity, not against discrimination. Focus on what you want, not on what you don't. Diversity is a beautiful thing. Each of us is unique, with our own gifts to offer. Recognizing our similarities and appreciating each other's differences is the way to create an environment that truly performs.

Know it is coming, that you already have it on order, and that it's on its way!

Act with intent, step forward, and take action as though you are already there. Maintain the attitude of gratitude. Use the principle of gratitude to appreciate your new situation. Nothing new can come into your life without gratitude. Care about the people with whom you interact. Be prepared to take action and make changes in the way you do business and watch your life and your business move to a level beyond your dreams!

168

About author.

Caroline Newman *has a Masters degree in Law and is an Attorney (England and Wales), an expert Diversity consultant, author of Legal Gold, trainer, coach, and international Professional speaker. She specializes in change management, leadership training, and personal and professional development in the legal profession. As a certified Life Success Consultant with Bob Proctor's company Life Success Productions, Caroline focuses on engendering a shift in thinking and performance.*

Caroline's expertise and experience is considerable. She is trained in mediation by Centre for Effective Dispute Resolution, is a certified Master Practitioner and Trainer of Neuro Linguistic Programming. She was the first person of African-Caribbean descent to be elected to the Council of the Law Society of England and Wales, and chaired the Law Society's Equality and Diversity Committee between 2002 and 2008, and was a member of its Management Committee.

Caroline is CEO of Lawdacity Limited and was presented with an award for outstanding services to the Legal Profession in April 2007. Email Caroline at **caroline@carolinenewman.com**, *and visit her Websites:* **www.carolinenewman. com**, *and* **www.lawdacity.com**. *Follow her on Twitter: carolinenewman1; Skype: carolinenewman1, and* **www.Facebook.com/CarolineNewmanLaw**.

Starting a Business When Funds are Low

by Larry Louzon

You had been a faithful employee for several years, but then the unthinkable happened. Your boss came in and told you that "Because of the poor economy, the company has to cut back, and can no longer use your services." While you were disappointed to lose the job, you were confident that with your background, you would soon be back to work.

Weeks turned into months, and hundreds of resumes and job applications later, it is obvious you will need to do something different. The thought of being your own boss comes to mind. You like the idea of being able to control your future. But, the obstacle standing in your way is not having much money to start a business. Your friends and family are not in a position to help you with loans. Well-established businesses are having problems getting loans from the banks, so with startups, they won't even bother talking to you. So what do you do?

To overcome this obstacle, the best thing to do is to begin with the end in mind so you can plot the course that will take you to your desired business and lifestyle.

Are you looking to start a business where you will have an office or retail store? Do you want a manufacturing facility? Or are you looking for a business that will allow you to work from home? Are you seeking time and financial freedom?

Knowing where you want to end up helps you to determine where you begin.

When working on a tight budget, it is generally best to start with a home business. However, just because it starts as a home business does not mean it has to remain there. Remember, Apple Computer started in a garage! A home business offers many advantages. You will not have the added overhead of operating out of another building. To rent a retail storefront, you will have the added store rental costs of heat, lights, and telephone. To maintain hours, you will probably need to have an employee or two. Then, you need to fill up the space with furniture and inventory. All this before you even open your doors! Once open, you will need working capital, the money that allows you to pay your many bills while waiting for sales to come in.

With a home business, you keep your business overhead to a minimum because you're already paying for home utilities. A cell phone for your business helps eliminate the need for an employee. The end result is that money from your sales goes into your pocket faster than if you were operating the traditional brick and mortar business where you must first pay for all your new overhead costs.

Knowing where you want to end up helps you to determine your strategy to get there. Ultimately, you want to be in a business where your passions are, where you look forward to being each day.

Let's look at some business models that let you start inexpensively.

The first is where you "own your job." This is where you operate as an Independent Contractor. You can do this in a variety of areas; one of the most common is where you represent a company in the selling of their products. You may be a bookkeeper or secretary offering your services to multiple businesses. If you have a skill or service that can be used by many types of businesses, but they do not need your help on a full time basis, here is an opportunity for a business that costs very little to set up, *and*, the work is often done on the client's premises. The downside is that these companies do not pay you benefits. You have no "sick days." And when you are not working, you are not earning any money.

If you want to build a brick and mortar business, there are a couple of different strategies you can use. They both start from home, and in this way, your startup cost are kept low.

You will want to build in a way that will minimize risk.

The first way is to create "mini incomes." These are small incomes that you can do on a part time basis. Each one by itself might not make a lot of money, but together they provide you with a steady income. This gives you the opportunity to accumulate your startup capital for your dream business, and it gives you an income as your business takes hold.

The second is to start your dream business in your home, and grow it until you are ready to move. If you are planning to start a retail or manufacturing business, you will have to be more creative. With a retail business, you are not going to be having the customers come to your home... your neighbors would probably not appreciate that very much. So, you will need to take the marketing to your customers, and you can do that by direct sales, or by setting up your store online. When your sales are sufficient enough to support a retail location, then you can move.

A manufacturing business can be more difficult to start in your home. If the actual manufacturing creates much noise or entails many delivery trucks coming to your home to drop off supplies or to pick up finished goods, you may not only encounter problems with your neighbors, but there may be problems with your local government as well. In that case, you would need to "job out" the initial manufacturing.

For many budding entrepreneurs, the home business is the perfect option. It not only provides low cost of entry, but it also provides a more comfortable lifestyle. Many home business owners find that having the flexibility to spend time with their family is priceless! They can attend school events for their children, they can work on a schedule that is best for them, and their commute to work is just a short walk down the hall.

Let's look at two of the best areas for a lifestyle home business.

The *Internet* has revolutionized the home business, allowing the home business entrepreneur to become an international entrepreneur. Not only has it become an invaluable tool for all types of home businesses, but the Internet can also be a business in itself. Through the creation of inexpensive blogs and websites, the home business entrepreneur has the ability to market to the world.

Another ideal area for creating a home business is network marketing. Network marketing also offers low cost of entry and a lifestyle business, plus, it offers free business training. Network marketers like to say, "While you are in business for yourself, you're not in business *by* yourself." They have a support team of others interested in seeing you succeed.

Many of the network marketing companies operate on a global scale while others are confined to just one nation. The companies represent a wide range of products and services; find one that appeals to you. You can choose from companies offering nutritional products, home care products, investment services, legal services, and much more.

Obstacles are opportunities in disguise... they will make you stronger.

When faced with an obstacle, approach it with a smile, knowing that there are hidden benefits waiting. The benefits will not always be obvious, so you will need to look at the obstacles with an open mind. When confronted with any obstacle, ask the question, "How can I make this work for me?" The more adept you become at overcoming obstacles, the more obstacles you will overcome. And as a result, you may find that your demand as a problem solver will increase.

We have taken just one obstacle of not having very much money to start a business, and shown that there are in fact, multiple opportunities open to anyone with an enterprising spirit who will seize a good idea and run with it.

The same is true of most obstacles. Obstacles offer opportunities for inner growth; you become stronger and with perseverance, continually find new opportunities for overcoming them.

Entrepreneurship is a wonderful way to be able to take charge of your life. To be able to provide you and your family with more income and quality time together.

Now go forth, face those obstacles, and make that new life happen!

About author.

Larry Louzon is a "Cypreneur," meeting the demands of the Cyber Age Entrepreneur. To learn more about entrepreneurship, please visit his websites: www.larrylouzon.com and www.homebusinesscompass.com. From there you can follow him on Twitter and Facebook, and you'll also find links to his other websites.

The Four P's of Good Crisis Management

by Judy Hoffman

N o matter what type of organization with which you are associated – a manufacturing facility, a service provider, a health care organization, a financial institution, a not-for-profit agency, or a small or large business you run as an entrepreneur – you must realize that every single day something could go wrong.

Accidents happen, and people get hurt or even killed. The environment could be damaged because of your operations or a transportation incident. One of your products could harm someone (or someone could allege it harmed them). A disgruntled former employee could return one day with a gun and commit violence. A competitor or an unhappy customer could start a smear campaign that spreads like wildfire on the Internet.

There is a cartoon in my office of an ostrich with its head in the sand while a big lightning bolt aims for its backside. The caption reads, "When you insist on burying your head in the sand, a lot of your anatomy is left exposed!" It is those businesses and organizations which say, "Nothing bad will happen to me," that are really pressing their luck. Certainly they are endangering their organization's good reputation, which can significantly affect their ability to attract and retain customers and employees. In the worst of circumstances, they may be gambling with their very existence.

I'd like to suggest that you sit down for a few hours with your senior staff – whether that is one business partner or an executive team of people – and put some serious thought into "The Four P's of Good Crisis Management."

PREVENT

The best way to deal with a crisis is to avoid it. This does not happen just by wishing. The best organizations spend some time brainstorming on the question, "What could go wrong?" They think through all of the crisis possibilities such as those mentioned above. I guarantee that if you put your mind to this task, you can fill up a number of flip chart pages! Don't let yourself stop after you've named the obvious, because it's the ones you don't think of right away that will put you behind the eight-ball fastest if you haven't thought about how to handle

174

them. What do you most dread hearing has just happened? What has happened to others in your type of business that brought unfriendly attention from the media or a bunch of angry customers to their door? Is there anything that someone could allege has happened in your organization (e.g., discrimination, sexual harassment, unethical practices, etc.)?

When you end up with a list of dozens of potential crises, it is easy to be paralyzed into inaction. Instead, I recommend you conduct a "vulnerability audit" to prioritize the crises. Simply draw a graph with a horizontal axis labeled "Probability" and a vertical axis of "Severity." Rank each one of your potential crises, placing a dot where each falls. (If you would like a copy of the chapter in my book that describes in more detail how to conduct a vulnerability audit and contains the rating graph, please contact me.)

Once you have ranked the possible crises, management can move to address those issues clustered in the upper right hand corner – those that are the most likely to occur or that would be most devastating to your company. For each one, a responsible party should be assigned to investigate what must be done. Is there a new procedure that should be instituted, equipment that should be purchased, or training that should occur? Yes, it may take time and/or money to do this, but spending a little now will be a tremendous investment if it results in avoiding a crisis that would cost many times more.

PLAN

You must have a written plan for crisis response. Don't be discouraged about undertaking this project. A simple plan is not that hard to do. On a sheet of paper make five columns entitled (1) Crisis, (2) Those to be Notified, (3) Contact Numbers, (4) Action Items, and (5) Responsible Party. While that form is still blank, make a lot of copies of it. (If you want a copy of the template for this plan and some more details on it, please contact me.)

In the first column, jot down the top-ranked crisis you identified in the vulnerability audit. In the second column, note those individuals (both internal and external) who would need to be notified if this should occur. Think of everyone who could be of assistance and those who would feel they needed to know what was happening (e.g., town officials, neighbors). You may need to talk to some folks ahead of time. (Do you know who you could call upon if you needed some grief counselors because your organization had been victimized by violence in the workplace? Right after a tragedy occurs is not the time to be thumbing through the Yellow Pages!)

The next column should contain every office phone, cell phone, fax, pager, beeper number, or e-mail address where you could reach those individuals, whether it is day, night, weekend, or on vacation.

Under "Action Items," list those things you should remember to do if you want to be perceived as a responsible and caring organization after an incident.

For example, if you had to institute a product recall, do you have plans in place that would allow you to utilize an 800 number immediately – and would you have people on call who have been trained to manage those phone calls competently and compassionately?

In the column "Responsible Party," assign an individual from your organization whose job it will be to prepare your organization to deal with this particular type of crisis and who must keep the information on the chart current so that it is useful when you need to put it into action. (If you are a sole proprietor and one-person show, your name will show up a lot, of course, but you might identify people on whom you could call in an emergency under a prearranged agreement.)

Pre-planning is necessary for all of this. It won't just fall into place if you haven't thought it through ahead of time. The media and the public will notice if you are able to implement a plan quickly and competently or if you seem to be stumbling around. And they will remember that impression long after they've forgotten the specifics of the problem itself.

PREPARE

Some organization leaders think that just by virtue of having successfully established an entrepreneurial business or achieving a high-level position in a larger organization they are prepared to take charge, make the right decisions, and communicate properly during a crisis. It ain't necessarily so! The good crisis managers I know are the ones who recognize that it takes a specialized skill set to communicate effectively in a crisis – especially when the media becomes involved. The best ones are willing to call in a crisis communications expert ahead of time to help them refine their skills so that they will be able to perform at the highest level when the time comes.

In a full- or half-day workshop, the senior management team can work together on basic techniques like (1) identifying who their initial spokesperson should be, (2) following the "10 C's of Good Crisis Communications," (3) recognizing the "Five Big Nevers" in dealing with the media, (4) identifying the most likely questions, (5) developing their key messages and learning to "bridge" to them, and (6) creating memorable "sound bites" that capture their messages in ways the media may repeat and the public can remember. Those involved in the training learn a great deal about how to act well as a Crisis Management Team.

PRACTICE

Olympic athletes and astronauts have to practice in order to excel. Those who are forced into being crisis leaders should do no less. Even if business owners and managers are usually good at thinking clearly under extreme pressure, they may not be prepared for how intimidating it can be when the TV camera lights go on. They may not realize that procedures that look good on paper don't always

176

work in actuality. The best way to discover the weaknesses in a plan is to drill on it. When TV host David Letterman asked former New York City Mayor Rudy Giuliani how it was that he seemed to know the right things to do and say on 9/11 and the terrible days that followed, he answered, "We DRILL on these things."

Every once in a while, you should – without warning – simulate one of your brainstormed crisis scenarios. Does everyone know his/her role? Is the needed equipment available? Are procedures in place? Do people have the necessary skills to carry out their responsibilities? Do the various groups coordinate as a team? Do communications break down? Theories of how to operate can be tested in active role-playing exercises which will challenge assumptions and clarify points that need to be strengthened.

In summary... do whatever you can to prevent a crisis. Brainstorm what could go wrong. Put in place a simple, basic plan that will allow you to be organized so you can respond properly. Take the time to provide crisis management and media training to your management team. Finally, put your plans to the test so you can identify your weaknesses in a low stress environment, instead of when you are in the midst of the real thing. When it is your organization in the glare of the media spotlight, and you are on the "hot seat," you'll be glad you did!

About author.

Judy Hoffman is a trainer/speaker on dealing with the media and handling angry people. Her book, "Keeping Cool on the Hot Seat: Dealing Effectively With the Media in Times of Crisis" is used by several colleges as a text in crisis communications courses. Be sure to sign up on her website at www.judyhoffman. com for her free monthly e-zine. She can be reached at 1-800-848-3907 pin 2145 or jchent@earthlink.net.

Building The Business of Your Dreams No Matter What!

by Louis Lautman

I have been outsourcing since 2003 when I started my first training company. I had a couple of people located in a few different cities around the United States who worked for me. I set up my business like that because I really didn't want to work from an office, and knew that it really didn't matter where people were located as long as they achieved results.

After several years of delegating work to my team nationally, my business began to slow down a bit as I had not scaled it properly, and I was looking at new ways to cut expenses and increase profits. I had a couple of friends that were outsourcing overseas because of the cost savings. In 2007, I figured I would give it a try.

A friend referred me to a company in Uruguay, and starting with an appointment setter, I actually began getting new appointments everyday to present my training services. This was great as it was costing me half of what I was spending on the guy I had working for me from his house in San Diego, a guy who had started underperforming.

I thought I had stumbled across my silver bullet. I started thinking about all the money I was going to make and how quickly I was going to start hiring more appointment setters, and then sales people, and then trainers… and was really getting excited! Things were great for about 3 days, and then the appointments stopped. I let that go for the next two days thinking that everyone has a bad day or maybe two.

The next week I was ready for my new appointments, but they didn't come. I spoke to the manager of that office and he told me that the appointment setter had quit. Over the next two or three weeks, they tried to get me appointments, but it never happened, so I stopped using that service. I did not give up on outsourcing overseas, though. I knew it could happen because I had tasted it; I just had to figure out how.

Over the next few years I began outsourcing all of the tasks that I was already outsourcing in the US, to different places of the world, from Russia to Czechoslovakia, to India, to Bangladesh, to Pakistan… and many places in

178

between. I had some victories, but unfortunately many more challenges along the way, the main challenge being the language barrier, and the integrity of getting work done on time.

As frustrating as it was for me, and with all the time I had put into this delegation process, I was committed to building the right system for me, as I had many colleagues who had effectively set up the same system that I so desired. Then, I heard about the pleasures of outsourcing to the Philippines because of the ease in communicating in English.

I gave it a shot and started researching ways to outsource to the Philippines, and found a couple of channels of locating people who could do my work for me. It was now 2009, and finally it felt good when talking to the people who were going to do my work. One of the challenges of the past was communicating with people in different countries and their level of English proficiency. I was getting closer to finding what I was looking for, since it was now easier talking to the people from this country.

I was still using websites where I had to write an ad, post that ad, filter through numerous unqualified resumes and responses, and then from those who I thought were qualified, filter through many more of them until I finally found someone to work with. Sometimes it would work out and some times it would not, mostly because the people I was working with just didn't communicate the way I wanted them to, or they just disappeared on me.

This was getting very frustrating to me as I was spending endless hours putting together a team that I felt comfortable with. But finally, when I had my team in place, things were getting done, and getting done well. By 2010, I had built a virtual team overseas that I felt was like my mini army – that I felt would finally get things done. But every now and then, I would lose someone and then had to start the whole frustrating process over of filtering through people to find someone who fit my culture.

I actually ended up hiring someone whose job was to hire good people for me. This was a little more expensive in the beginning, but in the long run it actually ended up saving me money, because it saved me countless hours of having to go through all those people myself, searching for the right worker. Plus, the people they placed with me seemed to stay.

My business started picking up, and many people started hearing about my victories in building a virtual team. In fact, many of my colleagues and associates started asking me to get work done for them. This became a regular occurrence because of their difficulty in finding the right people to do the jobs they needed to get done. At first I started helping my friends as a favor to them, until around the end of 2010. Then I realized that I was at the helm of a new business.

Welcome to the birth of Supreme Outsourcing. I had my virtual team put together all of my marketing materials and build my website, as well as start the

179

initial online buzz for my company. Next thing you knew clients started calling with money in hand, in need of our services.

I had a proven team for my projects and some of my friend's projects, but now it was time to take my systems to the next level and to serve more people. I was very excited to share the benefits with my new prospects, and most of them were very happy to receive them. On occasion, because I was not the one doing the work, we would let a client down and lose their account.

This was heart breaking to me, not because of the loss of money – even though I did not like that – but because the client trusted me and my company to deliver for them, and on the rare occasion we did not. What I also realized though, in this process, is that this was an excellent opportunity to grow and make sure these issues would never arise again, so I started implementing quality assurance systems. This allowed me to streamline a lot of our processes and deliverables to people, and soon enough we were a fine tuned machine that got things done for clients fast, at high quality and low cost, relative to value.

Most people would not have done what I did back in 2003: even consider delegating their work to someone not in their office, and probably would not have tried the overseas route that I did back in 2007. Many more would never have persisted with the challenges I faced for 2 years of working with a variety of overseas workers until I discovered the ease of working with Philippine workers. And even more would have gotten so frustrated in people not delivering results that they probably would have gone back to trying to do everything themselves.

This is what separates Supreme Outsourcing from all of the other outsourcing companies out there: WE GET RESULTS! Today I run the business of my dreams that allows me to work from anywhere, choose my clients, and that generates a significant amount of reoccurring profit for me on a monthly basis. If you are persistent and NEVER GIVE UP, you to will build the business of your dreams, and maybe you will learn to delegate more work, so you can start to work *on* your business instead of *in* your business.

About author.

Louis Lautman travels the world sharing his strategies with business owners and entrepreneurs from all walks of life, showing them how they can build the business of their dreams and do it in lightning speed. Louis is a master of figuring out what matters most and building systems to get all of the other things done. If you would like to find out more about Louis Lautman, go to www.LouisLautman.com or if you would like to find out how you can delegate work to Louis and his team, go to www.SupremeOutsourcing.com.

180

How to Get What You Want in Any Negotiation by Using The *Law of Attraction*

by Rick Otton

"When you give people what they want – from the Highest Good – your wants are returned to you in abundance."

Most people have needs and wants, and when they focus on what they want, the *Law of Attraction* comes into play. The *Law of Attraction* is created by focusing with powerful intent on a goal, then making it happen. Unfortunately, many people focus on what they DON'T want, and attract this very thing. I find when you consistently and joyfully imagine and visualize what you want, with powerful concentration, the universe answers by making it happen.

In any negotiation, if you use the *Law of Attraction* to fulfill the needs and wants of the other party first, you will get what you want in return. In traditional negotiations, most people are only interested in "giving to get," so they end up in a power struggle. In any relationship, whether business or personal, ask yourself:

"What will make the other party happy?" Then give them what they want first, and the *Law of Attraction* will create the outcome for you as well. You'll find that your return is often more than you could have asked for.

The *Law of Attraction*: The goals you focus on consistently, create your life.

Here's how I apply the *Law of Attraction* to my real estate negotiations. This process is traditionally a painful one in which no one achieves what they truly want. The power struggle often revolves around the sale price of the property. The seller's goal is to achieve the highest possible sales price, and the buyer wants to purchase at the lowest possible price. Yet, before negotiations begin, I stop and ask the other party this simple question: "What do you want?" You'll discover the answer is often not what you'd expect.

When I use the *Law of Attraction* to focus on a goal (the object), an opportunity is created. Objects have finite value; opportunity has *infinite* value.

As an object, vacant land in the desert has a finite value. It is worth about the same as the parcel of land next door. Yet, if oil is discovered on that vacant land, the object suddenly becomes an opportunity for the landowner. Opportunity has infinite value.

When a seller sells a property, it is not always about the price (object), it is sometimes simply about how easy the seller can make it for the buyer to purchase the property (opportunity). I find that if you satisfy the needs and wants of the other party first, the contentious issue of price becomes secondary.

When buying a property, ask the seller the following questions:

Why are you selling?

What are your plans for the future?

Do you need all of your money now?

Often people are not selling a property because they want to, but because they have to. Many times money is not a seller's prime motivation to sell. Actually, it's the outcome from the sale – whatever that is – that will enable the seller to obtain what they really want. Quite often what the seller wants is very different from what the other side might assume.

Let's say a retiree might be selling a property because they can invest the funds from the sale to earn an income in retirement, so the sale of the property is about fulfilling their need for an income stream. Knowing this, a buyer may choose to purchase the property and pay monthly payments for a set period of time directly to the seller, and get bank financing at a later date.

In return for the seller financing the buyer into the property, the seller receives market price for their property as well as a higher monthly income than if they had cashed out of the property in one lump sum. The buyer doesn't have to get immediate financing from a bank or mortgage lender.

How does object versus opportunity play out in this example? The house itself is the object, and if it is sold in a traditional transaction, it will remain as such. But, while having his or her own needs met, the seller can transform the house into an opportunity for the purchaser who will pay full price or more, because their roadblocks to homeownership have been eliminated.

A common roadblock in these situations is the real estate agent's inability to communicate well with both parties involved in a property transaction. Sometimes the agent may not wish to tell you what the seller of the property is ultimately trying to obtain. As a result, many sellers get disgruntled when they sell a property and ultimately do not get the selling price they were hoping to receive. Objects can only be sold as opportunities when marketed that way; otherwise, they remain objects and are given the same value as other objects.

182

When I sell a property, I'm not selling a house (object), I'm selling an *opportunity*. An opportunity is what you believe it is. You can positively affect the opportunity through the *Law of Attraction*. Most people focus on the negatives, so they mentally list all the mistakes that could happen. Instead, I choose to focus on the positive.

The *Law of Attraction* uses the Highest Good for every person in each negotiation. With strong positive intention, The *Law of Attraction* creates a positive outcome every time.

Consider this situation: John is selling his run down property for $295,000 – which is market value – so that he can move out of state to care for his sick parents. The agent tells John that the property will not achieve market price in its present condition (based on comparables with similar houses in the same neighborhood). The bottom line is that John needs to sell, but can't afford to remodel his house, which could be an obstacle. John advertises his house for sale in the newspaper. He can't afford to pay the agent's commission. John applies the *Law of Attraction*; he has high intent to sell his property. He uses this formula to visualize a positive outcome: $I \times V = R$ *(Imagination x Visualization = Reality)*.

Two buyers, Paul and Mary, see John's ad. They're currently renting, but want to own their own home. They do not have enough deposit to buy John's house. Using the *Law of Attraction*, Paul and Mary have high intent to own. They use the same formula: $I \times V = R$ *(Imagination x Visualization= Reality)* to own their own home.

Paul and Mary ring John and they meet at his house. John knows that he cannot sell his property the conventional way through an agent, and get the price he wants, because it's run down and needs to be remodeled. Yet, he can't afford to repair it himself. John knows that his house is an *object*. By creating an *opportunity* through giving the potential buyers what they want, his wants will be met and returned to him in abundance. John is coming from the highest good. A third energy is created by all of them "being in agreement" together. *This third energy, the act of jointly providing mutually beneficial solutions, ignites the Law of Attraction: Paul & Mary + John + Strong Intention = 3 Positive Energies.*

Paul and Mary embrace the opportunity of home ownership. They agree to remodel the property to bring it up to market value, which John supports. He knows that will increase the value of the property. John agrees to seller finance his property to Paul and Mary for one year. John receives the sales price that he wants, a monthly income, plus he's free to move and care for his sick parents, which gives him immediate peace of mind.

The new buyers, Paul and Mary, receive the opportunity of home ownership acquired through their sweat equity. The opportunity for Paul and Mary is that they can buy this property with no deposit, and they can renovate it to match their personal style. They'll also capture the future capital gain as the property increases in value over time. After Paul and Mary remodel their property, they can get a bank loan and cash out John.

The *Law of Attraction* is applied as if the positive future has already manifested in the present moment.

John, Paul, and Mary placed themselves in their positive future by imagining and visualizing their new reality, in the present moment. John "pictured" his house sold, and Paul and Mary "visualized" buying.

The facts are that the seller did not reduce the sale price of the property, because he was offering financing (opportunity). And the buyers didn't negotiate for a lower sales price, because they recognized they weren't just buying a house (object), they were receiving financing with the house (opportunity). Given the value of the opportunity, the issue of price becomes much less important in the eyes of the buyers.

During every negotiation, no matter which side I'm on, I visualize the seller or buyer in my mind, in the present moment. Using the formula, $I \, x \, V = R$ *(Imagination x Visualization = Reality)*, I picture each person benefiting from this transaction.

When I give people what they want – from the Highest Good – my wants are returned to me in abundance. I joyfully picture a positive outcome. With seller financing, you can see how an object with finite value (such as a house), transforms into an opportunity with infinite value when financing is attached. In any conversation, whether it is personal or business, ask yourself what it is that the other person wants. Then apply the *Law of Attraction*, and observe the positive outcome!

About author.

Rick Otton is the founder and CEO of "We Buy Houses," a leading property enterprise which Rick has successfully expanded into the international markets of America, the UK, New Zealand, and Australia. Rick's success has been achieved by recognizing that property profits can be maximized when you start to create strategies relating to the terms under which the property is acquired or sold, and not simply relying on price-led strategies. Rick buys, sells, and trades property using little or none of his own money, and he structures transactions to create positive cash flow. www.rickotton.com.

Lemonade From a Layoff

by Stuart Rosen (aka: Gurustu)

They say that when life hands you a bunch of lemons, it's time to make lemonade. When that lemon comes in the form of a pink slip, it's time to... well... make PINK lemonade.

I knew it was coming. The company had taken a horrific downturn. The industry itself was falling apart around us. The party was over, and it was time for the guests to leave. So when they said, "Can I see you a minute?" it didn't come as a shock.

"Your services are no longer needed."

Those are some shocking words to hear, especially after years of promotions and pictures taken at award ceremonies. Yet when they hand you a well groomed package with tiny token pay checks attached, it finally sinks in: "I'm being laid off."

I drove home that day with a huge mixed bag of emotions – concern, confusion, a little worry, and a little bit of relief as well. After all, as in "A Tale of Two Cities," it had been the best of times and the worst of times. And so that chapter of my life was closed.

I'm not alone. Not only were there thousands of others from my company, there were plenty of other people all around the country going through the same exact thing I was. Millions, in fact. However, it doesn't really matter if it's one person or one million people. If you're the one, that's all you can really think about.

So... when faced with this downturn in your career, how do you even begin to make pink lemonade? Here are some of the things I did....

Reach out for support
One of the first things I did was to reach out to the people I care about – if only to have someone who you can talk to, who will listen to you rant without judgment, and who can reason with you when planning the next phase.

Stop the bleeding

The first thing they teach in emergency classes is to tend to the most pressing problem. Get that under control and attend to the rest later. When it comes to being laid off, there are a bunch of technical things that need to get done, from filing for unemployment to changing insurance and health plans. There could be stock plans and retirement funds to deal with. While they can be heavy tasks right in the middle of your heavy heart, they have to get done in a timely manner. So just buckle down, set your emotions aside for a moment, and do what has to get done.

Take a break

Admit it to yourself, "That hurt." Losing a job is a major, major change. It's very high up there on the list of stressors, so the last thing you need to do is make decisions while you're right in the middle of it. Distancing yourself from the whole situation not only lowers your blood pressure, it gives you time to mentally get some breathing room and a fresh perspective.

Reflect

We never really fail, as long as we are willing to grow from every situation. The layoff might have seemed really bad when it first happened, but when you have time to look back, you may start to see that it may just be the best thing that could have happened to you. Take the time to see the good, the bad, and the ugly of the past. Think about what was done right and what you could have done better. Don't wallow in the woes of the past, but instead use it as a tool to figure out what not to do next time.

Dream

You may have forgotten how to, or might be afraid to try again, but now is the perfect time to dream. Go ahead, you've got time. It may not seem like it, especially with your mind on "I gotta get a job!" but if you don't take the time to do it now, the decisions you make at this point can result in less than desirable situations down the road. Pull out all the stops. Don't think in terms of what you did in the past. If you could do ANYTHING in life, what would it be? Now is a very good chance to at least head in that direction.

Take inventory

This is an excellent opportunity to reflect upon yourself now as well. If you've been in the job for a long time, like I was, you may discover that a whole bunch of skills got put aside in order to do the job. Maybe this is an opportunity to dust some of those off. Maybe it's time to stop doing some of the stuff you've just been doing out of habit or necessity. One of the things I did was to make two lists – one of all the things that I was good at, and the other of all the things I loved to do. Then I narrowed it down, and down, and down, until I was left with only a few choices. Ideally you should be left with one from each column, but don't beat yourself up if you have a couple extra.

Map it out

This is a new journey you are about to undertake. Just like you wouldn't think about heading out on a road trip without a map, you ought not to head out

186

into a new career without one either. Do you need special classes for this new career? Is there a list of people you need to contact? Are there special groups you need to join? The more laid out your plans, the more control you will feel as you move along.

Grow yourself
While you're planning your future, consider seeking ways to expand your skills. If there's some training out there that can help you get a better job, or even if there's something you just always wanted to know, now's the time to go to class. This little bubble between jobs might be just the time you need to grow.

Action!
Finally there's going to come a time that you're just going to have to do SOMETHING. When you do nothing, nothing gets done. Taking action will get the ball rolling.

Grow your network
When things start turning downward, it's very easy to turn inward. While that's a good thing in terms of reflection, it's not a good thing when it comes to rebuilding. The more people you know, the more connections you will have to finding that career you've always dreamed of. New people = new opportunities. So get out there and meet people! Join organizations, even volunteer – you never know where the next miracle is going to take place.

Have faith
You really don't have to know what every next step is going to be. In fact, you CAN'T know (unless you really are that good at predicting the future, in which case you should go pick up a lottery ticket instead). Just knowing what you want, with an idea of where you're going, should be all you need, for now. Every great explorer had to lose sight of familiar territory and venture out into the unknown, or else they never would have made their great discoveries. So become the explorer in your own adventure!

Be flexible
There are things that are going to work, and other things that won't. Don't get hung up on doing it one way, or staying with something that's just weighing you down. Be willing to try new things. Be even more willing to let things go.

Be persistent
There's a huge difference between giving in and giving up. Some things just take time and might seem like they're not working. That's the time when you need to keep at it – just one more step. If you know you're heading in the right direction, don't give up three steps away from the finish line.

Be patient
Along with persistence comes patience. Whereas persistence is action, patience is how you feel about those actions. Patience is a quiet form of passion. It's faith. It's really all of the above. I always say, "Pulling on the stalks isn't going to make the corn grow any faster." Just keep at it and let it do its thing. Everything

187

takes time, so take the time... and make the time. Because we live in time, time is really all we've got.

About author.

Gurustu *takes an enlight-hearted look at life, motivating others through inspirational articles, reflective daily thoughts, humorous cartoons and the ever-popular LifeWatch. Are you seeking words of wisdom on love, life, work, relationships, and enlightenment? Are you on a self-help quest for words of encouragement for a friend or loved one? Need to get motivated to make a life change? Come up the mountain at* ***www.gurustu.com***.

Arriving in the
Village of Abundance

Even if You are a Minority of ONE... The Truth is the Truth.

~ Gandhi

The Way of Success Sometimes Will Come Because of a Way of Struggle

by Vic Johnson

The following is an excerpt from an article in Napoleon Hill's magazine of 1921:

"Lincoln wrote the greatest speech ever delivered in the English language, on the back of an envelope, a few moments before it was delivered, yet the thought back of that speech was borne of hardship and struggle."

Overcoming obstacles can be some of the most important achievements you do in your lifetime. All down the road of life you will meet with obstacles, many of them. Failure will overtake you time after time, but remember that it is a part of Nature's method to place obstacles and failure in your way.

Every time you master failure you become stronger and better prepared to meet the next one. The moments of trial will come to you as they come to all at one time or another. Doubt and lack of faith in yourself will cast their dark shadows over you, but remember that the manner in which you react under these trying negatives will indicate whether you are developing power or slipping backward.

"And this, too, will soon pass away." Nothing is permanent. Therefore, why permit disappointment, resentment, or a keen sense of injustice to undermine your composure, because they will soon eliminate themselves.

Look back over your past and you will see that those experiences of yesterday which bore heavily on your heart at the time, and seemed to end all hope of success, passed away and left you wiser than you were before.

The whole universe is in a constant state of flux. You are in a constant state of change. Evolution is removing the wounds left in your heart by disappointment. You need not go down under any difficulty if you but bear in mind that "this, too, will soon pass away."

I looked back at my heavy load of grief and worry which crowded the happiness out of my heart only yesterday, and lo! they had been transformed into stepping stones of experience over which I had climbed higher and higher.

Source: Napoleon Hill's Magazine. September, 1921. Volume 1, number 5, page 9.

Your Circumstance is a Spiritual Lesson

"As a progressive and evolving being, man is where he is that he may learn that he may grow; and as he learns the spiritual lesson which any circumstance contains for him, it passes away and gives place to other circumstances." -As A Man Thinketh (*www.asamanthinketh.net*)

It has taken me a long time to be able to look at a problem I'm having as a necessary spiritual lesson. To be frank, I'm still not always real excited to be enduring the pain and frustration that negative circumstances usually cause. Some days I'd like to "play hooky" and skip the lesson.

But as I look back at my life, it is easy to see that the times when my wisdom and understanding grew to new levels – those times when I approached becoming the person I long to be – it was always the times that followed negative circumstances. The greatest growth you're going to have is going to come from the negative circumstance you have today that sometimes seems too overwhelming, too big to scale.

Writing in *Byways of Blessedness* (*www.asamanthinketh.net/byways. htm*), James Allen is strong in his call for us to embrace our circumstances. "Let a person rejoice when he is confronted with obstacles, for it means that he has reached the end of some particular line of indifference or folly, and is now called upon to summon up all his energy and intelligence in order to extricate himself, and to find a better way; that the powers within him are crying out for greater freedom, for enlarged exercise and scope.

"No situation can be difficult of itself; it is the lack of insight into its intricacies, and the want of wisdom in dealing with it, which give rise to the difficulty. Immeasurable, therefore, is the gain of a difficulty transcended."

Maybe that explains why it sometimes seems that I can't shake a particular problem, or I have one that keeps rearing its ugly head. Instead of fighting it, I need to jump in and gain the insight and wisdom to handle it. Then it would be gone, and I would be ready for the next lesson – only stronger, both in spirit and in wisdom!

My long-time hero, Emmet Fox (*www.asamanthinketh.net/EmmetFox. htm*) wrote: "It is the Law that any difficulties that can come to you at any time, no matter what they are, must be exactly what you need most at the moment, to enable you to take the next step forward by overcoming them. The only real misfortune, the only real tragedy, comes when we suffer without learning the lesson."

How to Set Personal Goals That Inspire You to Take Action

Remember when you thought you could do and be anything? The innocence of early childhood is perhaps the last time you were unencumbered by perceived limitations and labels. Personal goal setting was simple, and there was no doubt you could achieve anything. When asked, "What do you want to be when you grow up?" you would have responded with whatever struck your fancy that day, whatever you were "in to." You did not concern yourself with how you would do it, if you could do it, or if you should do it. Your dreams were based on what you wanted, pure and simple. You set personal goals based on wonder and curiosity, not practicality.

The dreams of childhood were big dreams. Travel into space, win a medal at the Olympics, become a rock star. Soon enough the dreams become modified to reflect what is practical and expected of us. This is precisely when most people start having trouble setting personal goals. The dreams are no longer larger than life, so why take steps to achieve them?

Big dreams inspire big action. When you set personal goals, they need to have huge payoffs for you in order for you to take consistent steps to achieving them. You need to feel excited – even giddy – at the prospect of seeing your dream come true.

How Dennis Walters Achieved the Goals He Set

Back in the early 1970s, Dennis was fresh out of North Texas State University, which he attended on a golf scholarship. During his senior year, he led the school to its fourth consecutive Missouri Valley Conference golf championship. That same year, Dennis was runner-up in the prestigious Tucker Intercollegiate Golf Tourney, and finished 11th in the United States Golf Association Amateur Championship.

Dennis' dream was to become a PGA touring professional. From all appearances, he was well on his way. To sharpen his skills, Dennis spent 1973 competing on the South African tour and in mini-tour events in the U.S. Shortly before the 1974 Tour Qualifying Event, Dennis went home to Neptune, New Jersey, for a visit and to play a few friendly rounds of golf. On July 21, 1974, he was riding a golf cart down a steep hill on a course near his house when the brakes failed. Dennis Walters was thrown from the cart and suffered severe spinal cord damage.

At a hospital in Morristown, New Jersey, he was diagnosed as a T-12 level paraplegic and told that he would never walk again, which also made playing golf highly unlikely, to say the least. However, at age 24, Dennis was determined to prove otherwise.

After five months of rehabilitation, Dennis went home. Immediately, he began searching for ways to make playing golf practical. He tried hitting the ball from his wheelchair, but found it to be unsatisfactory. He had trouble wheeling the chair around the course and could not venture onto the greens or into bunkers. Then one day he was struck with an idea. "Why not mount a swivel seat on a golf cart?"

Working with his father and a couple of friends, Dennis fashioned a seat that would swing away 90 degrees from a golf cart and allow him to play the game he loved. Everyone said it would be impossible, but Dennis defied the odds and was back on the course again. "I had to experiment and modify my techniques," said Dennis. "I basically tried to work on things I could do and not worry about the things I couldn't."

Dennis taught himself to hit sand shots and to putt one-handed while balancing himself on his crutches, and got his game to the point where he could break 80 on an average course. He continued practicing his game, and people started noticing what Dennis could do. Before long, pros were asking him to conduct clinics at their local clubs. "I liked to put on the clinics because they made me feel like I was preparing for a tournament again," Dennis says.

Those clinics evolved into "The Dennis Walters Golf Show" which Dennis has performed over three decades, with over 2,000 performances all across the U.S. and Canada. His program is not only one of golf lessons but also life lessons as he tells his story and challenges everyone in the audience to do something in their life that perhaps they think is impossible. The show becomes much more than a golf clinic as Dennis presents his positive motivational message and encourages all to reach for their dreams and to strive for excellence.

Dennis' remarkable repertoire of shots includes sending a 225-yard plus drive straight down the middle of the fairway while blindfolded; the "slook," where one ball slices and one ball hooks; hitting a ball off the crystal of his assistant's watch without leaving a scratch; his "death-defying swing through fire" shot; and his "3 iron," which is a one-of-a-kind club Dennis uses to hit 3 perfect shots at the same time. Dennis also hits pure shots with an assortment of clubs made from a fishing pole, baseball bat, crutch, and radiator hose. The finale to the show is his famous, rapid-fire machine gun shot.

In 1998 Dennis was chosen to appear with Tiger Woods at the first youth clinic conducted by the Tiger Woods Foundation. Since then Dennis has continued to be the opening act for Tiger at 24 additional clinics held all over the country. When asked about Dennis, Tiger replied "Dennis Walters has been nothing short of fantastic in his performance during the Tiger Woods Foundation junior golf clinics. His knowledge, skill, and performance bring delight to all."

In 1994, Dennis was awarded an honorary lifetime membership in the PGA of America. Only the fifth person to receive this honor, Dennis joined such greats as former President Gerald Ford, Gary Player, and Bob Hope.

"If there is something you really want to do – no matter how impossible it may seem – with enough hard work and perseverance you can do it," says Dennis.

By the way... Dennis Walters' story can be found in his book, *In My Dreams I Walk With You*. The forward for the book was written by Jack Nicklaus. The book details Dennis' remarkable comeback and 27-year career of touring the country, displaying golf excellence and encouraging all to reach for their dreams. Dennis' website is ***www.denniswalters.com.***

194

When you aspire to something that is less than what you really want, procrastination sets in. With a big dream in your sights, procrastination is a lot less likely to occur.

You may have heard of making a "life list" of places you would like to see, things you would like to try, and dreams you would like to see realized. Instead of making a list of goals based on what you think is attainable or would fit into your life, start your personal goal setting with a life list of the big stuff that really gets you going.

Here again, draw on the feelings of childhood for inspiration as you set personal goals. Remember the annual letter to Santa Claus? Even if you did not celebrate Christmas, you can imagine the wish lists sent to the North Pole were not full of realistic, practical requests. They included the biggest, best gifts a child could think of, because there was always the possibility that Santa would bring you exactly what you wanted.

Dreaming big has the added benefit of inspiring others to come to your aid in your pursuit of the goal. If your personal goal setting is limited, or "small," why would anyone want to help you achieve them? People want to be part of something special. Big goals motivate friends, family, and even complete strangers to help you reach them.

When you set personal goals, go back to those childhood aspirations. Sure, you may not want to be an astronaut anymore, but the old dreams can spark new life goals. Perhaps you would like to go to a grown-up space camp or become an amateur astronomer. Whatever goal you set, make it big. As the ancient emperor Marcus Aurelius said, "Dream big dreams; only big dreams have the power to move men's souls."

And that's worth thinking about.

About author.

Vic Johnson is an internationally known Internet infopreneur, author, motivational speaker, and creator of a host of personal development websites. Talk show host Mike Litman called one of his sites, AsAManThinketh.net, "The hottest personal development site on the Internet today." Subscribers hail from more than 90 countries and have downloaded almost 300,000 eBook copies of James Allen's classic.

Vic's other websites can be found at MyDailyInsights.com, mp3Motivators.com, Goals-2-Go.com, and ClaimYourPowerNow.com.

Ground Rules for Breaking Unproductive Behaviors

by Lee Milteer

Do you have obstacles in your life due to the fact that you procrastinate on taking right actions that would move you toward success? As a productivity coach I often hear people say: "I had this great idea but before I could act on it someone else did." Or, "I learned something from a book, coach, or seminar and I know that if I would take action I would benefit greatly, but I just haven't had the time to do what I need to do to utilize the knowledge." As entrepreneurs, it is in our nature to see possibilities, but the main difference between successful and average people is the ability to take action even when things are not perfect. Life and business change on a dime, and those of us who see opportunities and do not act on them often lose out, not only to the profits, but to the fact that others who take advantage of the opportunity or change will leverage themselves to a better market position or more income streams for their business.

Remember this: we all have LIFE GIVING personal life habits such as exercising, eating right, and taking time to relax. In our business, LIFE GIVING habits would be things like brainstorming with other like minds, marketing our business, educating ourselves, getting a good staff, and looking for new ways to expand our businesses without working harder.

We also have LIFE REMOVING personal life habits such as working too hard, not taking care of our bodies, not taking time with our loved ones, losing our temper, blaming others for our problems, negative thinking, excessive spending, overuse of mindless TV or computer time, lying, procrastination, being late, losing things, and various other unwanted habits that detract from enjoying life.

The old saying, "time is money" is true for you as an entrepreneur, so keep in mind: you only have 1,440 minutes per day. Are you conscious of how you are using your time and life energy? Are you aware of how much energy you waste on LIFE REMOVING personal or business habits?

There are proven strategies to help you overcome your negative habits, which prevent you from using your life energy in ways that assist you in becoming the creative, solution-oriented person you want to be, earning the money you want to earn, and living the type of lifestyle you want to live. For example, what types of habits do you have that serve you, and which ones hurt you?

Habits are a way of doing something you have comfortably taken for granted. Everything you do becomes a habit. Your successes and failures come from your daily habits. Society has reinforced our patterns of behavior, and it is difficult to change, even if we don't like the way things are. We are creatures of habit and these habits are familiar, easy, and routine. A change of habit means a disruption of emotional equilibrium. The new way of doing or thinking alters life's routine. We convince ourselves that it takes too much effort to change and that it is inconvenient because it takes too much energy. I am here to tell you, that isn't true! It's worth loving and honoring yourself to change old behaviors to get new results.

Because you aren't used to looking at or breaking habits from a broader perspective, you tend to hang on to traditions and ignore new ways of thinking. Whether you're swearing off cigarettes, kicking the procrastination habit, or marketing your business in a new way, it doesn't matter because you have the power to make these changes. Psychologists say that the resistance to change lies in the wall of inertia. Personality factors like old habits and childhood scars, contribute to this resistance to change, and although you've spent your entire life becoming the person you are, you expect to change in a weekend.

The bottom line is that you need to bring to your conscious mind – where you can take action – the pitfalls of allowing yourself to stay in a mode of procrastination. Taking action, as opposed to not taking action is what makes the difference in your bottom line and personal enjoyment of your business.

Ground Rules for Breaking Unproductive Behaviors:

- You must be honest with yourself
- You must sincerely commit to making changes in your life
- You must develop a deep passion to rid yourself of unwanted habits
- You must be open-minded to try new strategies
- You must be creative and resourceful in creating new behaviors to replace old, unproductive habits
- You must instill new habits of thought and actions.

Instead of relying on old solutions, make new choices to get rid of your procrastination behaviors. Become conscious of how you use your mental, physical, emotional, and spiritual life energies to create new, positive behavior patterns. After all, your thoughts, intentions, and actions create your future. We are self-fulfilling prophecies, and what we focus on, we bring into our lives. Stay motivated to make your desired changes by enlarging the repertoire of resources you have.

Empower yourself by realizing that you can choose a new response to any circumstance and thus, powerfully affect your future. Take responsibility for your life and alter the circumstance of your future for the positive. Our perception of the world determines how we interpret events, both inside and outside ourselves. In order to effectively deal with changing our life, we must question our perceptions. Because our perceptions filter our every experience in life, our strongly held rules can blind us to our unproductive behaviors. Resistance to new ideas rejects new ways of thinking before we've even given them a chance.

To be successful in overcoming unproductive procrastination behaviors, you need to step back and do an inventory on how you are using your life energy: mentally, physically, emotionally, and spiritually. Are you being as productive as you want to be? If not, why not? If you only have so much energy per day, where is your energy being spent? If you do everything the way you have done it, you are going to get what you have always gotten, and clearly if you are reading this, you want new results.

You must understand that your emotional and mental attitudes are shaped by your habits. If you have a positive outlook on change, you look forward to challenges and experimentation. If you're in a rut and don't want to try anything new, you reject new solutions and opportunities for growth. It's always your choice!

There are always consequences for bad habits and unproductive behaviors. An event occurs that sets off your procrastination or otherwise unproductive behavior. It affects you personally, emotionally, and physically, and also affects the people around you, such as your family, friends, clients, and customers. You must accept that your actions have consequences. Lay all of the cards out on the table face up so you can deal with your unproductive behaviors and how they affect you, your income, and the people around you. After you are able to see how your habits affect you and those you care about, you are empowered to make changes in your actions and attitudes because you have had the courage to write them down and face them.

You must gain an understanding of how your procrastination behaviors have affected your business success, income, risk taking, peace of mind, and family life.

There is a huge secret to making changes in our behaviors, thoughts, and actions. Record keeping is the most useful device for self-reinforcement. Always carry a notebook with you to record your progress. You should record your performance in such a way that you can see your improvements at a glance. Have fun and create a visual representation of your progress. Create graphs of your progress that can soften any feelings of failure or guilt caused by a lapse. These will let you see how much you have progressed in your journey of overcoming unproductive behaviors.

198

Ask yourself questions like:

> *"How does acting on my unproductive behaviors make me feel about myself?"*

> *"What are the reactions of my customers, clients, staff, or family?"*

> *"What financial consequences have I had to deal with relating to my unproductive behaviors?"*

> *"What are the areas where I currently procrastinate in my life?"* Identify them so you have a point of reference. Don't beat yourself up about the past because that is a waste of time and resources. Simply accept your past procrastination without judgment. By doing this, you free yourself to deal with it more objectively. You don't want to give it more power to work against you. Have the skill of awareness and as you approach your next project, monitor yourself.

> *"What are my typical procrastination behaviors?"*

> *"How do I feel when I procrastinate?"* How do you feel about the inferior work and missed opportunities that result from procrastination? How do you feel about late charges for payments you didn't send on time?

> *"What can I do to schedule free time for myself to help reduce procrastination?"*

> *"When is my best work time?"* You should take advantage of what comes naturally for you and schedule your heaviest workload for this time.

> *"What are my areas of strength, things I should focus my time on?"* List the things that you are so good at you can't be replaced. (One of the secrets of success is to only do what you are really good at and outsource everything else.)

> *"What things can I delegate or outsource to get things done in a timely manner?"*

You might also want to ask yourself exactly what motivation you have had in the past to keep acting on unproductive procrastination behaviors. Now knowing what you do, along with the new decisions and choices you have made for yourself, do old motivations still hold true for you? You can use new motivation to condition yourself and inspire your new, productive behaviors. Everyone has to take steps to keep themselves motivated toward the attainment of goals. Be creative and determine what steps will work for your personality and needs.

Whatever you believe about yourself will determine how much time you devote to trying new strategies, creating a support system, and creating positive habits to replace your old negative habits. Make a new decision to alter your life, and get what you want and deserve. Because we are all self-fulfilling prophecies, focusing on your new outcomes will help you overcome any challenge you may face while moving toward positive behaviors.

No matter how great your ability, how large your genius, or how extensive your education, your achievement will never rise higher than the beliefs you have about yourself. In the words of the late Henry Ford, "If you think you can or if you think you cannot, you are always right." This is an indisputable law of life. Many people go through life thinking that successes are out of their reach and don't realize that they sabotage themselves with these attitudes of self-depreciation.

Don't settle for less than you deserve. To change your beliefs, you must see these rewards and focus on the positive reinforcement by having a clear picture of why you want to do something. You must give yourself permission to believe in yourself. After all, this is one of the greatest gifts you have. The more you believe in yourself, the more you expect of your life, and "life" delivers!

About author.

Lee Milteer is a human potential speaker and productivity coach for the Millionaire Smarts™ Coaching Program for entrepreneurs. She is the author of the books "Success is an Inside Job" and "Spiritual Power Tools for Successful Selling." Lee also has educational CD and DVD programs to assist you to reach your career and personal dreams. Lee is available for limited speaking engagements. Visit www.milteer.com to download your free Time Integrity for Entrepreneurs report and other FREE Reports to help you reach your potential.

Lee Milteer, Inc.
2100 Thoroughgood Road
Virginia Beach, VA 23455
TF: 800-618-6780
Call: 757-363-5800
Fax: 757-363-5801.

Changing to a New And Wiser You

by Les Brown

Sometimes it's not about changing to become the person you want to be; it's about changing to become the person you need to be. There is a whole big, expectant world out there waiting on you, as an entrepreneur, to do the things you were destined to do – and the only obstacle in the way is YOU. Personal growth can help you conquer that obstacle, but you must first be a willing participant.

"Didn't I automatically become a willing participant, once I stepped out and started my own business?" you may be asking. Absolutely not! The fact that you got out of the starting blocks only means the race has just begun. And with this race called life, you have to go after it and live it as though it owes you every minute! You have to spend every last bit of talent and energy before your body is spent and your spirit summoned. You have to answer your calling.

I am blessed to know exactly what my calling – or purpose – in life is. My success as a public speaker confirmed that purpose. There are few things as important as answering your calling, whether it is to lead a national government or to care for children in your neighborhood. We all have a purpose, a reason for being here, our role in the greater plan. With that role comes the responsibility to pursue that calling with all the energy we can muster.

When entrepreneurs truly live up to their calling, they live dynamically. They are driven. They accept no defeat or setback as the final blow. Instead, they push on. They do what they have to do with fire and gusto, and most importantly, they don't just make a living, they live their making.

There is no doubt I was born to be a public speaker. The tools were all there, but I had to hone in on them and learn how to put them to their best use. I must have known this all my life – consciously or unconsciously. If I hadn't, where do you think I would be? What would have been the future for this poverty-stricken, adopted, slow learner, who was held back twice in grade school and kept in special education classes all through high school? Where would I be if I had not identified my calling and gone after it? I don't even want to think about it! What I do know is that I became a willing participant.

Now, once you have decided that you are that willing participant in your calling, follow these four easy stages of increased awareness to help you complete your journey to a "new and wiser you." Let's take a quick look at how 1) self-knowledge, 2) self-approval, 3) self-commitment, and 4) self-fulfillment intertwine to help you consciously win this race – taking your business from its current state to unlimited success.

First of all, in order to see yourself beyond your current circumstances, you must master self-knowledge. Simply ask yourself, "What drives me?" And then pause long enough to hear your response. Try to understand what outside forces – positive or negative – are influencing your answer. Many of us suffer from what I call "unconscious incompetence." That means we don't know that we don't know, which leaves the door wide open for others to tell us what we think we need to know. Therefore, before you can fully wake up and change your life, you must understand the frame of reference from which you view the world. Study yourself, study the forces behind your personal history, and study the people in your life. This will help liberate you to grow beyond your imagination.

The second and perhaps most crucial stage of personal growth is self-approval. Once you begin to know and understand yourself more completely, then you must accept and love yourself. Self-hatred, self-loathing, guilt, and long-standing anger only work to block your growth. Don't direct your energy toward this type of self-destruction. Instead, practice self-love and forgiveness, and watch how they carry over into your relationships, your work, and the world around you, opening up the possibility for others to love you, too. If you need help in boosting your self-approval, try these steps: 1) focus on your gifts, 2) write down at least five things you like about yourself, 3) think about the people who make you feel special, and 4) recall your moments of triumph.

When you are committed to taking on life, life opens up for you. Only then do you become aware of things that you were not aware of before. That is the essence of self-commitment. It's like the expanded consciousness that comes whenever I commit to a diet. Suddenly, everywhere I turn, there is FOOD! Or how about when you buy a new car? Suddenly you notice cars exactly like yours everywhere you go. Well, likewise, when you make a commitment – when your life awareness is expanded – opportunities previously unseen begin to appear, bringing you to a higher level. In this posture, you are running your life rather than running from life.

The fourth stage of self-awareness is self-fulfillment. Once you have committed to something and achieved it, you then experience a sense of success and empowerment, otherwise known as fulfillment. Your drive for self-fulfillment should be an unending quest, a continual sequence of testing self-knowledge, fortifying self-approval, renewing self-commitment, and striving for new levels of self-fulfillment. Once you have accomplished a goal and reached a level of self-fulfillment, it is then time to go back to the first stage in the cycle.

These four stages create synergy for a conscious awareness of your personal growth. Now, with this newly gained awareness, take a minute and

202

consider whether or not you are answering your calling. First of all, write down your calling.

Next, determine what the ultimate goal is that you can achieve with that calling. In other words, how far would it take you if you pushed it to its greatest level? The truth is, you probably have no idea how far it can take you because, as I have discovered, when you keep pushing all of your life to develop your calling, it takes you places you never dreamed you would go. But for now, write down five levels that you think you could achieve if you answered your calling. Try to come up with five levels that you might reach.

For example, my calling as a communicator has taken me to:

Radio deejay

State representative

Motivational speaker

Public television personality

Talk show host

The interesting thing about going after your calling and pushing and pushing it, is the way unexpected opportunities open up to you. As a young man, I may well have dreamed of being a radio deejay, but I never would have thought I would end up as a state representative, television talk show host, or the author of a best-selling book. Take one of your projected levels listed above and list three things that might grow from it. I'll provide an example based on a few opportunities that have presented themselves to me as side journeys along the way:

Syndicated national radio host

Network television co-host

Best-selling author

Now, make your projections of unexpected levels that might open up to you. Go ahead, dream big! Look inside and remove all obstacles that stand in the way to that new and wiser you!

About author.

For free inspirational and motivational minutes presented by **Les Brown**, *the world's leading motivational speaker, visit* **www.lesbrown.com**.

The Path I've Traveled

by Nordine Zouareg

Idon't believe that anyone who claims to be a leader can ask people to follow him – whether from New York to Chicago or from self-doubt and poor health to confidence and fitness – unless and until he's traveled that path himself. I've traveled every inch of the journey you'll be making with me in this book, and I daresay my path has been strewn with more detours and stumbling blocks than you can imagine. In fact, it's because I was able to surmount those obstacles and arrive at the place I am now that I know I can lead you, too, to a place where your body, mind, and spirit will be working together to give you a healthier, happier life.

I was born on July 1, 1962 to illiterate Bedouin parents in the back of a French army truck in Algeria. My mother was just 15 years old and my father was 29. Algeria was a French colony at the time, and the truck was part of a convoy taking Algerian Bedouins to vote on the question of Algerian independence.

As they were traveling through the desert, my mother went into labor. They finally had to stop the truck so that she could deliver her baby by the side of the road with the help of 25 elder women of the tribe. I weighed just about two pounds at birth, and my mother later told me that all she could see of me were my eyes and my stomach. I was literally nothing but skin and bones, and to this day it amazes me that I survived that journey, much less all that was to come after. And yet, my mother did manage to keep me alive.

We lived in a small town called El Houamed, which was the last oasis before entering the Sahara desert. For my mother, who was already living a difficult life in the desert, I presented a terrible dilemma. No more than a child herself, she was burdened with a sickly baby whom no one – including she – believed would survive. Finally, after about six months, the elder women held a "wisdom meeting" to decide, in effect, my fate. The problem was essentially this: "We don't think this baby will survive, but we can't kill him, so what are we going to do?" What they, in their "wisdom" decided, was that my mother should be sure I was fed and happy, and then she should leave me on a tombstone in the cemetery, turn her back, and walk away. But, the elder women told her, if she heard me cry she would have to take me back.

My mother did what the women had decided. She fed me, and when she left me on the tombstone, she said, I was happy. But the minute she turned her back to walk away – luckily for me – I began to cry. Of course, she went back for me. At that point, however, my parents decided that they would have to take me to M'sila, one of the larger towns about three hours north of where we lived, to get me proper medical care. It was only because of my mother's tenacity and dedication that I'd lived even this long, but both she and my father were about to show a degree of enterprising spirit that I can only attribute to the strength of character of the Bedouin people, who needed that deeply rooted spirit to survive at all.

When my parents arrived in M'sila, they took me to the hospital where they left me to be examined. When my mother arrived the next day to see how I was doing, the doctor who was treating me told her I had died. In fact, my vital signs were at such a dangerous level that the doctor and his colleagues honestly believed that they wouldn't be able to save me, and that it wouldn't be wise for them to try to prolong my life. To them, I was as good as dead, but I was still alive. And so, when my mother asked to see my body, the doctor believed he had no choice but to refuse. On the one hand, he believed that keeping me alive would only cause her more pain when I ultimately died – as he was sure I would – and on the other hand, he knew that if he let her see me, she would take me back and continue trying to save me.

My mother, however, wouldn't leave that town without seeing me, so she went to the police for assistance. An officer then returned with her to the hospital and told the doctor that my mother had every right to claim her baby's body and give him a proper burial. Of course, at that point, there was nothing for the doctor to do but to confess that I was, in fact, not dead – yet. He apologized profusely but said that he truly believed he had done the right thing. As he saw it, my mother was very young; she could have more children, and allowing me to die in what he considered a "proper" place was kinder than letting her watch me die in the desert, as I surely would.

Once more, my mother took me back, but both my parents knew I was in critical need of immediate medical attention. Their last resort, they felt, was to take me to France. (All Algerians were considered French citizens then.) However, my parents spoke only the Berber dialect, and they didn't have any money for the trip, so they collected the money from their fellow tribes-people, and speaking not a word of the language, set out to start what would be the second phase of their lives.

In France they settled in Roubaix (the end-point of the famous Paris-Roubaix bike tour), which is a major textile center about two and a half hours north of Paris and a half hour from the Belgian border, where there was already an established Algerian community. At the hospital there, I was diagnosed with rickets. After remaining in the hospital for some time, I was sent home and followed as an outpatient for the next several years. I also remember having terrible skin problems in the winter that caused me to scratch my feet and lower legs until they bled, at which point I was checked back into the hospital, where they painted me with gentian violet and bandaged me up to stop the scratching.

My health problems were not all that made life in France difficult. My father worked whatever jobs he could find to support his family, which, over the years grew to a total of 13 children – me, three brothers, and nine sisters – all living in a small two-bedroom apartment. At one time he was a trash collector, and then he went to work in a textile mill, working nine weaving machines at once.

In addition to economic difficulties, we had to deal with what was, at that time, extreme prejudice on the part of the French against all North Africans. It was so bad that people were literally being killed in the streets, and I remember walking with my father on several occasions when people stopped their cars just so they could spit at us. And, of course, what children learned from their parents they took with them – and took out on me at school. I was beaten up regularly, and had my lunches stolen as well as jackets and shoes. The school authorities knew about this but condoned it with their silence, and I was too ashamed to tell my parents. In retrospect, I realize that I was a skinny runt of a kid with absolutely no self-esteem, and that the negative energy I was putting out was virtually asking for the treatment I received. Nevertheless, I was miserable.

To comfort myself, I developed a ritual – and I call it a ritual rather than a routine for good reason. A routine is something you decide to follow or not follow while a ritual is something so deeply ingrained that it becomes soul-inspired and you do it without even thinking about it. My ritual was to come home from school and go to my room (which I shared at any given time with up to seven siblings), where I sat on the bed or in a corner on the floor, and cried. Sometimes my crying was so profound that I couldn't talk afterward, but it was cleansing and beneficial. It allowed me to purge the burden of pain I was carrying around every day, and it protected me on a spiritual level from my ordinary ego-based behavior, which was to be afraid. When I was done, I got up and went about my life for another day.

This ritual continued for years – all through high school in fact – until one day I came home to find the entire family sitting in front of the television watching a gymnastics competition. On my way to the bedroom to perform my ritual, I stopped to see what they were watching. I saw a guy performing the iron cross on the still rings. He wasn't big, but he was "ripped" and lean.

Normally, if you visualize yourself in a particular situation, it takes a while for that visualization to move from your conscious to your subconscious mind. But on that afternoon the pain in my heart was so deep that I was looking for absolutely anything to take me out of my misery. In that moment, I claimed that image on the screen for myself and anchored it in my subconscious. It became my true core desire to be that young man on the still rings, and having that desire unleashed a magic within me that I didn't even know I had.

You must understand that I was then 19 years old and weighed 108 pounds. My sisters were bigger than I was. But once I had identified my true core desire, I became unstoppable. I saw myself having the body of that kid on TV, and that in turn allowed me to use the power of my intention, which was to learn whatever I needed in order to fulfill my desire. At that point, I took what I believed to be an appropriate action plan – go to a gym and learn gymnastics.

I joined a local gym that had a gymnastics team of which three of my friends were members. And because my friends were good gymnasts, I was allowed to join the team as a favor to them. As it turned out, however, my initial plan was not appropriate.

I was too skinny, and I was still releasing negative energy, which resulted in my continuing to be treated as an outsider by the others in the gym. I was doing bench presses in a corner with an empty bar (because that's all I could lift) while the others were pressing weights. But I was there, and that's what counted.

I remember going to the semi-final meet that was to decide the French gymnastics championships. I fell off the pommel horse during my routine and broke my wrist. A judge told me that if I didn't complete the routine I'd receive a score of 0, which, when added to the team score, would effectively eliminate us from the championship. I was used to hiding my pain, so I got back up on the horse and finished the routine. My fear of losing was greater than my pain, and I scored a 1.5. My team took second place, but instead of praising me for finishing in spite of my injury, my teammates told me it was my fault they hadn't won! As a result, I wound up back in my room crying for a few weeks before I could make myself return to the gym.

The coach told me that if I ever hoped to succeed at gymnastics, I needed to "put on some weight," and so I went in search of a weight lifting gym. I remember walking in and seeing the owner/instructor coming toward me. He looked like a mountain that was growing bigger with each step he took in my direction. I turned and walked away.

My parents were always very supportive of whatever I wanted to do, but my father had also made it clear from the time I was a little boy that getting an education was my key to a better life. I had never given up on education, and I completed my schooling no matter how miserable I was. However, I knew that as long as I was feeling so much internal pain, my education wasn't going to help me. The only thing for me to do was apply my resolve and return to the gym.

Of course, my lack of self-esteem still kicked in from time to time. I would step aside whenever someone else wanted to use a machine, and I didn't dare ask to use a piece of equipment even if the others were just standing around talking between sets. So, if a session lasted an hour and a half, I probably got a ten-minute workout. However, at least by then I had arrived at an appropriate action plan.

Slowly I began to improve. I was building my body and was feeling better in my mind. As my mind focused in the right direction, I became more resolved to continue what I was doing until it became a ritual.

Three years later, in 1986, I won four bodybuilding titles – Mr. France, Mr. Europe, Mr. World, and Mr. Universe. As it turned out, however, my initial success actually derailed me from my path for a while. Although my original goal had been to get out of my misery, a goal that emanated from my soul, I became obsessed with my body and temporarily lost contact with my spirit. Truthfully, if you spend all day staring at your body and measuring your body fat, you won't have much time left over to devote to your spiritual well-being.

The fame and the money were very seductive for a poor kid who had grown up as I did. In fact, I was living in fear – fear that I wouldn't be good enough for my fans. And when your actions and decisions are ruled by fear, you can't be happy.

Happiness is something we all have within us. Unhappiness is something we create for ourselves when what we want to be is in conflict with what we are doing, and as a result, we are afraid. Fear is a lack of love for ourselves, and to love ourselves is to honor, respect, and trust what comes from within – our strong core desire. For a while, I lost track of that, and I needed to rediscover my inner truth.

In 1995, I was invited to come to the United States as "an alien of extraordinary ability" by a friend who was an American lawyer, because I would be able to promote fitness among the youth of America. I settled in Albuquerque, New Mexico, where another Mr. Universe lived. There I met Dr. Dharma Singh Khalsa, a medical doctor, yogi, and author, who is the president and medical director of the Alzheimer's Prevention Foundation, and whom I now credit for turning my life around.

I became the fitness director at Khalsa International and started to train Dr. Khalsa personally. He, in turn, began to teach me yoga and meditation. It was through meditation that I was finally able to get out of my body-obsessed mind-set, but it was a painful transition that often left me crying again as I had as a kid. Dr. Khalsa explained that my crying was an expression of the cleansing and purifying I was experiencing through meditation, and as I have come to understand, it was a way to get beyond my ego-based behavior and reconnect with a deeper level of spiritual consciousness.

In 1999, Dr. Khalsa introduced me to Joseph DeNucci (then general manager and now an owner of Miraval). My true "core" desire was to release the obsession with my body and reconnect with my soul. Mr. DeNucci, who was himself a yoga teacher and a very spiritual person, invited me to come to Miraval for a couple of days to see if I would like to create a fitness program for the spa. After those two days my energy was flowing, and I knew it was a place I'd be staying for a very long time.

What this journey has taught me, is that if I want other people to love me, I first have to love myself. Secondly, if I am acting out of love, I will be creating a positive flow of energy that's contagious, and other people will love what I'm doing as well.

About author.

Nordine Zouareg is an acclaimed International Fitness Coach, a former Mr. Universe, and the author of Mind Over Body: The Key to Lasting Weight Loss is All in Your Head, published by Springboard Press/Warner Books. He has helped thousands of people get healthier, be happier, and lose weight for good. And in the process, he's discovered something astounding: the mental work his clients do before they start their nutritional and exercise plan is actually just as important as the plan itself – if not more. Nordine travels extensively, taking his teachings around the world. You can visit his website or check out his book at www.avtarwellness.com.

Once You Have Faced Your Greatest Fear, Nothing Can Stop You

by Amy Jones

"**H**elp me! Help me! I think my brother's dead!" I'm screaming at the top of my lungs and running toward the highway – oblivious to my own injuries. The cars are stopping, and I'm pacing back and forth. I cannot look away from the sideways tangled wreckage that was our passport home only moments ago.

His hand, lifeless and covered with blood, is hanging out of the passenger window. I'm watching the firefighters rip the car open like a tuna can with the Jaws of Life... waiting for a sign that he survived. Then my brother's scream comes as if on cue... and I realize he is alive!

The car accident, the reading of his Last Rights, the ICU doctor telling us to say "good-bye," dozens of surgeries, nurses, wound changes, losing his leg, finding the strength to move forward – the memories of everything are now flooding in as I write this. What we had endured gave both of us hope as we learned we could overcome anything. This newfound strength was necessary, because a little later I had to tell my brother that our mom had committed suicide.

I was only 14 years old when I experienced my worst fear of losing my mom... and even younger when the accident happened. Each time, I was virtually all alone. My parents divorced when I was extremely young, and my father was not yet a strong influence in my life. My mother (when she was alive) was an alcoholic and continuously depressed. For years, I also was lost, depressed, and lived in complete apathy... not caring about anything. I was afraid to care because it appeared that anytime I did, the object of my love disappeared or was hurt.

This cavalier mindset caused me to always feel sorry for myself, with plenty of sympathy and pity. It also caused me to give excuses for everything I didn't follow through with. Integrity was the lowest on my list of priorities. After all, how many people could function with "abundance" thinking when the only parental influence around either committed suicide or was absent?

I had an even longer laundry list of why I was a victim, besides the reasons above, but these were inflicted upon me by myself... gangs, drugs, violence, bad schools, and countless other reasons I was "not responsible" for my life.

210

I moved in with my dad almost two years after my mom died. He was unwilling to listen to my victim stories and held me accountable for my brilliance and talent. One phrase he said that altered my life was, *"It isn't what you can do when you feel like it... it's what you can do when you don't."*

That phrase, and his taking the time to care, motivated me to complete my high school education with honors, obtain my business degree, and become the youngest general manager with Pizza Hut at only 20 years of age. I turned around multiple broken business units into the highest profiting stores. Later, I managed over $10 million in real estate, became a speaker/trainer at the age of 24, and a published author/CEO at age 25.

My point in telling all this is to illustrate that it doesn't matter in the least what your background is, what your age is, or where you came from. If there is something you "decide" without any doubt that you want, you can obtain it. Many have asked, "How did you accomplish all that you have at such a young age?" My advice is simple: make a decision with clear unwavering focus, and find a coach who will hold you accountable, one that will allow you to realize your greatness and not buy into your "woe is me" self-pity parties. You'll NEVER meet a successful "victim!"

Life is circumstances; choose how to utilize yours to make a difference for others. When you are of "contribution," miracles occur daily. Believe. Trust. Choose a vision and chase it with passion. And lastly, the reasons you "can't" are the reasons you "should."

That being said...

To manifest or create a new level of success, you will be required to question the majority of your beliefs or anything that you've ever known as real. You will be required to give up your self-imposed "false truths" in order to have access to something new... or you can keep what you've always believed, which will give you exactly what you have already gotten. Ultimately you must submerge yourself into a new thought process, and this is what will give you access to something entirely new. It is your life, of your design, and it is your choice.

I am going to give you access to the three major principles that shifted my life from being a receiver (victim), to one of responsibility, where the art of manifestation becomes a "daily activity" instead of just a good concept.

These three principles are:
1. Disappearing significance
2. Ultimate responsibility
3. Integrity is the only key

Disappearing significance – Let's start by looking at the importance of *disappearing significance* and what can happen if you do otherwise. When I personally was in the state of "being significant," I was in a survival mode and

211

lived in a world of lack. It was a world that I designed to protect myself, and believed only in my own existence. I had separated myself into a world of "Me"... and then there's "You." Nothing can create a greater hell. I would compare myself on all levels to see how I was doing against the other six billion individuals of the world. In this frame of mind I was competitive, playing to win, and fighting for my right to be known. I was fighting to survive and to increase that ability to survive. This isn't the way of abundance. There was only me living an ordinary life, being a victim of my circumstances, and fighting to survive. Putting this out to the world caused me to receive the same back. The cycle was an endless downward spiral toward ultimate destruction.

I was determined to be smarter, faster, better, healthier, richer, and more successful. It was all about ME and my ego. Granted, this model did work to a limited extent. I became very accomplished at a young age, but I was alone. I did not have partners, teamwork, or the ability to accomplish anything outside of my own means. What I did not understand at that time was that I existed in the perception of others. So although I had "things" and "accomplishments" to prove my own self-worth and how I was perceived by others, I was not who I wanted to be. I was bossy, driven, and valued success over relationships. For those of you who want a recipe for failure... follow the above guidelines.

Once I finally allowed my *significance* to *disappear,* I became a person of *contribution.* When it wasn't only about me, I was finally able to find myself. I could genuinely look at others and ask what support they needed without my own agenda attached. The way others perceived me, shifted to someone they could count on for support instead of someone who would use them. My networking circles increased rapidly. I began having an abundance of friends and support. An entirely new world of possibility opened up.

Ultimate responsibility – Do you "blame" or find "fault" in others? This is the way I was for a very long time until I found a way out. Every time you blame or find fault, please ask yourself the following question: "Is there something I could have done differently that would have produced a different outcome?"

If you begin to look at situations in this way, there truly is nothing beyond your means. By living in this definition of responsibility, it becomes impossible to be a victim of any circumstance. If you want to take *ultimate responsibility* to an even higher level... consider a child who is starving on the other side of the world that you've never met. This child also is your responsibility. That one child is starving because you have not done anything to make it better. Now please understand that you are not going to take the "blame" for that child's starvation. Just begin to acknowledge that it is within your capability to make a difference on the outcome of that one child's life.

This way of thinking is important because if I am responsible for a starving child that I've never met on the other side of the planet, then I can also be responsible and proactive for how much money I have, what circumstances are impacting me in the present, and everything in life – it is the ability for me to be in a position of power over my current and future circumstances. When I am the source of everything that is true in my life, then I have access to make it different. When I am the victim of circumstances, there is nothing that I can do except react to them. Being proactive or reactive is a choice.

Integrity is the ONLY key – Integrity is the foundational structure for creation and success. Integrity causes power to live behind communication and a belief in a future to occur that does not yet exist. It is the ability to speak things into existence, because others believe what is spoken.

So why did I choose these three principles as the key principles in manifestation? Because I know that who we are as individuals is created by how others perceive us. When "who you are" is someone of contribution, who is always responsible and has a high level of integrity, you can truly create anything and speak anything into existence. These are three things you cannot pretend to be. You have to know yourself as a contribution, be responsible, and be in integrity to be congruent. Also, hold confidence in your speech patterns and have your communication deliver results.

This is the art of manifestation in simplest terms. Be committed to the result and unattached to the way it arrives. You'll be amazed at what you begin to see. What you focus on expands. What you choose to see will be real for you. Your reality can only exist in your perception. If you believe something is true, then it has no choice but to be true unless you gather evidence to the contrary, altering your belief.

Now, the foundational key to manifestation: many people are at an understanding that they can, at least conceptually, manifest anything. What if everything is already manifested? With that in mind, this should take you back to the idea of *ultimate responsibility.* If you have manifested everything in your life the way that it is right now, then what would it have been like *if you had known* you were manifesting everything? Therefore... what can you create in your future when everything is already manifested?

About author.

Amy Jones is working diligently to transform the educational system to teach children life and success skills. For more information, please visit www. smartmentorsystems.com. Additionally, if this story intrigued you, you can read Amy's detailed memoir, "Growth Hurts: A True Journey of Breaking the Chain and Filling the Void."

Reasons, Seasons, and Lifetimes of Influence

by Allan Davis

As I begin to write these words, I do so with a certain sense of ambivalence, but mostly joy mixed together as one. For the past couple of hours, I've reflected back on my life, remembering the influences of a multitude of people who have helped to create who I am today. These words are written in order to ultimately inspire you to do the same thing. Take the time after reading this chapter and start writing down every person you can remember that had any type of life changing effect. The result will be profound. For me... it has been a healing force.

One of my personal obstacles to overcome in life has been in attempting to realize where I belonged that would fit my personality. A few years ago, I was hired by Linda Forsythe as a Graphic Designer. My purpose was to create most of the designs in the magazines and books that you'd see out there from Mentors, as its Art Director. I love what I do and have finally found a home for my passion.

I have been blessed (and sometimes cursed), because it hasn't been an easy journey to start my own business and work on a daily basis with some of the most prolific minds on the planet. The obstacles to developing a global business have been substantial, but also very instrumental in my own personal growth. I've had realizations of talents I never knew I had.

People who look at me now would never guess where I came from or what environment I was brought up in. Many tell me I'm "eccentric." This makes me smile, because I always thought that word was reserved for the very wealthy who had strange ideas. In fairness, I guess I've always had strange ideas and a unique way of acting. But being different was never an issue for me. I am who I am... and I'm a rebel entrepreneur. *(If you were to see me on the street, you'd observe a 6'4" guy with long dark hair, who appears like a Heavy Metal "Rocker"/Goth/Athlete. In some aspects all of this is true, but one thing that stands out most: I don't look my age and certainly don't act it. **wink**)* It wasn't until I was 37 years old that I realized the words "rebel" and "entrepreneur" were synonymous.

As I look back on the people who have come and gone throughout my life, I can see now how they've had a significant impact on me: how I think, act, the lessons I've learned, and how I've grown. Some people who came into my life caused a great deal of pain or difficulty, and it is from these that I had lessons to

214

learn in order to grow. There are also those who came, that were there as "passing ships in the night." Even though these contacts may have been brief, they still left an indelible mark. The more obvious impacts come from friends, family, and even enemies. Each meeting had its purpose in creating who I am today.

They say that we choose our parents before we are born, and as I look back on my youth, I certainly chose well for my guidance. My mother is a Registered Nurse and my father was the Labor Commissioner for Baltimore County. Both career paths demand a rigid adherence to rules, structure, and policy. Both are in a field of public service and a champion to help others in need. Since my father was an attorney representing "Labor Law," at a very young age I became familiar with many injustices practiced in the work place. There were times that my father had to receive a police escort to work (for his own protection) in order to fight for justice. Both of my parents practiced integrity and honor on a daily basis. This became deeply ingrained into my being.

Since my father was also a high profile figure in public service, I was taught early on how my performance in daily life would be closely scrutinized, and how public perception of me could affect his job. Therefore, I had to be "well behaved" at all times and closely follow the law. Public perception is very important when in a high profile situation. This is all well and good, "But, what about my need to just be me, and remain unique?" I wasn't what many call a typical "cookie cutter" all-American type of kid. I knew even then that I was a rebel... albeit a suppressed one.

Looking back on how both of my parents were members of the prestigious Brant Beach, New Jersey Yacht Club, and how I attended there on a regular basis with the entire family, brings back fond memories... but not for the reasons you might think. Again it was important that a certain public display was adhered to. This is where a balancing act of clinging to my unique style while maintaining public decorum came into play and probably caused my parents a great deal of grief. Ultimately I learned how to do both. This also had a positive effect in that it would prepare me for what would come in the future when I came into my own high profile position as an adult. But my success didn't come easily!

It took a long time to find my niche. I hated school and accomplished barely enough to get by, just so I could obtain my diploma. A teacher in the 11th grade felt I had a great deal of artistic and creative abilities, so she suggested I become a Graphic Artist. This brief advice started me on my career path to where I am today. But becoming a successful and well paid artist of any kind – especially as a lifelong endeavor – isn't realized by very many. That is an obstacle that I'm proud to say that I've overcome.

Probably because of all the things I saw my father fight against, I've had an inherent distrust of employers. Looking back, it is obvious that I was only subjected to the unusual bad happenings in the corporate world, and realize now it wasn't the norm. But because of these experiences with my father, the attitude that I developed toward employers is probably responsible for quite a few of the bad things that have happened to me in the work world. No matter how hard I slaved

215

or followed strict protocol, I always seemed to be thrown under the proverbial bus in each business. Every job that I lost – whether I was laid off or fired – taught me something. After many painful lessons, I ultimately learned that I needed to have my own business.

After a multitude of career heartaches in Maryland, I saved $8,000 so I could move to San Diego, California – which had always been my dream. With this huge decision came the reality that I was going to have to leave behind what I thought was the woman of my dreams. After much introspection, I realized that she had very different goals from mine, so I made the decision to listen to my instincts and make the move to San Diego. Looking back, it was the best decision I could have made, although a very difficult one at the time. She and I were meant to go on our own separate paths. Leaving behind my friends, family, and everything familiar was one of the toughest decisions of my life, but I just somehow "knew" it was my fate.

What made my decision more heart-wrenching was that my great lifelong friend, Larry – who was supposed to have come with me – died unexpectedly of a heart attack at the age of 31, just three days before we were to leave. We had such great plans for our journey, and what a perfect addition it would have been to have my friend join me on this adventure to a place where where I didn't know anybody. So, as I arrived at the Pacific Ocean at dusk, I stepped out of the car and felt his spirit with me. I looked at the spectacular sunset and thought, "Larry, we made it... I miss you buddy."

A few more career heartaches were in store for me in California, and I began to question my goals. I lost another job after four years, a job where I thought I had finally found my passion. Depression and despair set in and I wasn't sure what my next step would be.

After 8 long months of searching, I finally found a job at Mentors Harbor International. The path of this journey is still unfolding before me, but little did I know the transformation in my life that was about to occur! It was with Mentors that I realized I was an entrepreneur, and ultimately became Linda's business partner. The story of this evolution is worthy to be put into its own book, but lack of space prevents that from happening. I will say that I met some of the most prolific minds, celebrity speakers, best-selling authors, and spiritual leaders on the planet. These people have changed my thinking and my life. They've helped me to grow in many directions... even though I've only spoken with them for short periods of time.

The most pivotal time in my life came when we were putting on our very first 3-day seminar (Wealth Celebrity Summit in Los Angeles), with an all-star lineup of speakers. The planning and hard work, including a significant financial investment from all of us, transpired over a 3-month period. I couldn't have been happier, because this was to be a huge step for me and the business (of that time). For as long as I live, I'll never forget the phone call I received from my mother, the evening after the first day of our event.

The excitement and exuberance from the daylong activities were still fresh in my mind as I went upstairs to the hotel room and checked my voicemail. I remember thinking... "Wow, two more days to go of this!" As I sat down listening to the first message, my heart began to sink because of the tears I heard in my mother's voice: "Call me back as soon as you can because this is urgent." The second voicemail from my Uncle John wasn't much better as he told me to call my mother right away if I hadn't done so already. When I immediately called her, I still remember verbatim what she said while in tears, "Honey, your father died tonight... the love of my life... and I don't know what I'm going to do!"

My world crashed. Everything appeared to happen in slow motion after that. I did manage to mutter some words of comfort and tell her to remember that she still has a son, daughter, son-in-law, three brothers, and a mother who all love her very much.

I spent the evening remembering a lifetime of memories. It was my dad who showed up at the baseball games I played in and who gave me inspirational support my entire life. It was my dad who taught me about taking responsibility for my actions, to live with integrity, and not to always have excuses. It was he who taught me how to treat women with love and respect by watching how he treated my mother. Even though sometimes his love toward me had to be "tough love," it was always done with the purpose of teaching the right path. Because of my dad, I learned how to cope with many obstacles. Even though at the moment I felt "diminished" knowing that never again would he be there for me, his guidance would continue to live on and inspire me over and over again.

As I write about the times of my life that were pivotal, it now comes to mind how each person has served a purpose in preparation for what was to come. With all the twists and turns... any one of my decisions could have been different.

I'd like to reprint something here that was sent to me in an e-mail from a close friend, soon after my father's passing. This e-mail touched me to the core, and nothing can say it better than this, in my opinion. As you take the time to read, maybe it will cause you to reflect on the people you've met and the impact they have had on your own life. It certainly has on mine....

Reason, Season, or Lifetime

by: Brian A. "Drew" Chalker

What are you? Are you a Reason, a Season, or a Lifetime?

Pay attention to what you read. After you read this, you will know the reason it was sent to you! People come into your life for a reason, a season, or a lifetime. When you figure out which one it is, you will know what to do for each person.

When someone is in your life for a REASON... it is usually to meet a need you have expressed. They have come to assist you through a difficulty, to provide you with guidance and support, to aid you physically, emotionally, or spiritually. They may seem like a God-send, and they are! They are there for the reason you need them to be. Then, without any wrong-doing on your part, or at an inconvenient time, this person will say or do something to bring the relationship to an end. Sometimes they die. Sometimes they walk away. Sometimes they act up and force you to take a stand. What we must realize is that our need has been met, our desire fulfilled, their work is done. The prayer you sent up has been answered. And now it is time to move on.

Then people come into your life for a SEASON, because your turn has come to share, grow, or learn. They bring you an experience of peace, or make you laugh. They may teach you something you have never done. They usually give you an unbelievable amount of joy. Believe it! It is real! But, only for a season.

LIFETIME relationships teach you lifetime lessons, things you must build upon in order to have a solid emotional foundation. Your job is to accept the lesson, love the person, and put what you have learned to use in all other relationships and areas of your life. It is said that love is blind...

but friendship is clairvoyant.

About author.

Allan Davis is the Art Director and owner of SD Pacific Creations. He has a Bachelor's degree in Visual Arts with an emphasis in Graphic Design. He would be happy to provide you with any advertising needs if you send him an e-mail at ADavis923@aol.com.

Living a Life of Freedom, Not Excuses

by Bardi Toto

"Take the first step in faith. You don't have to see the whole staircase. Just take the first step."
- Martin Luther King Jr.

Do You Live a Life of Freedom, or do you allow excuses to control your life?

Have you ever complained that you don't have enough money, the type of relationship you want, or the happiness you desire? Whatever your complaint may have been... have you ever really done anything about it?

Why do we do this? Because we have been conditioned to have a mediocre life and feel we deserve less. Many times this will come about because of past incidences we allow to affect our thinking and perceptions.

For a long time, I was stuck in a phase of allowing the verbal abuse I received as a child to affect how I lived. I had a mother who was an alcoholic, unpredictable and believed in conditional love, not unconditional. How could I know what I wanted, when I was told I would never finish what I started, or never amount to anything. At a young age, I basically was led to believe that I would fail at anything I tried. Sometimes people cannot see the outcome of their dreams, because they are stuck in their past. I had a fear of failure and a fear of success.

My mother also told me almost every day that "we couldn't afford this" or how "poor we are," but then we moved to Hawaii when I was 13. Talk about mixed signals!

Based on my beliefs, I sabotaged myself in every way against success. I know there are those reading this that do not have my story, but you may have experienced some situations that caused you to feel as though you cannot even dream. You may feel that your dreams are out of reach, and I am here to tell you they are not.

219

"Try and fail, but don't fail to try."
- **Stephen Kaggwa**

Later in life I decided to become a nurse. My intensions were to help others and make a positive change in life, not suck all the money out of families and give pills, surgeries and procedures they did not need. When I decided that remaining a nurse wasn't for me anymore... I wasn't sure what to do next. I just knew I was finished. I no longer wanted to be over worked and under paid. Plus, I saw and experienced things in the nursing field that I knew were absolutely wrong. For two months, I sat in indecision regarding my next step, until one day I received a call from an old friend. He was the only one I knew that had ever succeeded in business. Bob had a mindset like nobody I had ever met; and the best part was he believed in me.

Parallel to my nursing, I had started a marketing company on the Internet in 1997. I had gotten ripped off by a company and decided I was going to go into business myself. One night, I had a dream, woke up at 3 am, went downstairs and wrote an advertisement about my company from the point as if it already existed. It moved on to become an overnight success and drew more work than I could handle. I eventually advertised for over 200 companies out there including Amway, Life Force, Alpine and Nu Skin, just to name a few.

NO MORE EXCUSES!

Looking back after going to my "First Steps to Success" with Dani Johnson in Dallas, Texas, I realized why I attracted people in my life who made excuses, and why they failed. I was living a life of excuses; therefore I attracted people who made excuses. Even when I became successful, I still made excuses. To be honest I was scared to death. I was told I would fail at everything in my life, so why try, and why dream? So excuses about what I perceived as negative effects were the way I handled everything.

My friend Bob sat down with me one day and showed me how much money I could have been making had I just moved forward with some simple actions. My fear of failure had cost me a great deal. I learned from Dani and others that... you won't compromise with excuses when you write down your goals.

I've learned to live a life of urgency every day by pursuing my goals. My past existence was of a woman who was verbally abused, and told she could never do anything right. I am now re-born and live a life of freedom.

GOALS WILL MAKE YOU GROW

Give yourself permission to DREAM BIG, I mean HUGE! The biggest reward I have received is not the materialistic things, but about whom I have become through pursuing my dreams. The Investments I have made for myself were in reading motivational books, going to instructive seminars, listening to self-help CD's, and learning how to outsource by hiring people who knew how to do things better than myself.

In the seminar I attended with Dani Johnson, she had us do an exercise I'll never forget and will share it here with you:

If you had no fear of rejection and knew you would not fail, what would be some of the things you would do?

Take yourself back to age 5, when you had that mindset of a persistent child. Remember when you would ask for anything and would do everything without fear of rejection? What Happened? You can change your existing limitation and overcome your obstacles by changing a few of your beliefs. Write Down Your Dreams and Goals.

Once you are clear about what you want, you turn Your Dreams into Goals and Objectives. Turn your dream list into a measurable objective. For instance, use the words "I will weigh 120 lbs. by July 24," not "I want to lose weight." Saying I want to lose weight is a vague want – not specific enough. As Dani says, "Nothing can become Dynamic until it becomes Specific."

You must take each and every part of your vision and turn it into an objective. Make a comprehensive list. Once you have done this, you are ready to go on to the step of turning your dreams into a reality.

Because of a few simple changes in my belief system, I went from a single mom of two children, and a burnt out nurse of 14 years, living paycheck to paycheck... to earning over $200k my first 8 months on the Internet with NO prior Experience at all!

No longer live by finding an excuse for a mediocre life or non-existent results; start being willing to find a way.

About author.

Bardi Toto is a #1 Best Selling Author and world renowned Social Media, Personal Branding Strategist and Attraction Marketing Specialist. Sign Up for a FREE Newsletter 1:1/Group Consulting, Training, FB, YouTube, Social Media Courses, Become a Facebook Fan. Visit Bardi at:
BardiToto.com
1-540-867-2530
www.facebook.com/realsocialmediaguru
Twitter: www.twitter.com/bardi_toto
LinkedIn: www.linkedin.com/in/barditoto

If I Can Do It, Anyone Can!

by Glenn Brandon Burke, M.A.Ed

I'm often asked, "Glenn, you're a Motivational Speaker with two college degrees and a million dollar sales company, but you were once a high school dropout. What made you go back to school and do all you've done?" Since this is so often asked, I thought I'd put it here for all to read. Please allow me to break it down for you as simply as possible (an abridged version).

I was kicked out of high school when I was 16 years old. Being ignorant back then, I thought it was cool. It allowed more time for a venture that made me money – although it wasn't legal. (Someone told me about the GED, which I took – twice – in order to pass. Oh well, at least I passed.) When I was 19 years old, I was seeing this college chick who said, "If you couldn't even get a high school diploma, then you're stupid!" It bothered me that she said I was stupid. I said to myself that I'd show her! I went to an adult education school which was a branch of the Poway Unified School District in California and told them I wanted to receive my high school diploma.

Based on how well I did on my GED, they said I had enough units to graduate, but in order for them to issue me a diploma, I would have to take one class at their school. I did, and 16 weeks later I had my diploma. Well, the girl was long gone, but hey! I now had both a GED and a high school diploma. In reality, I learned two valuable lessons that have served me well in life.

Lesson 1: If I want something BADLY enough, then I WILL achieve it!
Lesson 2: The girl was gone... I really did it for myself!

For the next several years (until I was nearly 23) I continued my life of illegal activity. It was then that a business associate of mine was gunned down to death during a raid at his home, and it was only 15 minutes after I left. I realized then that I had been doing so many wrong things and could've been in prison or dead!

I sat alone for the next couple of days trying to decide what I should do. All I knew was that I needed a new life. Monday morning I flushed all my illegal substances down the toilet, went to see a Navy recruiter, and enlisted for five years. Since I had 45 days until I had to report to boot camp, I moved to my Father's house and worked out daily so that I would be in shape for the physical activities I would endure.

Long story short... toward the end of my enlistment, while working directly for the unit commander, he called me into his office one day and said, "As your commanding officer and direct supervisor, it's my job to encourage you to reenlist for another five years. However, to do that to you would not be doing you a service. Based on what I know of you over the past two years, I think you'd be better off getting out, going to college, and one day running a corporation."

He saw "something" in me, and it was "something" I hadn't seen. What he saw was enormous business potential. So, I left the Navy at the age of 28 and began my first college class. I was on a mission! I completed a four-year degree in 36 months – all while going through a marriage, a divorce, my father's death, and working full time.

I now have two college degrees (B.A. Communication & M.A. Education), am an adjunct instructor at a college teaching Oral Communications/ Public Speaking, an advice columnist with The Student Operated Press *("www. TheSOP.org")*, a motivational speaker *("www.GlennBrandonBurke.com"),* and an author.

In all honesty, I am no different than anyone else – just an average person who set his sights on the bigger picture and went after it with all I had! And if I can accomplish what I have... ANYONE CAN! ESPECIALLY YOU!

You just need to do the following:

1. Prioritize
2. Manage time effectively
3. Focus on the task(s) at hand
4. NEVER forget why you're doing what you're doing
5. Be willing to forego some things to accomplish what you truly desire
6. KNOW that at times it will be hard, and you may lose sight of the goal, but if you stay with it, I promise... IT WILL BE WORTH IT!

Bottom line, it's simple... it comes down to CHOICES! The RIGHT CHOICES can take you to the right places, and the wrong ones... well, you know where they lead. Success isn't always about dollars and cents. It's about what makes you happy! But hey, we do live in a monetary world. Make it work for you!

SUCCESS is a CHOICE! (Education * Life * Career)

About author.

Glenn Brandon Burke, M.A.Ed., *should not be where he is today! Statistically speaking, Glenn should either be dead or in prison. Glenn made the choice not to become a victim of his circumstances, and you can too! Initially a high school dropout who sold drugs, Glenn overcame the adversity in his life and chose to succeed in the U.S. Military, College, Career, and especially Life! Now, Glenn is a Motivational Speaker / Author / Advice Columnist / Educator / and CEO of a Las Vegas based sales company. Glenn uses his past experiences to Motivate and Inspire all walks of life to Succeed with their* **Education * Life * Career** *so they, too, can live the life they desire!*

"If Glenn Can Do It, ANYONE CAN! Now get up, and do whatever it takes to live the life you desire!" – gbb

Book Glenn for Your Next Event. Mention This Book to Receive 25% off His Regular Fee *Publically Funded Incarceration Facilities – Call for Special Rates* ***www.GlennBrandonBurke.com****.*

Overcoming Judgment, Anger and Hatred

by Michael Skowronski

Recently I was talking to a woman about the need to overcome anger. She was surprised that I thought it was necessary; I was surprised at her surprise. I explained that anger causes us to think, say, and do things that create experiences we do not want.

Certainly there are people who live in such adversarial circumstances that they have found anger to be their friend, protecting them from harm, but these are extreme circumstances with an ongoing amount of suffering that they have become almost numb to. Even these people can use the *Law of Attraction* to change their circumstances and get to a point where they can understand the harm that anger causes.

Likewise there are plenty of people in the world who believe that there are circumstances where judgment and hatred are justified. It is natural to form an opinion about some action, event, or thing as in wanting it or not wanting it. It is also natural to strongly dislike certain actions, events, or things. But to hold condemning judgment and hatred will certainly cause you to suffer, and your life experience to be more painful than it needs to be.

Judgment, anger, and hatred are unnecessary and can be overcome.

These three mental-emotional states cause us to say and do things that frighten, offend, and harm others. There are even those who would think, "Why does it matter if we harm someone else if we get what we want?" The truth is that harming others will eventually come back around to harming oneself.

There is such a thing as the *Law of Karma*. We are all one being, so anything we do to another is done to ourselves. In some cases karmic payback is swift, and in others it takes some time. However, those who have been observing life will confirm that what goes around, comes around.

If we repeat a thought or action many times it becomes a habit. Habits come out at the most unexpected times. They come out when we are stressed and at moments when we let our guard down. So even if you are clever and sneaky

225

in doing harm to others, there will come a time when it just slips out and you are exposed. The harm will come back to bite you. There will come a time when you are no longer in the position of strength – you may grow old or sick, or lose your wealth or position of power... then you will not have the skills to acquire what you need, because you have only developed the skill of taking or doing what you want from an unfair advantage.

There is another way that judgment, anger, and hatred harm us. The *Law of Attraction* says that "like attracts like," and if we are in these vibrational states, we will attract something to judge, something to be angry about, and something to hate. We will even create it out of nothing if need be. We have all had the experience of thinking circumstances were one way, when in fact, they were exactly the opposite. This is the *Law of Attraction* at work. We create our experience based on our thoughts. Thoughts become habits when they are repeated. Thus, if we create the habits of judgment, anger, and hatred we will continue to experience the negative emotions that go with those habits of thought, no matter what the outer circumstances are.

There really is no way around it... judgment, anger, and hatred cause suffering in those who engage in such. If you allow these into your mind under some circumstances, they will harm you every time you engage in them through negative emotion. They will create more such experiences through the *Law of Attraction*, and they will become habits of thought which will continue to affect you. They are like Chinese thumb cuffs: the more you struggle and pull to get out, the stronger they grip onto your thumbs and trap you.

We have to change our thinking if we want to get out of this trap. Acceptance, love, and other thoughts that make us feel good are the answer. Emotions are caused by our thoughts. Emotions serve us by indicating if our thoughts are on or off track toward achieving our heart's true desires. Negative emotions tell us we are focused on thoughts that are taking us away from our desires. Thus, it should be clear that we should focus on anything we can that makes us feel better.

This may seem like the wrong approach. Our tendency is to want to wrestle a problem to the ground. But as with the Chinese thumb cuffs, we must make an opposite movement to free ourselves from our suffering. Every master on this planet has told us that this is true based on their experience. I, too, tell you this is true based on many years of my own experiences.

One day while I was living in the state of Kerala, South India...

I have ideas of what a safe and considerate driver should be, based on my experiences in America and Australia. Indians do not drive the way I would like. When I first arrived in India I liked the freedom from over-regulation that Indians enjoy, but too many drivers drive very dangerously or without consideration for anyone else on the road. Coming only inches from being hit by a driver who is traveling in the opposite direction at very high speeds is a common occurrence. Having someone cut a turn right in front of you with no time to stop is a common occurrence. People walking in the street with no regard for their own safety, animals, large rocks, other objects, and large potholes all add to the stress of driving in India.

I took my wife to a doctor's appointment in Kottayam, which was a three-hour drive from our home in Kumily. We left at 6:00 a.m. It was a trip we had made every week for many weeks. I had plenty of time to build up some habits of judgmental, angry, and hateful thoughts, and the *Law of Attraction* had plenty of time to deliver to me experiences that matched those thoughts.

On this particular drive home, I had three different drivers get in my way for no reason while I was trying to pass them. They were going slower than I wanted to go (I drive at a safe but brisk speed), so I signaled with my horn as usual. They responded by moving into the middle of the road, preventing me from passing them. There was no apparent reason for doing this. There were no blockages on their side of the road, these incidences did not occur at curves, and there were no oncoming vehicles. What I was trying to do was usual and expected driving behavior in India. I believed they were blocking me on purpose, and I got quite angry. I began accumulating these offenses and thinking about pulling one of them over, yanking them out of their car, and beating them in the street. I spent a fair amount of time thinking these kinds of thoughts, never really intending to do so. On top of this I was accumulating judgment about all of the other oncoming busses, trucks, and cars that were driving in my lane when there was plenty of room in their own lane. The anger in me built up.

Then it happened... I was passing a bus in a very safe manner on wide open road. I had nearly gotten past the bus when I heard it lightly hit the left rear bumper of my car. I flew into a mad rage! If I had thought about it, I would have known it did no damage to my car – it did not affect my course of driving at all. But all of that built-up emotion enraged me. Somehow I grabbed the parking brake lever and pulled it up. I never use that, except for parking and starting out on a hill. I don't know why I pulled on it. That type of break locks into place. You have to push a button to release it. Because of the speed we were driving, and not really understanding what I had just done, I did not have the presence of mind to release the break. This caused me to spin my car and land on the side of the road in tall grass and weeds, up against a hillside.

I got out of the car in a furious rage. I went over to the bus driver's window (he had stopped), climbed up, reached in, and smacked him on the face. I didn't slap him very hard, but it was insulting. Then I broke one of his windshield wipers off and threw it in the street. He got off the bus and I threatened to beat him. About twenty other men got off the bus and they were all threatening to beat me. I am sure they did not even know that the bus driver hit me. All they knew was that I spun my car, and then smacked the driver for it and continued to abuse him verbally. It was really crazy. Eventually my wife Shyni got me to calm down, and we left. Thank God there was no real damage to our car or to us.

I felt justified in my mind that their actions were wrong and that my ideas about driving were right – until this event occurred. After that I realized that God had been prodding me through that bus driver and all of the other drivers, too. It became very clear because the bus driver really did nothing to me, nor did the other drivers. My desire to police Indian drivers attracted the worst drivers into my path. My judgmental thinking made me slap a man, which is something I just don't do. My anger nearly killed Shyni and me when I spun our car, and nearly got me beaten by a mob of angry men from the bus.

In my life I have learned, more than once, and in more than one way, that if I expect the world to change, or even any single person or event to change, because I did not like it or because "I was right and they were wrong," that I would make myself miserable. Unless I catch each thought of judgment and criticism and change them, then those thoughts will slowly build up and eventually flare up in anger at some specific person or event that probably did not even deserve it.

It is a big job, but we must watch each and every thought, and change the ones that do not serve us. Even if it is possible to evoke a change in the outer world, we must still let go of the judgment, and go about changing it from a place of love and the sincere desire to be of help. I so wish I could change Indian drivers, but I cannot. There are millions of them. If I change one, or even fifty, still more will come until I have wasted all of my energy, and still they will keep coming. We must use logic and reason to convince our minds to let go of its judgment, anger, and hatred. We must come to recognize where our true safety lies, and that is in God. There are no random events. Nothing happens in our reality that we have not earned or created with our energy.

So now when something I don't like happens on the road, my practice is to remind myself, "Nothing really happened, I made it safely. God is watching out for me. Dear God, bless them with awareness of how it is they are driving and how dangerous it is. Help them to learn to drive safely." When I catch myself moving into judgment, I remind myself what happened and what could have happened. I remind myself of the power of my mind and stop my mind from creating violent, vengeful thoughts.

The Miracle – This worked… and very powerfully so! I made at least ten more long-distance drives like that in India after that incident. Each time I was able to maintain this practice. Each time I kept my peace of mind. Before starting on a long journey I even paused in the driver's seat long enough to set my mind clearly on the thought process I wanted. I prayed for all the drivers on the road to drive safely while in my presence. I prayed for them to be aware and courteous. I reminded myself that I no longer needed to police them, not even in my mind; I gave that up to God.

It was a miracle! That is exactly how my drives have been since that time. I am sure those same crappy drivers were still on the road doing the same stupid things, but not while I was around. The real world changed as a result of changing my mind. This change persisted in every single drive I've made since that time, of which there have been many. The difference in driving experiences was so remarkable that every family member who has ridden in the car with me has noticed. Certainly they noticed how much calmer I was, but more than that they noticed that the outer world changed, too.

Making that change had a ripple effect in my psyche. I now calm down much quicker in other situations where anger is rising in me, even if I feel justified in my perspective. We shall see what else Life has to reveal to me and in what other ways anger might try to find expression in my life, but for now I know a dramatic change has taken place within me, and it is a welcome one.

One by one, piece by piece, we whittle away at our unwanted personality traits and develop new ones that serve us in ever more powerful ways.

About author.

*Michael Skowronski is the author of the book, **Unforgettable: A Love and Spiritual Growth Story**, which demonstrates the Law of Attraction at work through equally amazing true-life experiences. Unforgettable is more than a book of great wisdom, it is a true and inspirational story of romance, spiritual transformation, healing miracles, and dealing with death and cancer. You will find many in-depth lessons on the Law of Attraction and Spiritual Growth on Michael's free blog site at www.gr8Wisdom.com. For more information on his book, please visit www.unforgettablebook.com. You can contact Michael at Michael@gr8Wisdom.com.*

"Serendipity" and Overcoming Obstacles

by Lydia Proschinger

The word "serendipity" was coined by Horace Walpole who was one of the most gifted authors of his time, known primarily as a great letter writer. He creatively applied the word "serendipity" (making fortunate discoveries by accident) to situations that three princes encountered in the story called "The Three Princes of Serendip." The story goes as follows:

Once upon a time a king had three sons. When the king became old and desired to retire from his throne so he could relax, enjoy life, and live comfortably and peacefully in his royal abundance, one by one he asked each son if he would like to take over rule of his empire, and one by one, each son declined his generous offer. All three stated that they felt inadequate to fill the king's shoes, and that they could never be as great a leader as their father had been.

Clearly, the three young men were all having a bit of a self-esteem problem. Their limiting thoughts, small mind sets, and spirit of cowardice provoked the king's fury. He reacted by expelling all three sons from his kingdom.

The gist of the story (I won't spoil the tale for you if you plan on reading it) is that by expelling his sons from his empire, the king was sending them on the road to maturity. As it turned out, after all their adventures, all three sons did indeed end up as kings, and as in most fairy tales, they became husbands to beautiful princesses, matured, made great leaders, and mastered all obstacles.

Of course the sons were not always in the most fortunate of circumstances, encountering various obstacles while on the road to maturity and to becoming kings of their own lands, but they were able to use what they had and move beyond their perceived limitations. And what the sons had was what money can't buy: eagerness to prevail and a keen perception of the path including all the signs alongside the road. They were equipped with a gift to make connections between seemingly unconnected events and people or concepts, and all based on pure logic.

Serendipity Jane

I chose the nick name "Serendipity Jane" because I felt it was truly fitting for me. No, I'm no princess, but more like a Bond-girl gone Indiana Jones, the real life female version without the mud-slides and safaris. My explorations and expeditions are into the mind, finding options and being a catalyst for real life decisions that people who come to crossroads may need to make. Along my journeys, I have been able to provide real options for many people; I would be the person others would call to get help for whatever challenges they had to face.

Through trial and error, and by learning from my mistakes, I have found what works for me. Serendipitously through these experiences I have found my direction in life, which is my passion and vocation: life coaching. It was after having my three children that I discovered I had developed an entrepreneurial mindset, and because I so eagerly wanted to start my life coaching, it became more and more difficult to remain employed.

Being a Life Coach is about the ability to see what's on the other side of the coin. You never know what is going to happen because when you toss the coin once, it may show up heads, and when you toss it again, it may show up as tails. What makes the difference in life is our mindset and how we respond to experiences which we judge as being a challenge. In my practice I help people make changes in their lives using humor, creativity, and the active re-conditioning of their mindset that they will adopt and maintain.

When all things are going well in life we are cheers and smiles, and the average person sits back and relaxes to enjoy the good times. Only seldom during these periods do people actively seek new challenges where they consciously work on themselves to improve, expand, and grow.

What are Obstacles Really?

Obstacles are windows of opportunity that you haven't managed to open yet, and there may be a number of reasons why. It may be due to your limiting beliefs, or it may be because you have been busy looking in all the wrong places for solutions, or it may even be that you have been asking the wrong questions.

An obstacle obstructs growth, hinders a path, blocks a passage, and what more does it do? It can make you feel anxious, panicky about change, insecure, and fearful.

Slip Through the Windows of Opportunity.

When you set out to identify what is hindering your progress in life, you go on a mission... the search and destroy kind of hunt for clues to indicate what you can do in order to advance in your personal development. Sometimes you have to make choices in life that, upon reflection, make you wonder if you had been temporarily insane or if some joker had sent you on a wild-goose chase. At times it feels like you're losing ground, or on a wild-water boat ride or flying on a huge wave in the ocean. What matters during these unsettling moments is to create enabling thoughts and a positive mental attitude.

Learn All There is to Know.

My own father was an alcoholic and my mother, a workaholic. I fell into the gap of parental absence of support and guidance during a time in my life, when it was most needed. I felt completely alone. At various times in the ensuing years, my mom went into a severe depression, fell into a coma, and survived breast cancer, not only once but twice! Once I fully realized what horrendous trials she had been through, I felt that I had no excuse for not making a success out of my life.

In 2002, I discovered *Serendipities: Language and Lunacy*. In this book, Umberto Eco, the well-known Italian medievalist, semiotician, philosopher, and novelist helped me to understand two things: the importance of language and our unlimited ability to learn. Between 1995 and 2004 I learned French and Dutch, and added Italian and Spanish (which I'm still practicing regularly). I made it a habit to stretch my mind beyond my comfort zone, making change a constant in life. When I was in school, I felt that I would never need French, but this of all the languages I have come to need in order to survive in a multi-lingual international environment.

Serendipity played a part in how I streamlined my life to fit in the self-study and to persevere so that later I would have the expertise needed to function in the employment market. Since I had three kids, I created my own "curriculum" so I could study at home. I studied everything there was under the sun that seemed would enable me to learn and develop coping strategies for making life easier.

Along the road to where I am today, I experienced the break-up of my 10-year relationship, which landed me in the situation of being a single mom of three with little money to survive on. However, keeping my focus on what I wanted, I continued studying in the evening while working full time during the day, creating the background from which the obstacles I was encountering became windows of opportunity for development, growth, and greater fulfillment.

In my case, what didn't help was that I had a tendency to perfectionism, procrastination, tiredness, and a few physical problems, one of which was a herniated disk of my cervical spine that left my left arm numb for a while. Fully convinced that this was the fire I had to pass through to be refined, I knew that giving up was just not an option.

Enabling Thoughts Keep You Afloat.

In your daily routine, when you feel everything needs to be done at once and you can't do it all, you quickly get overwhelmed. "Just another one" would be my line to overcome procrastination, and I would feel the achievement, checking off every bullet point on my To-Do list of things needing to get done.

Another line that helped me was, "It's not perfect but I accept myself and what I have started now, anyway." That was an enabling thought which helped me overcome the initial terror barriers of starting something new, things like learning French, having to be on my own raising my kids, and the double pressure that comes from having to be on a job while tackling health issues.

Today I am enjoying my life and I guess I have attained my objective to have a "normal and happy life." What that means to me is doing what I enjoy and creating the balance and serenity that I feel is needed as a single mom raising kids.

My Formula for Overcoming Obstacles is:

- Look at serendipity and take your focus off the obstacle.
- Slip through the windows of opportunity and think "enabling" thoughts.
- Learn all there is to know and "be like water" (I borrowed this line from Bruce Lee), which means to always be perfectly flexible, to adjust and adapt your approach to any changes, unforeseen circumstances, or challenges.
- Adopt the mindset of a master of the martial arts.
- Incorporate and allow for serendipities. Don't just look to the outcome at the end of the horizon, look at the crumbs that fall to the side of the table. Actually, don't dismiss anything as unimportant unless it really is.
- Develop the capacity to turn obstacles into windows of opportunity. How? Let me take you through the L.O.V.E. process – a simple method that teaches you how to face fear and discomfort but keep going as you perceive a shift in perception.

L - Letting go of limiting beliefs
O - Opening up to empowering beliefs
V - for Victory (not for Victim!!)
E - Emerge beyond your comfort zone

I would really like to hear from you and how you have been able to overcome your own obstacles, and of course if you feel that I can help you with overcoming your current obstacles. Regardless, if you're a self-starter, highly motivated to change an unsatisfactory situation, interested in self-development, and keenly want to develop a mindset through personal growth... surely my serendipitous life coaching is for you.

Get started now. Be committed to your success. Keep that sparkle!

About author.

Lydia Proschinger is a human potential developer, advanced Emotional Freedom Techniques Practitioner (EFT Level 3), trained in Matrix ReImprinting, and NLP. She's an international coach, author and speaker who specializes in helping spiritually-oriented entrepreneurs, executives, and high profiles overcome internal blocks to create amazing lives. Her L.O.V.E. process has empowered hundreds of people to achieve emotional freedom and return to optimal health, prosperity, happiness. Native of Germany, Lydia overcame debilitating physical pain and depression before emerging as one of the world's most effective coaches. She is an intuitive expert in restoring the mind-body-spirit harmony, empowering people to experience the unlimited nature of their potential.

Lydia Proschinger
Life Pro Coaching
Christophstrasse 4
88662 Überlingen
Phone: 0011 49 7551 9 89 36 19
Mobil: 0011 172 7 60 19 90
http://lydiaproschinger.com/,
twitter.com/Daily_Sparkles,
www.facebook.com/Lydia.Proschinger.Fans,
www.xing.com/profile/Lydia_Proschinger,
de.linkedin.com/in/lydiaproschinger.

Transforming Fear Into Faith

by Cynthia Gardner O'Neill

"Faith is to believe what we do not see, and the reward of this faith is to see what we believed."
- St. Augustine

Is fear the obstacle you must overcome, or is it the *blessing* that brings you closer to faith? I began my adventure of transforming fear into faith before I took my first breath to live this human experience. My human adventure is providing me with experiences to initiate me into a higher consciousness, a loving consciousness. This love is who I am and it is who you are, too. Love is creation, the co-creators of life, you and me, my brothers and sisters, the I, the One, the All. I and the mother and father are one. One cannot BE without the other.

You have forgotten that the masculine and feminine energies, yang and yin, light and dark, faith and fear, complement one another. Everything is within us. You have been conditioned to compare, criticize, and you have been told you must pick one over the other. You have been taught that if you are more left-brained you are smarter, and if you are more right-brained you are more creative. Yet, there is knowledge that you can live, feel, and experience for whole brain balance, wholeness, harmony, and peace. Your brain is balanced through your heart.

You and I have been conditioned and educated in a left-brained masculine world, leading us down the path of fight or flight, defensive, and fear-based experiences, which lead us into war, illness, disease, resentment, road rage, domestic violence, child abuse and fear. The majority has not been taught balance and harmony, and that you have free will and choice to "FEEL" peace within yourself.

How do you begin to choose what you feel? Humanity has been conditioned, programmed, educated, and guided by thousands of years of generational beliefs that say you can't change what you feel. Love has been the most misunderstood expression of who you are in life. Love is not just a feeling; it is who you are! Love is life in action. Love is the gold of the earth! It is what created you. You are LOVE!

235

The Masters who previously walked the Earth taught the importance of love. Theirs was a simple message. In practice, however, centuries of fear-based conditioning obscured a true understanding of what love is. Therefore, it is not an easy task to shed the old conditioning and live as the Masters taught. It's not enough to simply want a loving world. You must *become* the love and be it with every aspect of your being. This you are learning in a process over time, the human experience. *Being* love is what transforms fear into faith. Love transforms consciousness!

The Adventure

Today was a day of transformational growth, from fear into faith. I learned that I love myself enough to stand in my own truth, stay in a place of harmony within me, and to let go of other's fears, anger and discordance. The ways in which we view the world begin and end with our own minds and the meanings we choose to embrace. As we move on our spiritual paths we are able to see the positive aspects of our experience, even the difficult ones.

The Lesson in the Adventure

We packed up the horses and headed up trail. Everything was green, sparkly, and buzzing with life. As we began to reach the summit on a very slim trail, Joe lost the lead rope to the string of horses that were loaded with all the camp gear. As he returned to grab the rope, the horses pushed back onto the narrow trail where I was in the rear. All of a sudden, the last pack horse of three stepped off the trail, which lead down to a steep slope.

"Rocky" was thrown as if rearing up, but there was no ground to support his motion as he lost his footing. He flew backwards towards the slope, and let out a bellowing horses nay. Rocky, who was almost 30 years old, seemed headed for disaster. He lay on the slope, head facing down, with the sawbuck tucked under his body, along with the packs full of camp gear. I was standing with 4 horses: the one I was riding, the one that my beloved Joe had been riding, and the 2 other horses who were packed and tangled in the trees, all on the narrow path.

It was a surreal experience as I watched the moment unfold before me, but I was amazed at the calm of the moment within me. There were several hikers on the trail, and they were freaked out by the sight of the horse going down the slope. Some were screaming and asking if they should call wilderness rescue. I asked them to calm down, step away, and continue on their path.

Joe had gone down to comfort Rocky, and I was to figure out how to get the other horses to safety. An older couple in their 70's who had never been around horses asked what they could do to help. I asked them to walk the two riding horses up to safety while I got the other two packed horses untangled from the trees. They were hesitant, but I assured them the horses would be an easy walk up the short distance, and that I would be right behind them. All went well as the horses were lead to safety and tied to a fence to the entrance of the West Elk Wilderness.

Still, the hikers were upset, and I again encouraged them that the safest thing was to stay calm, because the horses will feel the calm. If we vibrate fear or discordance it would only bring more of that. A few looked at me with awe and wondered how I could be so calm; I knew it was the best thing to feel in that moment, it supported what was for the highest good.

With the four horses tied and safe, I went to Joe and Rocky's side. An older horseman joined us, and we observed the environment to see what would be the safest least traumatic way to untangle Rocky from the sawbuck pack so that he could move and stand up on his own power. With the peace and calm of the three of us collaborating and working together, we accomplished the task of freeing Rocky from the possibility of injury. This task was not easy standing on a vertical slope while the horse's body was pointing downhill with blood rushing to his head. I believe the comforting words that Joe spoke to his horse, the calm loving voice, and the love in his heart vibrating with every breath, let the horse know he was safe.

As we pulled the sawbuck and packs away from Rocky's body, it allowed him to move more freely. And as we began to encourage him to get up, he began kicking his legs and forcing his body to roll to the point where he was able to stand up. A big sigh could be heard from all of us as Rocky balanced himself on all four legs.

I hugged everyone in celebration of this incredible life affirming moment. I had learned that faith and trust in the moment is key. If we lose faith we create our own reality of struggle and pain. We have a choice. Choose harmony and love and the love shall set you free!

I walked Rocky and checked him out, providing him with a dose of flower essence for trauma, a loving massage, and I held my heart to his body in gratitude of his courage for providing a lesson in faith. We loaded him back up with the supplies and off we went to continue our adventure. *Harmonize with love, love transforms consciousness.*

Faith is the Adventure

This adventure provided me with the opportunity to transform fear into faith. I am re-learning what I already know: my very own nature, the nature of self! If Christ were to return to Earth, would he be pleased by what he'd experience? I say yes, for he would see us as whole and complete, without judgment, and through unconditional love, the love that we all are!

So why should we see ourselves as any different than what Christ saw in us, as himself? I paraphrase, "Love thy neighbor as thyself."

When you disconnect from the flow of Love and move into fear, you are the sole source of that disconnection. It is your hand that is turning on and off the faucet, the flow of love. You are in control of your own destiny. Knowing and trusting this is FAITH! Not knowing and distrusting this is FEAR!

Each time I have come to this Earth I have transformed consciousness. If I have been labeled, then I have created a new thought, a unique experience that causes human thought to take notice and wonder why I have seen life differently than most others. I let go of the past and am grateful for the experience, good or bad. One complements the other, so I can choose my experience and create my own reality.

You, too, can change the past, simply by changing how you feel and perceive the past. When you change your feelings and perception, you change your experience with life today in the present moment. Faith is your adventure! Faith is a quality that emanates from the heart! Passion for life is what will save you.

Balancing the left and right brain for higher consciousness and whole brain balance, returns us to wholeness, peace, and loving consciousness. Accepting and honoring the uniqueness within all of humanity, and knowing that one complements the other – instead of comparing ourselves and thinking we need to be a certain way – *is* the way.

You are *the way* to BE in this world, for only you have that unique way of Being. It is time to harmonize life with love, for love transforms consciousness. Love yourself and have faith that YOU are transforming fear into faith and love!

From Cynthia with Love on this beautiful day! So be it! So it is!

About author.

Cynthia Gardner O'Neill is a Life Coach, Wellness Educator, Adventure Guide, and Intuitive Wise Woman. Her service is to revitalize the human spirit with loving consciousness. She has been a wellness educator, illuminating the wellness that flows within humanity through wellness education, life coaching, and intuitive loving services for 30 years. Visit Cynthia's websites: The Center of Loving Consciousness: www.LovingConsciousness.com, and www. FromCynthiaWithLove.com.

Use the Law of Attraction to "Let Your Millionaire Out®"

by David Koons

It seems that you're presented with the *Law of Attraction* and must decide whether you believe it or not. Declaring "Attraction" a "Law" is a pretty strong statement. Quite frankly, the concepts taught about Attraction don't meet the standards of scientific proof necessary to be declared a law. The word "principle" seems a more accurate description. However, I suggest not getting hung up on whether it is a law, principle, proposition, or concept. Instead, let's focus on the word "Attraction" and its meaning. For this reason, I'll refer to the teachings of the *Law of Attraction* simply as "Attraction" to keep the focus where I feel it belongs.

First, let me acknowledge your willingness to read more about Attraction. Some may be turned off by the concept entirely because they don't think it's a law, feel it conflicts with their religious beliefs, or because it seems a little "out there." As you will read shortly, it does none of these things. So, by focusing on Attraction, we can focus on the core elements of what Attraction is all about.

Regardless of whether you think Attraction is a law, principle, proposition, or concept, you are now free to integrate the tips in this article to attract what you want. And ultimately, isn't that what this is about, getting what you want? I ask that, regardless of where you stand right now, you keep an open mind while reading and don't judge anything good or bad, right or wrong. Just consider for the next few days what you read here.

What are your reasons for reading more about Attraction? Perhaps you're curious and want to learn more from books you've read or movies you've seen. Perhaps you're a student of Attraction seeking to expand your understanding, or you're someone interested in a tool that can be used to help you overcome your personal obstacles. This article should help you with all of these.

I have helped thousands of people transform their lives and achieve results that had previously eluded them. Many of the tips, tools, and strategies I shared were based on the concept of Attraction. Basically, I teach people to make money doing what they love. My own life has benefited greatly from these strategies, but it was years before I learned about and mastered them. You see, for years I was a classic under-achiever. I felt frustrated about what could have been. I knew I was capable of so much more and felt bad that I wasn't realizing my full potential.

Ultimately, I felt like a failure and reached a point where I was sick and tired of feeling "sick and tired." In that moment (or crossroad) I made the decision and committed to the mission of finding and mastering strategies to overcome my obstacles and leave behind the pain of "what could have been." I have used these strategies to build multi-million dollar businesses, complete numerous Ironman® triathlons, and serve for eight years in an elite special operations unit of the US Marine Corps.

Now my mission is to share these strategies with you to overcome your obstacles and to help *"Let Your Millionaire Out®."* You see, I'm known for saying: *"You have a Millionaire inside fighting to get out, and the only person holding this Millionaire back is You!"*

Over the years of helping thousands of people just like you achieve phenomenal success, there was a commonality between those who achieved the success they desired and those who didn't.

The successful individuals were able to attract the situations, resources, and people necessary to propel them to their next level of success, while the unsuccessful ones attracted situations, resources, and people that repelled the results they desired.

Attraction is about drawing to you the situations, resources, and people to manifest (to make real) the results you consciously desire. According to the *Law of Attraction*, your circumstances are a direct result of your vibration. So, the good news is you are already using Attraction. The trick is to use it consciously to make your results match your conscious desires.

Quantum physics teaches that every particle in the universe is vibrating at a certain frequency. Everything from your emotions to money to the people in your life has a certain vibration. The results in your life represent the manifestation of your vibration and all that is attracted to it. If you don't like your results (health, relationships, money, etc.), then change your vibration. That's the basic premise of Attraction.

What is not always so evident is that beyond thinking about what you want, you must also take right-action and follow through on your intentions to manifest the results you desire. This is what hangs up many people. It is not enough to think about something, it is necessary to take right-actions to ultimately achieve it. I'll address the thinking side of things because determining which

240

are right-actions is beyond the scope of this article. The *"Let Your Millionaire Out®"* Success System was designed to help you take right-action.

In order to shift the direction of your results, it is essential to possess a burning desire to be, do, or have different results than you are currently experiencing. The most common description of a burning desire is inspiration. This is the feeling of being divinely guided. It doesn't involve struggle, you're not trying to figure it out, and it tends to cause an increase in your energy and vibration. Imagine a time when you were around someone who seemed to be inspired. Weren't you drawn to that person? You may even have thought, "I want some of what he's got."

Conversely, if you are coming from the energy of obligation, you are coming from a disempowered and needy energy. How does it feel when you say, "I have to go to work?" Do you feel excited or obligated? Is it something you would do if you didn't have to? In this case, whether Attraction is a law, principle, or proposition is irrelevant. You know that your energy decreases and becomes non-supportive. Think of the last time you were around a real "needy" person who complained frequently and blamed others for their circumstances. Is this someone you were attracted to? Is this someone you'd want to hang out with often?

Now imagine business and financial scenarios. If you're coming from the energy of obligation, what kind of customers do you think you'll attract? If you're coming from the energy of obligation, what kind of financial circumstances are you going to attract? You see, the reason I and others teach Attraction is that we know from our experiences that when we come from an inspired and empowered place, we attract resources, situations, and people that help us achieve similar outcomes. We also know from experience that when we come from the energy of obligation, we attract resources, situations, and people who unconsciously help us achieve uninspired (and undesired) outcomes.

How do you avoid obligation and come from inspiration? First, recognize that you don't need to do anything. Everything in your life is a choice. You don't need to go to work, pay your bills, or take out the trash. Sure, there are consequences, but you don't have to do any of those things. A simple exercise to assist you is to draw a line down the center of a sheet of paper. Down the left-hand column, list all the things you think you need to, have to, or should do. Next, review your list, and then down the right-hand column, rewrite the statements using either "I choose to" or "I choose not to" do each of the items.

The next element to consider when utilizing the power of Attraction is clarity. Are you clear about what you want in all areas of your life? There are people who seem to be experts on what they don't like and don't want in their life. However, few are really clear about what good health, healthy relationships, or financial freedom means to them. Understanding Attraction, it follows that someone focusing on how out-of-shape they are will naturally feel out-of-shape. Someone focusing on the unhealthy relationships they continue to experience will, no doubt, continue to attract unhealthy relationships. And someone focusing on their debt seems to find they continue to attract more debt.

We know from studying the brain that what we focus on expands in our awareness. Your brain's reticular activating system goes to work subconsciously looking for evidence of what you consciously (or unconsciously) tell it to look for. The common example of looking for red cars demonstrates this. Once you hear red cars mentioned, you start seeing red cars everywhere, whether you were consciously looking or not.

In the quantum field, we learn at the subatomic level that what we see is based on the observer. If the observer changes (the individual or their perception) then what they see will change. In other words, when you change the way you look at things, the things you look at change.

Rather than focusing on what you don't like or don't want, imagine what you would attract by being clear about the characteristics of your ideal customer. Do you want customers that pay in a timely manner? Do they enthusiastically recommend you to others? Do you want customers who appreciate the quality of your product or service? What other considerations would make for an ideal customer? Wouldn't it make sense that you act this way toward your customer?

If you're an employee, think of the customer as the people or person directly benefited by your work. How would you like them to act or behave toward you? Do they respect and appreciate your efforts? What would it look like to be valued? Imagine others within your organization speaking well of you behind your back. Would you like others to be respectful of your time, giving you ample notice of deadlines whenever possible? What other considerations would make them an ideal customer? Get clear about what you want and refine it as necessary. And be sure to demonstrate the behaviors you want returned.

As you're reading, you may be thinking of areas of your life that could benefit from more clarity. With your health, you can get clearer about what "healthy" means to you and what you "choose" to do when it comes to living a healthy lifestyle. With relationships, rather than describing what you don't like about your partner (or previous partner), describe an inspiring picture of what you would like in a partner. With money, rather than focus on debt, get clear about how you'd like to handle money. Does it multiply while you sleep? Do you attract it effortlessly? Is your net worth growing?

Understanding the quantum field, neurological processes, and the requirements to declare something a law, you may begin to see the complexity of proving the teachings of Attraction. What we do know is that everything is energy. Energy is a vibration. Energy, through vibration, is emitted from all things and affects all things. Therefore, the vibrations you emit and receive have a profound impact on yourself and others.

Consider the language you use. You may have described someone as having a "good vibe" or a place as having a "bad vibe." Vibe is short for vibration. Without even recognizing it, you are communicating about Attraction. You may have said things like, "I just don't like the energy of this place." Perhaps you've had a gut feeling about someone or something. These are all examples of your subconscious understanding of Attraction principles.

By now it may not matter to you whether Attraction is a law, principle, concept, or idea. You may realize that you would not be risking much by consciously harnessing Attraction concepts and putting your energy into thinking, feeling, and acting in line with the results you consciously desire. The key is consciously choosing what you focus on, during the many decision points you experience throughout each day.

It takes courageous action in these daily decision points, these crossroads. Every day the decisions you make either attract resources, situations, and people that move you closer to your desired outcome or attract things that move you farther away from what you consciously choose. One thing is certain: you don't stand still – it just doesn't work that way.

Here's the best part: it doesn't matter what happened 5 minutes, 5 days, or 5 years ago. Right now you're at a new crossroad and get to choose again. I can tell you, when I was in the Marines it was easy. Life or death, it was a clear choice. But what about you? Each day you're faced with choosing between supportive or non-supportive thoughts, feelings, and actions. You will attract what you consciously desire or push it further away. When you choose to come from inspiration, you are taking another step to *"Let Your Millionaire Out®."*

You can choose to put this book down and move on to something else, or you can begin using the power of Attraction to achieve results that, until now, may have eluded you. You're at another crossroads right now. Which direction will you choose?

About author.

David Koons is the founder of "Let Your Millionaire Out®" Success System featuring programs, products, and support for individuals and organizations seeking to overcome their obstacles and achieve new levels of success. David combines success habits with the latest in neuroscience and quantum physics to translate tactical concepts into achievable steps that anyone can follow. You can begin applying the principles of Attraction in your life by signing up for the free "Let Your Millionaire Out®" Success System. The free system guides you step-by-step to effortlessly integrate and apply the elements of Attraction (and other success strategies) in your life. Visit www.LetYourMillionaireOut.com to begin attracting new results into your life.

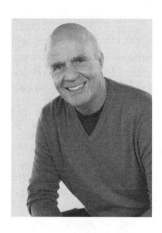

Making Intention Your Reality

by Dr. Wayne W. Dyer

Below are 10 ways to practice fulfilling your intention to live your life on purpose from this day forward:

Step 1: Affirm that in an intelligent system, no one shows up by accident, including you. The universal mind of intention is responsible for all of creation. It knows what it's doing. You came from that mind, and you're infinitely connected to it. There's meaning in your existence, and you have the capacity to live from a perspective of purpose. The first step is to know that you're here on purpose. This is not the same as knowing what you're supposed to do. Throughout your life, what you do will change and shift. In fact, the changes can occur from hour to hour in each day of your life. Your purpose is not about what you do, it's about your beingness, that place within you from which your thoughts emerge. This is why you're called a *human being* rather than a *human doing*! Affirm in your own words, both in writing and in your thoughts, that you are here on purpose, and intend to live from this awareness at all times.

Step 2: Seize every opportunity, no matter how small, to give your life away in service. Get your ego out of your intention to live a life of purpose. Whatever it is that you want to do in life, make the primary motivation for your effort something or somebody other than your desire for gratification or reward.

The irony here is that your personal rewards will multiply when you're focused on giving rather than receiving. Fall in love with what you're doing, and let that love come from the deep, inner-dwelling place of Spirit. Then sell the feeling of love, enthusiasm, and joy generated by your efforts. If your purpose is felt by being Supermom, then put your energy and inner drive into those children. If it's felt writing poetry or straightening teeth, then get your ego out of the way and do what you love doing. Do it from the perspective of making a difference for someone or for some cause, and let the universe handle the details of your personal rewards. Live your purpose doing what you do with pure love – then you'll co-create with the power of the universal mind of intention, which is ultimately responsible for all of creation.

Step 3: Align your purpose with the field of intention. This is the most important thing you can do to fulfill your intentions. Being aligned with the universal field means having faith that your Creator knows why you're here, even if you don't. It means surrendering the little mind to the big mind, and remembering that your purpose will be revealed in the same way that *you* were revealed. Purpose, too, is birthed from creativeness, kindness, love, and receptivity to an endlessly abundant world. Keep this connection pure, and you'll be guided in all of your actions.

It's not fatalism to say that *if it's meant to be, then it can't be stopped.* This is having faith in the power of intention, which originated you and is within you. When you're aligned with your originating Source, then this same Source will aid you in creating the life of your choice. Then, what happens feels exactly as if it was meant to be. And that's because it is! You always have a choice in how to align yourself. If you stay focused on making demands on the universe, you'll feel as if demands are being placed on you in your life. Stay focused on lovingly asking, *How may I use my innate talents and desire to serve?* And the universe will respond with the identical energy by asking you, *How may I serve you?*

Step 4: Ignore what anyone else tells you about your purpose. Regardless of what anyone might say to you, the truth about your feeling purposeful is that only *you* can know it, and if you don't feel it in that inner place where a burning desire resides, it isn't your purpose. Your relatives and friends may attempt to convince you that what *they* feel is *your* destiny. They may see talents that they think will help you make a great living, or they may want you to follow in their footsteps because they think you'll be happy doing what they've done for a lifetime. Your skill at mathematics or decorating or fixing electronic equipment might indicate a high aptitude for a given pursuit – but in the end, if you don't feel it, nothing can make it resonate with you.

Your purpose is between you and your Source, and the closer you get to what that field of intention looks and acts like, the more you'll know that you're being purposefully guided. You might have zero measurable aptitudes and skills in a given area, yet feel inwardly drawn to doing it. Forget the aptitude-test results, forget the absence of skills or know-how, and most important, ignore the opinions of others and *listen to your heart.*

Step 5: Remember that the all-creating field of intention will work on your behalf. Albert Einstein is credited with saying that the most important decision we ever make is whether we believe we live in a friendly universe or a hostile universe. It's imperative that you know that the all-creating field of intention is friendly and will work with you as long as you see it that way. The universe supports life; it flows freely to all and is endlessly abundant. Why choose to look at it in any other way? All of the problems we face are created by our belief that we're separate from God and each other, leading us to be in a state of conflict. This state of conflict creates a counterforce causing millions of humans to be confused about their purpose. Know that the universe is always willing to work with you on your behalf, and that you're always in a friendly, rather than hostile, world.

Step 6: Study and replicate the lives of people who've known their purpose. Whom do you admire the most? I urge you to read biographies of these people and explore how they lived and what motivated them to stay on purpose when obstacles surfaced. I've always been fascinated by Saul of Tarsus (later called St. Paul), whose letters and teachings became the source of a major portion of the New Testament. Taylor Caldwell wrote a definitive fictional account of St. Paul's life called "Great Lion of God," which inspired me enormously. I was also deeply touched by the purposeful manner in which St. Francis of Assisi lived his life as exemplified in the novel "St. Francis," by Nikos Kazantzakis. I make it a point to use my free time to read about people who are models for purposeful living, and I encourage you to do the same.

Step 7: Act as if you're living the life you were intended to live, even if you feel confused about this thing called purpose. Invite into your life every day whatever it might be that makes you feel closer to God and brings you a sense of joy. View the events you consider obstacles as perfect opportunities to test your resolve and find your purpose. Treat everything from a broken fingernail, an illness, to the loss of a job, to a geographical move, as an opportunity to get away from your familiar routine and move to purpose. By acting as if you're on purpose and treating the hurdles as friendly reminders to trust in what you feel deeply within you, you'll be fulfilling your own intention to be a purposeful person.

Step 8: Meditate to stay on purpose. Use the technique of Japa, and focus your inner attention on asking your Source to guide you in fulfilling your destiny. This letter from Matthew McQuaid describes the exciting results of meditating to stay on purpose:

Dear Dr. Dyer,

My wife, Michelle, is pregnant by a miracle-a miracle manifest from Spirit using all of your suggestions. For five years, Michelle and I were challenged by infertility. You name it, we tried it. None of the expensive and sophisticated treatments worked. The doctors had given up. Our own faith was tested over and over with each failed treatment cycle. Our doctor managed to freeze embryos from earlier cycles of treatment. Throughout the years, over 50 embryos had been transferred to Michelle's uterus. The odds of a frozen embryo successfully initiating pregnancy in our case were close to zero. As you know, zero is a word not found in the spiritual vocabulary. One precious frozen embryo, surviving minus 250 degrees for six months, has taken up a new home in Michelle's womb. She is now in her second trimester.

Okay, "So what?" you might say. "I get letters like this every day." However, this letter contains proof of God. A tiny drop of protoplasm, as you have so eloquently written on many occasions, a physical mass of cells alive with the future pull of a human being, turned on in a laboratory, and then turned off in a freezer. All molecular motion and biochemical processes halted, suspended. Yet, the essence of being was there prior to freezing. Where did the spiritual essence go while frozen? The cells were turned on, and then turned off, but the spiritual essence had to prevail despite the physical state of the cells. The frequency of vibration of the frozen cells was low, but the vibrational frequency of its spirit must be beyond measure. The essence of the being had to reside outside of the physical plane or mass of cells. It couldn't go anywhere except to the realm of spirit, where it waited. It waited to thaw and manifest into a being it always has been. I hope you find this story as compelling as I do, as nothing less than a miracle. An example of spirit in body, rather than a body with a spirit.

And now for the million-dollar question. Could this one embryo survive such hostile frozen conditions and still manifest because I practiced the Japa mediation? Just because I opened my mouth and said, "Aaaahhh"? I had a knowing, no question about it. Japa meditation and surrendering to infinite patience are daily practices. During my quiet moments, I can smell this baby. Michelle will thank me for my conviction and faith during the dark times. I praise your work for guiding me. Thank you. Now, nothing is impossible for me. When I compare what I have manifested now in Michelle's womb to anything else I might desire, the process is without effort. After you truly surrender, everything you could ever want just seems to show up, right on schedule. The next amazing manifestation will be to help other infertile couples realize their dreams. Somehow, I will help those who feel there is no hope.

> *Sincerely,*
> *Matthew McQuaid*

Many people have written to me about their success with staying on purpose through the practice of Japa meditation. I'm deeply touched by the power of intention when I read about people who use Japa to help achieve a pregnancy, which they felt was their divine mission. I particularly like Matthew's decision to use this experience to help other infertile couples.

Step 9: Keep your thoughts and feelings in harmony with your actions. The surest way to realize your purpose is to eliminate any conflict or dissonance that exists between what you're thinking and feeling and how you're living your days. If you're in disharmony, you activate ego-dominated attitudes of fear of failure, or disappointing others, which distance you from your purpose. Your actions need to be in harmony with your thoughts. Trust in those thoughts that harmonize, and be willing to act upon them. Refuse to see yourself as inauthentic or cowardly, because those thoughts will keep you from acting on what you know you were meant to be. Take daily steps to bring your thoughts and feeling of your grand heroic mission into harmony with both your daily activities and of course, with that ever-present field of intention. Being in harmony with God's will is the highest state of purpose you can attain.

Step 10: Stay in a state of gratitude. Be thankful for even being able to contemplate your purpose. Be thankful for the wonderful gift of being able to serve humanity, your planet, and your God. Be thankful for the seeming roadblocks to your purpose. Remember, as Gandhi reminded us: "Divine guidance often comes when the horizon is the blackest." Look at the entire kaleidoscope of your life, including all of the people who have crossed your path. See all of the jobs, successes, apparent failures, possessions, losses, wins – everything – from a perspective of gratitude. You're here for a reason; this is the key to feeling purposeful. Be grateful for the opportunity to live your life purposefully in tune with the will of the Source of all. That's a lot to be grateful for.

It seems to me that searching for our purpose is like searching for happiness. There's no way to happiness; happiness *is* the way. And so it is with living your life on purpose. It's not something you find; it's how you live your life serving others, and bringing purpose to everything you do. That's precisely how you fulfill the intention that is the title of this chapter. When you're living your life from purpose, you're dwelling in love. When you're not dwelling in love, you're off purpose. This is true for individuals, institutions, business, and our governments as well. When a government gouges its citizens with excessive fees for any service, they're off purpose. When a government pursues violence as a means for resolving disputes, it's off purpose regardless of how it justifies its actions. When businesses overcharge, cheat, or manipulate in the name of profit-making, they're off purpose. When religions permit prejudice and hatred or mistreat their parishioners, they're off purpose. And it's true for you as well.

Your goal in accessing the power of intention is to return to your Source and live from that awareness, replicating the very actions of intention itself. That Source is love. Therefore, the quickest method for understanding and living your purpose is to ask yourself if you're thinking in loving ways. Do your thoughts flow from a Source of love within you? Are you acting on those loving thoughts? If the answers are yes and yes, then you're on purpose. I can say no more!

About author.

Wayne W. Dyer, Ph.D., is an internationally renowned author and speaker in the field of self-development. He is the author of more than 20 books, has created many audios, CDs, and videos; and has appeared on thousands of television and radio programs. Four of his books, including "Manifest Your Destiny," "Wisdom of the Ages," "There's a Spiritual Solution to Every Problem," and the New York Times' bestseller, "10 Secrets for Success and Inner Peace," were featured as National Public Television specials; the book, "The Power of Intention," has been showcased there as well. Dyer holds a doctorate in educational counseling from Wayne State University and was an associate professor at St. John's University in New York. Visit his website at: www.DrWayneDyer.com.

Article excerpts reprinted from the book, "THE POWER OF INTENTION: LEARNING TO CO-CREATE YOUR WORLD YOUR WAY" by Hay House Inc. Copyright © 2004 by Wayne W. Dyer. Used here by permission.

Life is Rigged in Our Favor

by Patricia Dietz

Life is all about overcoming obstacles. From the day we are born, gasping for our first breath, until the day we exit our life's journey, life hands us one challenge after another to wrap our energy around and master. The ability to overcome all challenges that present themselves in our daily travels is a built-in mechanism that we all possess; however, the awareness of or belief in that ability to overcome these obstacles is what distinguishes the successful ones from those who choose to remain floundering in the dark.

For me, the challenge was climbing out of the pit of depression, low self-esteem and personal despair. While my physical needs for food, clothing and shelter were met as a youngster growing up, there was a complete absence of emotional, mental and spiritual stimulation coming from the main influences in my life.

I grew up frustrated, overwhelmed and unable to express myself very well. I walked around with a big lump of pain in my throat, constantly arguing and fighting, angry, and possessing a bad attitude in general. There was no outlet for me to express what was going on inside of me, no one who "understood me," no way for me to help myself except by throwing myself into the arms of nature or by hanging out with friends to soothe my tormented soul. I did anything I could to be somewhere other than inside my house, because that was where the pain was most intense.

Some very challenging inner dramas colored much of my adult life, and rather than allowing those challenges to crush me completely, I slowly learned how to turn them into personal successes. Along the way I have picked up some personal wisdom that I'd like to share with you throughout this article.

For all of us, the early years of our lives establish the platform we use for stepping into our independence. Whether we were provided early on by our caretakers with effective "tools" to use in establishing our new independent selves, or whether we were offered much challenge and confusion as to who we were and what we were "supposed to do," all of us emerge onto the adult stage with what we have to work with.

Even for those who appeared to "have it all" while growing up, once they got out there in the adult arena of life, they were on their own, same as the rest of us, struggling and making mistakes. And we all make mistakes. We are bound to be rudely awakened often by the seeming harshness of reality. Life engages us in ways that totally confound us, and while we are not necessarily in control of what life throws our way, we are in control of what we do with it. We do have the ability to build an inner network of knowledge and resources that we can rely upon to get us through any situation.

But, you must feel yourself worthy to even begin the process, and that can be tricky to do for some of us. Those who suffer from depression or low self-esteem must find a way to engage in supportive self-talk that will allow them to take the initial steps to help themselves out of their personal pit of despair. It can be done.

The truth is, we are ALL worthy of the best that life has to offer. We ALL have the inner mechanism necessary for helping ourselves through any situation we might find ourselves in. We ALL are made of the same stuff. It is a matter of arming ourselves with knowledge and of taking responsibility for making decisions and choices.

Life can be looked upon as a game. And the game is winnable! There are strategies that can be used, techniques that can be mastered, and there is an entire host of help everywhere one turns. Gift yourself with allowing your mind to believe this to be true, and begin the process of becoming aware that you have a great deal of power to influence the direction of your personal life.

Being aware of your thoughts and beliefs, of the way you talk, of the things you do, of the attitudes you possess, of the perceptions you hold… being aware of what is transpiring inside of you in these basic ways is vital for the process of becoming self-realized. Overcoming obstacles helps us learn more about ourselves in these ways – truly a blessing in disguise.

Many diamonds cross our paths throughout life. Many synchronicities and serendipitous events present themselves to us that we could never have foreseen. And they reveal themselves to us at the perfectly appropriate moments. These are synchronicities and serendipitous events that we have unwittingly prepared ourselves for through our ongoing self-discovery process. That is why becoming more aware of yourself daily is so important… as you do so you continue refining your platform for engaging in life, and you attract new situations that bring new solutions to help you overcome your latest conundrums.

There will always be challenges and obstacles to face. There will always be new opportunities for personal growth. Mastering what goes on inside your being is the key to influencing what occurs on the outside of it. As the title of Wayne Dyer's book so aptly states: *"You'll See It When You Believe It."* Believe in yourself, that you are a wonderful creative being, continue listening to all the signals, insights, guidance and information stemming from within your heart, arm yourself with knowledge, experiences and personal wisdom, and you will be sitting pretty to elegantly overcome any adversity that shows up at your door.

Already situated inside our personal arsenal is everything we need to create the life of our dreams. Life is truly rigged in our favor! For our part, all we need do is remain light-hearted, keep the focus positively on what we want, become a slayer of obstacles, and keep steadfast in the face of any fear that looms large and threatening, while continuing to chart a forward trajectory throughout our lives. Life does not have to be a burden to bear. Enjoying the process is an art that can be passionately embraced.

Life is a gift from the Creative Intelligent Source of all things. Uncover the diamonds hidden in plain sight on your path and you will thrive; you will continue to expand in your personal wisdom and knowledge. By engaging in all that makes you joyful, by creating peace of mind for yourself and harmony in your environment, you will be in the wonderful position of being able to offer your gifts to those walking a few steps behind you.

About author.

Patricia Dietz is Editor-in-Chief of this publication of Mentors Digest's ~ Overcoming Obstacles. She has known Linda Forsythe for several years and has worked as Assistant Editor for other Mentors Harbor publications. She is a self-taught writer who has been writing inspirational and personal growth articles for over 30 years. Please visit her website: www.thisearthgig.com for further delving into personal growth and the spiritual side of life.

SECTION V

Exclusive Mentors Magazine Cover Story Interviews

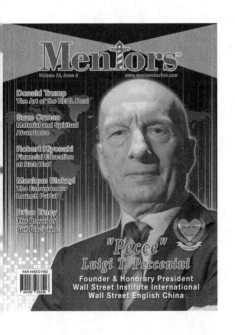

Note: These same interviews and many more are available on Audio, MP3, and downloads to iPod or disc.
ALL are available at
www.mentorsharbor.com

Bonus Section!!!
Exclusive Cover Story Interview

"*Pecce*"
Luigi
T. Peccenini

Brought to you by ...

Interview with *Pecce*
(Luigi Tiziano Peccenini)
Founder of Wall Street Institute
& of Wall Street English (China)

by Linda Forsythe

"MENTORS MAGAZINE™"
(Transcript from LIVE Interview)

Linda Forsythe: Welcome back to Mentors Magazine, here on this beautiful sunny day... brought to you LIVE from San Diego, California!

Today, I am extremely honored to have as our guest, *Luigi Tiziano Peccenini,* (though everyone from his close friends and employees to even Presidents of the United States call him *"Pecce"* [pronounced pe-chē] for short). And, as you may have already guessed... he is Italian.

Pecce with President G.H.W. Bush at a Wall Street English Center in Beijing, and with President Clinton at the Universidad Europea de Madrid.

Pecce is not so well-known in the States and other English speaking countries, but he is something of a celebrity elsewhere... especially in China. And there is a good reason for that! Wall Street Institute, the company he founded 40 years ago, teaches people to speak English, and all its learning centers – which number over 450 – are in non-English speaking countries. To date, Wall Street Institute has taught over two million people in 27 countries and territories – and it's expanding rapidly in China.

Today, Pecce holds the post of Honorary President of Wall Street Institute International and Wall Street English (China). But he devotes most of his

255

time sharing what he has learned as an entrepreneur, and as a man, with our future leaders. He does so through giving seminars, particularly at universities in China, and through the books that he is currently writing. He is Guest Professor at Shanghai International Studies University and Hunan International Economics University, and Adjunct Professor at Shanghai Jiao Tong University.

China, 9 May 2012: Pecce sharing his philosophy of business and life with nearly 3,000 students at Hunan International Economics University.

He lives between Barcelona, Beijing and China's beautiful island of Hainan, set in the tropical waters of the South China Sea, which is where we have caught up with him today.

Welcome, Pecce, to this month's Mentors Magazine interview. This is truly an honor to have you with us today!

Pecce: *Nice to be with you, Linda.*

Linda Forsythe: Well, Pecce, I don't suppose many of our listeners/readers will have heard of Hainan. Can you explain where this is on the map for us?

Pecce: *Hainan, as you rightly said, is in the South China Sea, and belongs to China. It's a beautiful island... and it's very big. It is between Hong Kong and Vietnam. In fact, it's an hour and a half's flight from Hong Kong. The best time to be in Hainan is from December until March, because during the winter you get 24°C (75°F) and upwards, so it is really a paradise. That's why I spend most of my time in winter here.*

The tropical island of Hainan lies in the South China Sea and enjoys an average temperature of 22-26°C (72-79°F), with over 300 days of sunshine a year.

256

Linda Forsythe: You have become a success, Pecce, beyond most people's wildest dreams. When they listen to this interview, they will probably want to know, "What do I have to do to achieve the success that you have had? Are my dreams even big enough? Am I up to it?" – and so on. Quite a few more may be wondering why they have never heard of you. *Laughs* What I am hoping today, Pecce, is that you are going to be able to unearth your secrets to success.

Pecce: The business I created is all about teaching people English, and is entirely located outside the United States. I would hope, though, that if you stopped a young professional on the streets of Beijing or Shanghai and mentioned "Wall Street English" to them, they would not only have heard of us, but may even have learned English in one of our centers.

We currently have 15 centers in Beijing, 17 in Shanghai and a further 32 in China's other largest cities. When you think that an average-sized English school elsewhere in the world has maybe 500 students at any one time, our largest centers each have up to 3,000 students enrolled!

If I was to walk you around our flagship center in Shanghai, I think you would be astonished – it still amazes me! It takes up the entire third floor of China's most prestigious building, the Jinmao Tower – one of the jewels of modern architecture. The tower is shaped like a pagoda that has been stretched 88 stories into the sky – 88 because 8 is a lucky number in China. It tapers all the way up to the Hyatt Hotel which occupies the top 34 floors. Our center is at the bottom, where the floors are the largest.

The Shanghai World Financial Center (left) and the Jin Mao Tower (right).

That gives us the room to provide the sort of facilities students could normally only dream of, like a cinema to watch English films, a Social Club area, and English Corner, where they can practice English with friends. In fact, the students enjoy such a degree of comfort that many prefer to spend their days in a center rather than in their own home! I feel very strongly that the space you learn in has a deep effect on how effectively you learn, so no expense has been spared!

Linda Forsythe: The environment you describe in your centers sounds truly inspiring! It's not difficult to see why Wall Street has enjoyed so much success. You said that you have sold the company bit by bit over the years... can you tell us more about that?

Pecce: *I have always been a one-man show, and a one-man show cannot last forever. There comes a time in the expansion of a company, especially one that needs a lot of capital investment up-front for new centers, developing online learning, and so on, when the opportunities for growth far exceed the cash available to finance that growth. I have hit that point three times in the life of Wall Street Institute.*

The first time was in 1986. A couple of years earlier I had invested all my money in developing learning materials especially for the new learning methodology I had designed. But I was unable to recoup my investment. There just weren't enough schools in Italy to spread the cost over. So the business went bankrupt.

I knew the business model was sound, though, and was determined to start again. But I desperately needed an investor. So I used my last dollars to buy an advertisement in a Swiss newspaper. Luckily, a Swiss business angel came forward, and his investment allowed me to launch and expand the network in Switzerland.

The next time I needed capital investment was in 1997. This time a large American company, Sylvan Learning Systems, offered to buy the whole business. By then Wall Street Institute had expanded through Europe and to Central and South America. Knowing that they would secure its future and enable it to grow more quickly than I could alone, I sold them the business.

Then the final time was in 2006. I had launched Wall Street English in China, this time as a franchisee. I had grown it to a point where it needed to make a quantum leap in expansion.

Just think – there are now nearly 3,000 people working for Wall Street English in China! There comes a time when you have to do what is going to benefit your staff, secure their jobs, and keep students coming through the doors. So I sold the franchise to The Carlyle Group, who had already bought the rest of Wall Street Institute from Sylvan Learning Systems. Carlyle, in turn, has recently sold the whole of Wall Street Institute and Wall Street English (China) to Pearson, which is both the largest education company and the largest book publisher in the world.

You know Pearson very well, I'm sure. They started out as the publisher Longman, which was founded in 1724. They also own Penguin Books, Addison-

Wesley, *and many other famous companies, as well as the* Financial Times *and 50% of* The Economist. *Importantly, they did not acquire Wall Street Institute and Wall Street English (China) to resell them but to keep them, and are planning to invest very large sums in taking the business to the next level. That's why I am satisfied with the situation now, and I'm helping them with that in a small way. They are already improving the business with new complementary products for our students. So the situation today... I think it is ideal for the two companies that I founded. They found their best destiny.*

Wall Street Institute learning methodology was devised by Pecce 40 years ago in Milan, Italy.

So you see, Linda, we all know that failure brings problems – and I have had my fair share of those – but growth, and especially lack of capital to grow, also brings its problems. Of course, they are usually better problems to have! But if not handled correctly, they can, if not destroy your business... they can see it relegated to the sidelines. At any of these points, had I not sought and accepted investment, Wall Street Institute could have ended up a mere footnote in the history of language learning... and people would still perhaps be laboring to learn English in the old and inefficient traditional ways!

Linda Forsythe: So, it was your confidence in your business model that carried you through the difficult times in the 1980s. Your confidence must have been infectious because you obviously managed to convince people to invest in it, including two very well-known companies, Sylvan Learning Systems and Carlyle. That's what we all dream about… coming up with an idea that is a game changer in an industry! It sounds, from what you say, that that is what you did, and I know our audience would just love to hear about how you invented a new business model. It must have been something special to have attracted the big players to your door!

Pecce: *Well, let me say that frankly, 40 years ago, it turned the English teaching world upside down. It was very much ahead of its time and is only now being introduced into the school system in the United States. Before my method, learning was teacher-centered. Afterwards, it has gradually become student-centered.*

Previously, you went into a classroom, and you had the teacher giving you a lesson together with maybe 10 or 20 individuals. And then you went home. You would maybe study homework, and then you would go back for the next lesson the next week. So what was the problem? In fact, there were a number of fundamental problems.

First, students in a traditional class would have different levels of fluency – I'm talking about the typical adult evening class, not a class in school, although schools are not immune from this problem. It is very difficult for a teacher to teach students who are at different levels of ability, and it is very frustrating for the more advanced students to have to slow down for those who are struggling. No one is really very happy – not the teacher, not the able students, and not the students who are lagging.

What makes this worse is that not every individual has the same skills for learning, whether it is mathematics, physics, history, or a language. You know, learning is not just a matter of intelligence; it is above all a matter of aptitude. Do you know that Einstein, at the age of 17, didn't pass his French exam because he wasn't very good at it? So if you put Einstein to study with someone who had a great aptitude for learning French, he would look stupid. People with an aptitude obviously move ahead of the rest.

Secondly, with a fixed timetable, students ended up missing some classes. Imagine if today's Einstein can't make it to all the classes and so falls even further behind. You can see how he would act as a drag on the class. These factors accentuate the differences among students over time. Clearly, getting people to sign up for a fixed course of classes at 7:00 p.m. on a Wednesday evening for 10 evenings is a recipe for dissatisfaction.

I realized there just had to be an opportunity behind a problem as annoying as this was. I needed to create a method that put students at the same level of fluency in front of a teacher, time after time after time, without exception. And that's essentially what I did.

260

Linda Forsythe: How did you finally manage to accomplish this?

Pecce: *Well, I had to deconstruct the process of learning a language. Like reverse engineering a car ... taking it to bits and seeing what makes it work. I realized there were essentially two aspects to learning a language: first you learn new vocabulary and grammar, and then you practice it so it's ingrained.*

With that in mind, I eliminated classes as we knew them, and I abolished the fixed timetable course. Instead, students would pay to achieve a result, a certain degree of fluency. They were then free to use the resources of the center as much as they liked, usually over a year or a year and a half. They would begin by learning vocabulary and grammar at their own pace by themselves in our language labs, using all the support we could provide. In the 1970s and 80s, that meant books and a tape recorder, whereas now it means a computer, of course. In addition, they can summon help from a lab assistant who is an English-speaking native of their country.

Then comes the bit that really makes a big difference. When they reach a certain point in the curriculum, they need to practice and reinforce their learning with a teacher before moving to the next level. One student might need one day to reach that point, another student four hours, another student six hours spread over two weeks, and so on. Well, rather than having to go to a weekly class with the same teacher, they head to the reception area of their center to book a small-group lesson with a teacher and a maximum of three other students.

The Reception Area at the Wall Street English Oriental Plaza Center in Beijing.

There they find a schedule of all the lessons for the next few weeks. They will see the lesson they're looking for repeated three or four times a week, maybe at 10:00 on Monday morning with an American teacher, at 4:00 on Wednesday afternoon with an Australian teacher, at 8:00 on Thursday evening with a Scottish teacher, and on the weekend with an English English teacher! They then put their name down for the time that suits them. This way they get accustomed to different accents.

Now, if they miss their lesson because they suddenly have to go away on business, and they cannot attend, then the next week they simply continue from the point they left off when they get back, in a week, a month, or whatever. Furthermore, if one lesson with a teacher is not enough to reach that point, then they can do it again – at no extra charge!

So you can have a thousand students in one center, and even if they all started at the same time, they won't all finish at the same time. Everyone (and this is the key) is going at his or her own speed. So courses are self-paced. This was the big revolution in language learning.

Our method today it's really very, very successful. It has become known as blended learning, in that it includes both technology and teachers in the mix. In China, we are the leaders – number one without any doubt – and in many other countries, too.

*Editor's Note: For anyone interested in how far ahead of its time Pecce's learning methodology was, see how this same concept is *only now* being hailed in education as "the new big thing": http://www.ted.com/talks/salman_khan_let_s_use_video_to_reinvent_education.html

Linda Forsythe: I know that our audience is going to be very eager to hear how a young boy from Italy ends up living in a tropical paradise and has built an organization of such a magnitude as you have. I also love how you have taken the English language and been able to sell it to the world. Some would say that that is incredible! Others would say that only a non-English speaking person can truly appreciate the value of being able to speak English. What was it that led you to enter the English language learning arena in the first place?

Pecce: *It's interesting how it all came about. Because sometimes things happen which you would like to take credit for, but actually they happen almost by accident!*

Linda Forsythe: *Laughs* I personally don't believe in accidents. But, with that being said… I'd love to hear your story.

Pecce: *The whole story is that before I started Wall Street Institute in 1972, I was running another company, called Computex. I had set it up in 1968 in Italy, when I was 29. It was while running Computex that I devised the methodology that I later used in Wall Street Institute. Computex was the first company to do computer training in Italy. This was the time when computers, like the IBM 360/20, used punch cards and were the size of a large American refrigerator!*

I remember in 1968 that some computer companies had just started up in Italy: IBM, Siemens, Honeywell, and General Electric. But there was no one training programmers, analysts, and computer operators. So I set up Computex. Actually, before I set the company up, some people said, "Are you crazy? IBM is already training people to use its computers. Are you competing with IBM?" Well, IBM and the others were doing free training because when they sold a computer they had to train their client's staff. It occurred to me that it wasn't their core business to do training. They were obliged to do it. And in a few years, training would be done by other companies. In fact, that is exactly what happened.

262

*Two men operating an IBM 360/20, one of the computers for
which Pecce's company, Computex, provided training.*

Linda Forsythe: What did you do after you first had the idea?

Pecce: *I moved forward to make it happen. The first ad that I published
was in the* Corriere della Sera, *the number one newspaper in Italy. Linda, I had a
queue at the door of people coming to enroll, despite the fact that the training was
very expensive! Expensive because I have always targeted excellence: the best
service, the best teachers, the best academic material, and so on.*

*And you know how it worked? I borrowed manuals from IBM and other
companies. They called it "Programmed Instruction." So, in effect, you had a
self-training handbook with multiple-choice questions, and you had the answers
at the end of the book. So trainees could check if they were answering the questions correctly.*

*What I did was this: I took the manuals, I eliminated the answers at the
end, and I replaced the checking process with a teacher. So the student would
study a manual at home in their own time, and at their own pace. There were none
of the multimedia tools we use today. Then when they were ready, they would
come to my school to have the lesson with the teacher. One student might need to
study at home for three hours, another 10 hours, another three days, and so on.*

*So, you can see how the methodology created in Computex came to form
the basis of the Wall Street Institute methodology. Of course it became more sophisticated in Wall Street Institute, with the advances in technology.*

Linda Forsythe: How come you went from computer training to English training?

Pecce: *Well, I always had a passion to study languages. I have to take
you back to the time when I was just over 20, and I had left my small town, Ferrara, in the north of Italy, and moved to Milan. In Milan I was working full time,*

and in the evening I went to the Swiss consulate because they were offering les-
sons in German, and I wanted to learn German. But that didn't work out very well
because one evening I'd be too busy to attend the course, and then another eve-
ning, and another, and I was always missing lessons. I then tried with the Goethe
Institute, but it was the same story.

And then I said to myself, "There must be a better way because this isn't
working for me."

Pecce founded Wall Street Institute in 1972 in Milan, in the north of Italy.

So, moving forward 10 years or so, when I'd finished with Computex,
and I was 33, I reflected back on the difficulties I'd had learning German. And I
wondered, "Why can't I apply the methodology I developed for computer training
to learning languages?" Well, I tested the methodology for 9 months with 15 peo-
ple in Milan. After 9 months I thought, "It works!" And I launched the company.

I then set up a school for English, yes, but also for French and German.
And this is why I say my career has been accidental. Because it took me a year of
trying to sell French and German courses to realize that most of my business was
coming from teaching English. From that moment on, it was Wall Street Institute,
School of English!

That experience – of starting a language school offering three languag-
es, finding it was a failure at selling two thirds of its product line, but then seeing
the potential in English – was one of a number of times in my life when I could
have failed, but managed to see an opportunity behind the problem.

Linda Forsythe: Mentioning your failures reminded me, Pecce, of when
you and I met for lunch in Chicago with Sharon Lechter (who is the co-author of
"Rich Dad, Poor Dad"), and we were all having a conversation.

You and Sharon were both talking about your history... how you started
your businesses and the failures you had overcome, and how you both had come
to realize that there's an opportunity behind every problem. You also spoke about
one problem, one obstacle in particular. I would love our audience to hear that
conversation.

Pecce: *That was one of the six lessons that I wrote in your first book,* "Walking with the Wise"*: Behind a problem, there is always an opportunity.*

Many people know this. But how many people turn it around in their heads so that it becomes a guide in life? In other words, until I come up against a problem, I won't have a chance of seeing the opportunity behind it! I have to seek out problems to find the most opportunities.

In doing that, I inevitably court failure because I am pushing the boundaries, trying new things, which make failure more likely: starting a new business, expanding to a new territory, inventing a new product, and so on. The reason I was eventually successful with Wall Street Institute was not so much because I did some things right, but because I was prepared to keep failing.

My first business failure was in my mid-20s, in the pre-Wall Street days. Everyone blamed my partner, but I knew I had to take responsibility for having chosen the wrong partner. I realized, at that early stage, that the more one blames, the more one loses power and control over one's own life.

Much later, in 1985, came my big business failure and my resulting bankruptcy. It was the worst time in my life, and it was the best, because from that failure I learned how to be successful and never failed again. I analyzed it, and I admitted I made "this mistake" and I made "that mistake," and I resolved to start again and try not to repeat those mistakes.

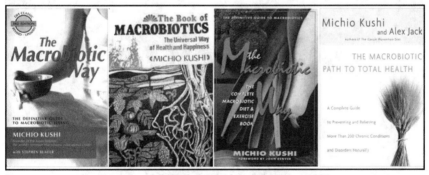

Pecce has followed a macrobiotic diet since 1985, based on the principles expounded in "The Macrobiotic Way."

Linda Forsythe: Were there other "failures" during your journey?

Pecce: *In 1985 my health failed with my business, and I nearly died. But thanks to that serious illness, I discovered a new style of life, which I have followed ever since. It's made up of fundamentally three things: one is the right nutrition, the second is exercise, and then the third is peace of mind. I try to keep body, mind and spirit in shape.*

From that time, I have followed a macrobiotic diet as advocated by Michio Kushi in his book "Macrobiotic Way."

Nutritious food, in my opinion, accounts for about 60% of the benefits of my health regimen. And exercise for another 30%: 2 hours before dinner, 20 minutes of swimming, and walking half an hour nearly every day. The remaining 10% has to do with something in the mind... it's that I have never thought in my entire life that "I am old." I always think that "I am young." When I stick to those three things, then peace of mind follows.

Linda Forsythe: I know that saying you think of yourself as young is not just words, Pecce. I have heard somewhere that you still play football (soccer, for us Americans)!

Pecce: *Hah! I guess you've seen the photos on my website! In fact, the last match was three months ago in Shanghai. We are all young guys, and play seven against seven. Normally when you play seven against seven, you play for half an hour, and then you have a 10-minute break, and then you play another half an hour. But we were crazy! We played for two hours without an interval, without a single break!*

The two members of Chinese rock duet Yu Quan playing football with Pecce.

Linda Forsythe: Wow! You know, Pecce, you have spoken very candidly about your ups and downs and different obstacles that you have had to overcome in life, and there are many in our audience who will be able to relate to that. Americans, in particular, will remember Fred Astaire and Ginger Rogers singing "Pick yourself up, dust yourself off, and start all over again," but it is not always that easy. What was it in you that kept you going when many others would have given up? What kept you going, Pecce, when things were tough?

Pecce: *I think there are a couple of things that kept me going when times were tough, and still do. The first is that my character was forged in adversity. I came from a modest family, so from early childhood onwards, I was used to the notion that we had to work for what we get – and indeed I helped the family by getting jobs during the school holidays. There was no money to send me to university, so I went straight to work once I left school. I was used to encountering obstacles. And I was used to overcoming them, plus I was doing so mostly on my own because I was an only child.*

It's like people who go to war and afterwards are more prepared to face problems, because their character has been tempered... like steel in a furnace. Of course when you have a tough life, two things can happen: you survive, or you succumb. But if you survive, then you are all the stronger for it. There is a quote from Nelson Mandela who stayed in prison for 25 years, and he said, "Tough times make people strong." I think we all know this.

The house where Pecce was brought up in Ferrara, Italy.

So, when my business failed in 1985, it was very painful, very difficult, very tough. I had a family, I had two kids, I had no money. Really I had nothing, and practically zero possibilities. But I could pick myself up because I was used to facing problems – nothing heroic, just a response that was second nature given my upbringing.

The second thing that has helped me through has been a mindset I have adopted in order to deal with the various downturns along the road. My approach to failure has been, "It is my business that has failed, not me personally." It was that mindset that has given me the confidence to dust myself off and start all over again.

267

Linda Forsythe: Despite what you say, not everybody has the chutzpah, so to speak, to be able to overcome obstacles and continue moving forward. That's rather a rare trait, which is sad. In America we have the saying, "What doesn't kill you will make you stronger."

Now, Pecce, there is one thing that you have mentioned to me in the past about "choosing the right partner," and that has been an important theme in your life. With hindsight, do you think it's possible to know in advance whether someone is going to make a good partner or not? I mean, are there any particular signs that you look for? For instance, even in personal relationships, some will look for those born under the same zodiac sign. And especially being in China, if you were looking for a partner today, with the benefit of having had good ones and not-so-good ones in the past, what would make you choose one person over another?

Pecce: *You know it's not my way to use the zodiac. I think the recipe for choosing the right partner has two ingredients: an understanding of human nature, and instinct. If you really take an interest in people in your life and you pay attention to your relationships, you begin to understand what makes people tick. I have always wanted to understand people, and like anything else, the more you try the better you become.*

I was as bad at it as the next man when I was young. In fact, I was given a lesson in instinct, when I was 25, by my fiancée, who later became my wife. I'd met a man (a 35-year-old) with whom I was planning to start my first company – the company I mentioned earlier. I thought he was brilliant, intelligent, a good speaker. Anyway, I introduced him to my fiancée. It was only a quick introduction, in passing: "Nice to meet you, and bye-bye." Later I met up with her and she said, "I don't like that man." Well, I was upset, Linda. I said, "How can you say that you don't like that man when you have only met him for a couple of minutes?" I was really perplexed. Then later in life I understood. She had a gut feeling, an instinct that that the guy was wrong. As it turned out, she was right, because one year later, his lack of care for customers brought the company down. We had two departments: my department dealt with education, his department was involved with machinery. But it was one company. My department was not so brilliant, but it made a profit at the end of one year. But his department was a failure. And because it was one company, we failed. Because he didn't care about people. He didn't care, and it was something I hadn't spotted.

I've improved over the years, for sure, but whatever my ability to assess people, I have always obtained help from friends and colleagues when hiring for senior roles. Sometimes appointments are just too important to rely solely on your own instincts. For example, ten years ago when I hired David Kedwards as COO – David is now the CEO of Wall Street Institute – I got every one of the nine senior managers to interview him and give me their take on him. All but one were very happy with him. The one who wasn't happy, funnily enough, was the one manager who I had had reservations about. When David told me afterwards that he was

268

impressed with all the managers bar this same one, it was confirmation to me that David had good instincts, and that the errant manager had to go!

David Kedwards, right, at the annual Wall Street Institute Conference, 2012.

It reminds me of a very interesting book called Blink *by Malcolm Gladwell, whom I was lucky enough to meet at a forum in New York. He explains in detail in his book the importance of instinct. He says that in a fraction of a second, in the blink of an eye, you can tell if a person is good or bad. I'm sure he's right, but it's a skill one has to work at!*

It helps if you are fond of people and study them. Then you develop a better understanding of human nature, and that is something that I developed over time.

Linda Forsythe: When I interviewed Donald Trump a couple of years ago, he said the exact same thing. He said that the people, who many times were very successful, are successful because they have that gut feeling – that instinct as you say, or "street smarts," is another way that he put it. So having that gut feeling and following it, I think, is very important to listen to. Now, Pecce, I'd like to talk a little bit about China, if you don't mind.

Americans, in fact many westerners, find China a little bit mysterious. You have had rare insight into how the Chinese people think and what they are like. And you've spent hours with senior figures there and even more time with university students at China's top universities. So, you must know about the culture and what is on their mind. I am sure that there are many questions that the Chinese ask you, which may give you a bit more insight. If you could sum up the essence of the modern Chinese culture, what would it be? And are they really that much different to us in the West, or are we all pretty much alike?

269

Pecce: *You know, I've been fortunate enough to live and work with people of quite a few countries. I've lived a few years in the States, I've lived in Switzerland, I've lived in France, and I now live in Spain and China. What I've discovered is that beneath the surface, human beings are the same everywhere. I know from the question and answer sessions that I hold at the seminars I give in China that they have the same needs, the same wishes, the same dreams.*

Pecce's Q&A sessions at his seminars in companies and universities show that Chinese people's dreams are no different to our own.

Talking about China... of course it's a different country. It's very different, and I'm sure some of your readers would like to know how to do business in China.

The thing to remember is that, although as human beings we are all the same, the culture within which people live can be very, very different. And so, to have the best chance of getting along with people, one must take the time to understand and respect their way of doing things. I have tried to immerse myself in the Chinese culture, and as a result I have been gradually accepted, almost as if I were a distant cousin.

People who fail to understand the culture get short shrift. I'll give you an example. Seven or eight years ago, when I had just started my business, I had a meeting in Beijing with the general manager of the municipal Education Commission. I was attending together with my Chinese partner, and there were other participants around the table.

One of the other participants introduced his organization to the general manager saying, "Well, we want to do more business in China and we have already done this and that." And he kept blowing his trumpet louder and louder: "We have already invested five million dollars in China," and so on. Well, you know what happened, Linda? The general manager, who was sitting next to me, suddenly stood up, looked at the "trumpeter" and said, "Are you just here to tell me that you invested five million dollars? Our meeting is over, goodbye." He then

270

gestured for me to accompany him to the door, and privately he said, "I know what you have done and what you are doing in China, and you are welcome here."

So, you can go to China, and even if you go as part of a large company, if you behave in a way that could be considered arrogant, then you and your company will not be welcomed.

Linda Forsythe: I know everyone would love to know more about Chinese culture.

Pecce: *When you want to start your business in China, be aware that the government is watching. Then, if you do the right things, and they understand that you are really doing things with quality, and you care about people, and you do things with excellence, they will support you. This is what happened with my company. I did the right things, I invested for the people. I didn't care about immediate profitability. Then, gradually, very gradually, I started to make profits. So, first you have to show in this country that you are doing things really for the people. You know, whereas in the United States or in Europe, nobody really watches you, in China the government is watching. So you have to pay attention, and you have to do the right things. So come, but don't act like an American or like a European; try to understand the culture and the way they live, and then you can really be successful.*

I should add that I get to meet a lot of business people and students in China because of the seminars I have been giving in companies and universities here, and they are really eager to understand and learn from foreigners. They are fascinated by what we can teach them. They have so many questions about life and everything. They are so alive, these people.

Yet, fundamentally I don't find any difference from students in Italy. They are very dynamic, and when you really create confidence, create trust, you can speak with them like I am speaking with you now. So, if you do the right thing when you get here, they will accept you with open arms... and maybe you will be invited onto their television to explain our Western ways, as I have been!

Pecce being interviewed about his business secrets and way of life on China's CCTV-9 "Up Close" television show in November 2009.

271

Linda Forsythe: I can honestly say that I also am very eager to learn about the Chinese and hold out my hand in friendship. As another point, Pecce, I know that you hand out other people's books at your seminars for free, because you've learned a great deal from writers, particularly the Chinese sage, Lao Tzu. What else do you think we can learn from the Chinese, and what else have you learned that has impressed you so deeply about Lao Tzu that you can pass on to us?

Pecce: *Well, Linda, the book by Lao Tzu you're referring to is called the* Tao Te Ching, *and I'm sure many of your readers will know of it. In it you can find the answer and advice for anything you want to do in life, whether in business or in private relationships, whether it's about friends, life, death, or anything else. It is such a fantastic book, and it's one that I want to bring to the attention of the Chinese, because believe it or not, a good few have not come across his writings. (Which is why I talk about it and hand it out at my seminars.)*

By the way, I discovered the Tao Te Ching *not when I came to China, but rather 35 years ago when I was still living in Italy. That's when I learned about Feng Shui, Taoism, and Buddhism – when I was 35. As a result, I practically never use Western medicine. Indeed, my doctors in Barcelona and Germany follow the Chinese way of medicine.*

Linda Forsythe: How did you come across the *Tao Te Ching* so many years ago?

Pecce: *Nobody gave me the book. I think a book finds you. I was in an airport and picked up a book and it was the* Tao Te Ching. *It was in this book that I found the wisdom for everything. It says, "If you know others… you are intelligent; but, if you know yourself… you are wise." I think that if foreigners read this book they will begin to understand Chinese culture through it.*

Linda Forsythe: That is very good to know. I have always wanted to see China. You are truly blessed. Now I know that another of your most favorite books is *The Power of Now* by Eckhart Tolle.

Pecce: *Yes, exactly, yes.*

Linda Forsythe: And there is a lot of information in there that you very much live by and believe. Why don't you pass on to our readers what you feel are the most important things to take away from that book and how you have applied these to your life?

Pecce: *Well, you know how it is when you pick up a book and it says things that you have been thinking all along, and gives you reassurance that you're not alone on your path? This book was like that. It was a confirmation for me because I've been living in accordance with Tolle's philosophy for a long time.*

272

I think I can answer your question with an interesting example from one of the seminars I've given, where we talk about everything: about business, health, life, study, family, love.... Well, one lady in her 40s asked me a question. She said, "We see you as a successful businessman, a successful person, and you are a very solid man on your feet. Are you afraid of death?" That was a good question.

I said, "I am not afraid of death. Death does not exist!" I said, "Let me explain. We are talking, you and I, in this moment, so this is the only moment we are living. And this is the present. So I am alive now. Death belongs maybe to the next minute, but I am not in the next minute, so why should I be afraid of something that does not exist in my life right now?"

What I am afraid of is sickness. Many people are lucky – they die in a second from a heart attack. But many others get sick and they suffer. Some people say to me, "Pecce, why are you so interested in being healthy? Do you want to live 200 years?" Well, to live one second or one million years, it's the same to me. And really it is the same because you can't go back to the last minute, and you cannot go to the next minute. I want to try to be healthy, not because I want to live long. I just want to live, to try to really live my life until the last minute of it, healthy.

I usually ask university students and business people in my seminars to tell me, in just one word, what is most important in their life. And I write their answers on the white board. One person will say "friends," another one will say "love," another one "money," another one "success," and another one "career." You know what is the most important of all of these? Something that sometimes they don't even mention at all: health! If you are not healthy, you'll find it difficult to obtain the other things you want. If you cannot be healthy, you simply cannot be happy. Health allows me to control my life.

Linda Forsythe: There's an old saying: "If you don't have your health, you have nothing." And on that note, I think that it is time that we have to end our interview. It has been absolutely fascinating and inspiring listening to you, Pecce! I have learned so much from our conversations together and during this interview. And I want to thank you for taking time from your very busy day to get together and talk with me today. I've known you for many years now, and each time we meet, you've always managed to inspire me.

Pecce: *Thank you Linda. If this interview can really be useful to your readers, then I will be very happy.*

Linda Forsythe: Well I know it will be useful! Pecce, before we sign off here, would you please tell everybody what your website is so that they can visit and learn more about you?

Pecce: *Yes Linda. It is half of Peccenini... it's **www.pecce.com**.*

Linda Forsythe: Well, thank you again for visiting with us today, with your wisdom and your accomplishments. Learning how you have overcome obstacles and how you live on purpose… that is something that many of us really need to learn more of in order to follow your example. We're going to sign off this evening by saying thank you with the Mentors Magazine motto: "Move forward with boldness on your quest, and mighty forces WILL come to your aid." Good night everybody!

If you would like to know more about Pecce, please visit his website at: __www.__ __pecce.com__.

274

Bonus Section!!!

Exclusive Cover Story Interview

Hari Harilela

Brought to you by ...

Interview with *Hari*
(Dr. Hari Harilela)
Founding Member of the
Harilela Group (Hong Kong)

by Linda Forsythe

"MENTORS MAGAZINE™"
(Transcript from LIVE Interview)

Linda Forsythe: This month I have the rare privilege of interviewing Dr. Hari Harilela from his beautiful palace in Hong Kong.

(Hari strides across his spacious office with a vigor that is rare for a man in the ninth decade, but then again, this businessman and patriarch has always been different. He sits down after shaking my hand, giving me his famous infectious smile.)

Hari: Thank you so much Linda. It is an honor to be interviewed.

Linda: Hari Harilela is a philanthropist and also known as the richest Indian in Hong Kong. But, his riches are not all financial. His kind and giving heart with strong family values are what gives balance to a life filled with opulent wealth. As a business tycoon, Hari has an empire spread across the globe. His rags-to-riches story is a saga of hard work, determination and the ability to know how to overcome many obstacles along the way. Hari, why don't you start out by telling me how old you were when you began in business?

Hari: I started work as a hawker on Peddler Street when I was 10 or 11 years old (he says, with eyes sparkling). I soon realized that all the Indians in Hong Kong were in the same business, so I decided to choose tailoring, (which nobody was doing back then). In the Indian caste system, a tailor was considered the lowest of the low. But, sometimes when you do what works and take your ego out of it... then it can turn into a blessing.

Linda: You started so young! What also amazes me is the size of your family and how close everyone is. In fact, you live with over 100 members of your family in this luxurious palace that sits alongside Kowloon Tong's Waterloo Road. We will talk a little more about that in a minute. In the meantime Hari, you have only six family members at any one time on the board of your many global businesses. What made you decide to do it that way and how has it worked in solidifying the success of the business?

Hari: Well, with six brothers running the company professionally, if you put a multitude of family members into the company, it won't work very well. For instance, if my nephew went into the hotel business and he misbehaved, no one in the hotel would inform me. So the idea was, "we save and nourish the family, but not place them in the business." Family members may not interfere in the hotels. But, if they want to go into the hotel business, they can go into the hotel business... just not in my organization. What built us to be so strong is the six brothers make all the decisions, but all our businesses are run professionally by highly professional people.

Linda: How can you maintain harmony among so many blood relatives and in-laws living together?

Hari: (Hari smiles.) It requires a great deal of understanding, sacrifice and tolerance, but, it also demands some basic rules. As mentioned before... there are only six family members on the board of the company (The Harilela Group) at any one time. So nobody is allowed to bring in all their offspring, making the company bigger and bigger. If that were to happen then... nobody would work!

There is also a statute for newlyweds. They can choose to leave Casa Harilela, or stay within the clan's embrace. If it's the latter, they must commit to staying for at least one year. In the first year, every marriage has problems, but then it settles down. We had one wife who didn't like anybody and wanted to leave. She wouldn't talk to me for three months. But after a year she became one of the best sister-in-laws we have ever had!

(Hari's only son and heir to the real estate and hospitality empire, Aron, recently married; and in accordance with what Hari said, Aron and his beautiful wife Laura, have chosen to live outside of the mansion, in an apartment in a building located directly behind the family mansion.)

Linda: Family insiders say those who live under Harilela's roof appreciate the fact that everybody tries to respect each other's privacy.

Hari: We practice non-interference. If I want to see a brother or sister-in-law, I call them first to see if they're available; I don't just barge in. And, we don't ask people how they spend their money. If they are doing wrong, we let them do it because it is their own concern. Most families interfere and that creates arguments or jealousies. If you don't interfere, that makes everyone realize that they have all the freedom they need – plus the protection of the family.

Linda: From what I hear, much of the Harilela harmony flows from your marriage of six decades to Padma, your beautiful wife. Both of you are the rock and backbone of the family home, (which currently encompasses three generations). But, the Kowloon Tong retreat wasn't always so peaceful. I understand that about thirty years ago, the men who ran the Harilela Company decided it was time they made their own homes elsewhere.

Hari: I was against it and told them, "When we were in poverty, we were together, and now we make money you want to be separate? I can't and won't do it." Eventually, we decided we should go our own ways, and then we came home after a very unpleasant meeting. All the ladies were there, so we told them the news. But then the ladies said, "You can go ahead and leave but we are not going." The way they stood there with arms crossed, broke all the tension. We all started to laugh and nobody left.

Linda: What is it that you value the most in your life? You've accomplished so much!

Hari: My wealth is my family, not the cash I have in the bank. Once you have the kind of love you get from your family, the greed leaves. Nothing is more important than family. I only hope there will be harmony among the generations to come. That is my dream, that after me, my family will not be broken.

Linda: There is another thing that has intrigued me, (I know our listeners and readers would also love to know!) You have a truly astonishing, "rags to riches" type story. Why don't you tell us more about that? As mentioned earlier, you started as a "hawker" on the streets of Hong Kong at the age of about 10. What changed that took you from such humble beginnings to where things are today? You survived World War II, thrived under British rule, and did even better after the Hong Kong 1997 handover to China. Today, you are sitting atop an empire with interests in hotels and general trading. Let's talk more about your story.

Hari: Well you see... my aim was to spread the name of Hari Harilela around the globe by leaving a legacy that made a difference for good. My second goal was to put the family back together (which was always my mother and father's wishes). I worked for both of these things very hard. I had my vision and direction. When you have vision and direction, then the most important step is to keep your focus while taking action. And you know, with the help of my brothers, we slowly, VERY slowly made it up the ladder. But Linda, so many times we would fall back down again!

The Bio channel on television has done a history on our family and that will show you how we came up in this world and how we went back down two or three times. The lesson from all of that is to learn from your mistakes, dust yourself off and get back up again. We all have setbacks. Everyone does. But for some reason, many people won't get back up and try again. One of the things I always remembered was my father's philosophy: "Don't cheat and don't be greedy." Those two words are very important in my life. We must be fair with each other. Of course money is important because we all need it to live. But greed is one thing that destroys the family fiber.

Linda: That is beautifully said, Hari. There have been several experiences over the decades which could have taken you in a completely different direction than what transpired, but yet you thrived. The first was during WWII. Can you give us a little background on how you were affected by it and how you managed to thrive?

Padma and Hari Harilela at Hari's 88th Birthday Dinner

279

Hari: *I always believed that building any business ... essentially is a noble pursuit, so I kept on building businesses, but I learned the hard way about the importance of diversifying. Many people depend on you when a business is built. So, not only is it is very important that it be done correctly, but you must protect what you've built with diversification.*

We were the first Indians in Hong Kong to establish a tailoring business. We supplied to the British Army and to the U.S. Armed Forces in this area at the time of WWII. That is how we made our start. Then we went on to diversify into real estate and finally into hotels. I sincerely believe if a man chooses to stay in one business, he'll become stale. With our six brothers, some stayed behind to look after the clothing business; I went forward into the real estate and hotels. Then, I went into many other businesses like computers. As for today, we only do hotels and real estate.

Linda: I see... ONLY hotels and real estate? Well, that's still quite a bit! Especially, since they are located all over the world. (Laughs) Very impressive!

Hari: *Thank you. The only way anything was ever accomplished from day one was to keep the goal in mind and not allow anything to keep you down when you fell. Falling sometimes can make your story more interesting.*

Linda: In the lead-up to the handover in 1997, many business people in Hong Kong left, or shall we say "fled" for fear of the unknown, but you stayed and thrived. Was there ever a moment in time when you made a decision to stay in Hong Kong, that you didn't have any fear? What made you stay?

Hari: *Very simple. You see, when Hong Kong was attacked by the Red Guards, it was just like a tidal wave of people and businesses leaving. I kept my cool because I knew that whatever happened, they would need an economy that had good businesses. That was my faith and why I stayed here. I didn't panic. "Not panicking during a crisis" is the major key in how to get through it.*

Linda: I see. Well how is life now in Hong Kong after 1997? Is it to your expectations?

Hari: *I think so. Being taken over by China did not change anything in Hong Kong. All the civilians, all the government officials stayed. They only changed the flag. So Hong Kong was still running the same as during the British time. We still have British laws here in Hong Kong. And for the next 50 years, (until 2047), we have a special administration region of China, and China does not enter into Hong Kong affairs.*

Linda: How do you manage to maintain an almost seamless balance between your incredibly busy and hectic schedule, family and down time? It's quite an accomplishment!

280

Hari Harilela, with wife Padma, and son, and heir to the Harilela real estate and hospitality empire, Aron, Sir David Li (Hong Kong banker and politician) and Penny Li; at Hari's 88th Birthday Dinner

Hari: *You see, our ladies of the family, (my sisters-in-law and my wife) help us enormously to keep the family together at "home." We (meaning myself and my brothers) are so busy in business matters, that the ladies of the house organize and control the entire clan to keep them all together. It's a lot of tolerance, understanding, and sacrifice.*

There is one thing that I've noticed in the world, and that thing is, "money divides people." Now if you don't make money as your basis for everything, it can change an entire climate. For example, let's say my brother is in trouble, and I choose to give part of my money to him. It wouldn't make any difference to me because that isn't what I base my life on. In my mind, I'm not going to get poorer, but the family unit will be retained. Now, if you don't put money as a priority against the harmony and love you get from the family and the unity, and the moral support, you get to grow... so I think we have to make our priorities: family first, money second.

Linda: That is profound Hari. Many of the most successful people in the world with whom I've had the pleasure of interviewing have said that an important aspect in their life is finding time each day to meditate or pray. Is this something that you also incorporate into your life, or do you have other methods to help you relax, bring peace or help you to find answers?

Hari: *Well, I think that meditation as a word is widely respected, but meditation or prayer is not the only ultimate thing. It also has to do with taking action after guidance. Plus, I think the best thing in life is, knowing how to find balance in whatever you do. Meditation might help to remind you of that, but if you organize a balance of one third of your life for your family, one third of your*

281

life to business, and one third for giving back to the community, it is a strong foundation to build on. Giving back to the community doesn't have to be all about money... it can be about the giving of your time or expertise. The whole idea of life is the true meditation. Divide your life into three parts that will entail giving to others: business, family, and community. It is that balance mixed with love and fairness that will create a fulfilled and peaceful life, not only for you, but everyone around you.

Linda: That's beautifully said. Over your years I'm sure you have faced quite a few obstacles in your life and business. How have you been able to rise above and overcome such situations? This is going to be one of the more important questions that people are really going to listen to closely about what you have to say.

Hari: You see, every set-back in life is a blessing in disguise. It improves you and it keeps you on your toes. Set-backs are always a good thing for people to realize if they learn from their mistakes. If you keep on climbing without quitting, then you will realize success eventually. I think every set-back is basic, and that teaches us how to behave and take another step forward. That's how we learned to walk in the first place as children. It's no different as an adult.

Linda: As you are aware, there is a serious financial crisis going on in the world with many people, and some are even saying this is close to what happened in the 1930's from the Great Depression. Quite a few people today have never had to face hardship to this degree, and some of them are very lost in knowing what to do in this new climate. So many things have changed! With your history and understanding of crisis, obstacles and experiences, what advice would you give the people of the world right now who are facing so many unknowns? Most who are living in fear…. What would you suggest that they do?

Hari: Many people think of the 1930's and use that time as a comparison, but they're wrong! Remember one thing, at that time we didn't have this high technology. Now we can communicate with each other within seconds, so I think 1929 should be forgotten. I think in that era, we had no power or insight to see what was going to happen the next day. Today, I do agree we have crisis, but the evolutions of a cycle come and go very quickly in comparison to then. Maybe every four years you have a success, and one year, a down trend. It's a cycle that goes on and on, because you cannot keep on rising. I've seen in my life that every three or four years a crisis comes, but because of modern technology and understanding complications, we will go back into a position of prosperity much faster than in the time of the 1930s.

Also, remember what I said about "Not Panicking." In fact back in history, they used to call these economic downturns "A Panic" because that is what people did. That is what happened in Hong Kong years ago, but I kept calm. Those who keep calm and take inspired logical actions... will not only get through this crisis, but will thrive because of it.

282

Linda: That is the first time I've ever heard anybody point out the difference in technology between now and the 30's... and it is so true!

In all your years in business, and as a husband, father, grandfather... if there was one single thing, or even a few words of wisdom that you could pass on to others as your legacy, what advice would you give to them as inspiration?

Hari: *Yes. The most important thing is family. If you have a family, you must not be so judgmental. As an example, in a family of five, one is very smart and progressive, the others are not. But, remember, a family is just like a hand. If you are a thumb, you will need four fingers to work, and those four fingers are virtually useless if the thumb is not there. So I think you have to have more tolerance and understand that each person has a different quality and talent in life. Each has an importance purpose for the whole unit. And, I think it's very important that don't reject any member of the family member as not being as good as you.*

When you have down the basic foundations for a good healthy family, then you will find those principles will automatically apply to other areas of your life, such as in business, or other projects. Knowing how to have a healthy family unit is key to so many things. If you have your own house in order, then you will know how to put your life outside of the house in order.

If you are going through a difficult time, have tolerance and have faith. Look toward the future you want to see and don't look back. We have such a short time on this earth. If yesterday is a dream and tomorrow is hope... work and plan today by planting seeds now, for tomorrow. No good or bad thing stays forever, because the earth was made to have cycles. So, have faith, have tolerance, have love for other people, and have a peaceful life. I think that is how we should lead our lives. It is certainly how I tried to live mine.

Dr. Hari Harilela is a founding member, along with his brothers Peter and George, of The Harilela Group, which was established in 1959. Hari is considered by many to be a financial genius, and The Harilela Group is one of modern-day's most successful family businesses.

The Vision of a
Village of Abundance

www.facebook.com/groups/VillageOfAbundance

The Love of One Person…
(A Fictional Tale Based On True Events)

by Linda Forsythe

"**A**n Obstacle is what you see, when you take your eyes off your goal." Remembering the wise words from her mentor, Carol pulled the rubber band out of her hair and let the tresses flow freely in the wind. Weighing only 101 pounds and a little over 5 feet tall, she was tired of being looked upon as insignificant. She had always been small in size, but with an indomitable spirit to get a job done… usually. Today, however, she felt overwhelmed and defeated again.

"I guess I took my mind off my goal," she thought while pumping the pedals harder on her bike. Over the rise and now with the added momentum, she breathed in the fragrant mountain air that rushed by. There was nothing in her opinion more releasing, than riding with abandon down her favorite dirt trail. After pushing herself harder to make it over the next hill, she stopped and walked toward the edge to look at the valley below. Still breathing hard and covered with a healthy sweat, she walked a little farther to park her bike and sit in the grass under a large shade tree.

Carol had lived in Colorado Springs all of her life, but the view that stood before her still managed to take her breath away. The green rolling hills, with swaying prairie grass, and the wide expanse of earth that held colorful rock tower formations were panoramic. Rushing rivers and bubbling streams below snaked their way through the valley, while cool breezes caused the leaves to shimmer. A few puffy clouds sailed by lazily. This and the sounds of chirping birds did wonders to ease away her tensions, on this warm summer day.

She almost forgot about her problems until she noticed the campfires of five more homeless families in the distance by the river. She sighed. Couldn't she go anywhere without seeing that?

The memories came flooding back from yesterday as she remembered trying to raise additional funds for the homeless shelter she was setting up. There was an old school building where she could arrange a refuge with food, showers, daycare services and sleep for those who lived on the street. It was all planned out and ready to go, except she didn't reach her financial goal. Quite simply, "no money" meant "no building," and the city of Colorado Springs wasn't willing to donate it. The city was known to donate some land to large established charities, even those from out of state to draw them in, but not hers. She was too small, so she had to raise her own funds.

Sighing, she remembered four years earlier when becoming homeless with her little girl, "Char." Her husband had left to pursue "A Better Life," and left rent and all of his debt on her shoulders. Carol had become pregnant, and married with parental consent at age 16. Dropping out of school, she had been completely dependent on him and didn't have any friends. Her parents didn't want anything to do with her anymore, let alone another baby.

Recent statistics stated that many people are only three paychecks away from being homeless. Well, considering there wasn't any paycheck or child support, she was out on the street in only one month.

Carol remembered living on the street for two weeks, standing in food lines and always looking for someplace to sleep. Life was certainly a challenge as a homeless person. Everyone looked at you differently. It brought tears of humiliation to her eyes as she remembered standing on the corner with a sign, asking for help as her daughter sat by her side. She honestly didn't know what else to do. Some people were kind and gave cash or food, but many ridiculed her. Because Carol was new at this, she didn't know how to obtain some of the services offered by the government. Others on the street had their own stories, but not everyone had problems with mental illness, substance abuse, or mental retardation as was the popular assumption. If she had a baby-sitter, or a place to clean up, she could then start to bring in an income, but that wasn't the case. Nobody offered because most assumed she was nothing... until one day a miracle happened.

An elderly lady, who used to live in the house next to her, drove by and happened to notice both of them standing on the corner with their sign. She was appalled that Carol hadn't said anything to her. Her name was Nora and encouraged them to stay in the extra bedroom in her basement. She helped Carol go back to school while she watched Char during the day. After obtaining her GED, Carol went on to receive training as a Nursing Assistant and then helped Nora financially pay for rent. With Nora living only on Social Security, it was a great help. Char fell in love with her immediately and liked to call her grandma. Nora hadn't been this happy in a long time. She had always wanted children, but never married. Now she had a family to call her own.

Carol sighed again. Closing her eyes and tired of reminiscing, she leaned her back up against the tree. What could one girl, especially with her background, do for so many anyway? She felt hopeless.

Slowly, with the chirping bird above her and the sound of rustling leaves, she began to be lulled to sleep. Letting the blissful feeling of peace surround her, she allowed herself to succumb.

As she started to dream, a man who appeared to be a homeless transient stood in front of her. She felt herself startle awake and looked up at him in a puzzled way, wondering if she were still dreaming. It was strange because she couldn't speak or move. He remained standing, looking down at her with a kindly smile. Carol wondered what he wanted. Then, after some time he finally spoke.

"Have you ever wondered what life would be like without charity? In order to have charity, you have to have love because they are the same. Do you know what life would be like? You were wondering how one single person could make a difference, especially with your background. What do you think life would be like right now, if others such as you had felt the same way?"

He paused, looking at her as if waiting for a response. When she didn't answer, he waited a while longer before speaking again. *"I'm here to give you a gift, a gift of insight into the past. Do you trust me?"*

Carol strangely enough felt absolutely no fear, but a sense of peace and warmth. The withered old man seemed to be able to read her mind so she thought, "Who are you?" He turned and answered, *"I'm a messenger for change. Now are you willing to look with me into history on what it could have been like without the love of one person?"* She nodded her head, being somewhat awestruck by the situation. "What a dream!" she thought.

In a vision, she began seeing life as it would have been without charity. Various countries and time periods would fly by as all humanity looked after their own needs. The illusion of being separate from one another was the normal feeling. Actions taken to hurt others, wasn't a concern as long as you were able to help yourself. Feelings were instinctive and predatory. Emotional comfort didn't exist, unless it was acquired by the taking. Killing, rape, pillaging, and hate were everyday occurrences. Life was survival. No one or nothing else mattered because of continual war, poverty, sickness, starvation, and homelessness. The few who were wealthy, were the strong. When their strength waned, someone stronger came along to take all of it. Pain and misery were everywhere because no one cared about their fellow man.

People were nothing more than animals. The sickly died in the street, and children slowly starved or wasted away with disease, and the population was significantly less. The children who survived, grew up hardened, learning at an early age what to do in order to live. Anger and fear along with extreme possessiveness enveloped everyone. Hope was nonexistent. What was there to hope for, except the fleeting possibility that maybe somehow, someone could care? No one cared. And the mere thought of looking beyond personal problems and helping out another, wasn't even considered, let alone done.

287

The old man patiently waited while Carol reflected on what she saw. After a while she thought, *"So how does this have anything to do with me? There were many thousands of people throughout time who have worked together for peace, hope, and even love. They worked as a team. How could any one person clean up the mess that so many lives are in? It's hopeless! It would have to be a team effort or someone has to figure out their own problems."*

The old man nodded and said, *"While working together as a team is necessary... the process does have to begin somewhere. All it has ever taken throughout history is one inspired soul to start the process. If the inspiration is right and one person is determined to see it through, others will follow, a team will develop and the ripple effect will extend for generations."*

He then pointed off to the right. The year of 1842 appeared in her vision. Dorthea Dix was a lone single woman who did something when she was appalled to see the way the mentally ill were treated on one of her trips to England. "Confined in cages, closets, cellars, stalls, pens... people were chained, naked, beaten with rods, and lashed into obedience." The mentally ill were thought of as inhuman. As late as 1815, the citizens of London could pay a penny to tour Bethlehem Hospital and gawk at the seriously mentally ill. Along with the club wielding guards, sightseers considered it great fun to taunt and provoke patients into states of frenzy. Less severely ill patients were dressed in black robes with white stars as a badge of identity and sent into the streets to beg for food. Dorthea Dix fought hard for vocational training of the mentally retarded and did much to ease the plight of the mentally ill along with changing their surroundings and treatment in America.

The old man pointed farther north to the year 1860 in Illinois, where Jane Addams was born. She became one of the first social workers. In 1889 she moved to the Chicago slums where she opened "The Hull House" for impoverished immigrants. She transformed one of the nation's notorious ghettos into a community of hopeful, self-motivated citizens. This inspired similar institutions across the country.

Around the same time, in another part of the world, a lone woman by the name of Florence Nightingale changed health care by transforming hospitals into a place to recover and get well, instead of places to die in squalor. At that time nurses were generally thought of as prostitutes and not very well regarded. She left her gentle and wealthy upbringing behind her in order to create change along with controversy.

Carol was drawn to look south. In 1859, Jean-Henry Dunant was inspired on June 24th when he saw the French and Austrian troops clash at the Battle of Solferino in Italy. He stated, "More than 300,000 men stood facing each other, the battle lines more than five leagues long, and fighting lasting more than fifteen hours. When the smoke cleared, 39,000 dead and dying bodies littered the

288

battlefield. The wounded were left to fend for themselves, which was the custom of the time." After doing what he could by soliciting the local townspeople to help the dying in the battle field, he went on and founded The International Red Cross. He later founded the YMCA.

The American Red Cross was founded after the Civil War by Clara Barton, an army nurse who later led the fight for women's suffrage, her part of a lifelong battle against ignorance and prejudice.

Da Yu was the legendary first Chinese monarch of the Xia Dynasty, best remembered for teaching people flood control techniques to tame China's rivers and lakes. Identified as one of "The Three August Ones and the Five Emperors," he took up researching and finding ways to control the floods. His techniques were effectively applied when a dam was conceived and built by the monarch. Remembered as an example of perseverance and determination, he was the perfect valued civil servant of his time that continues to save many lives.

One after another, Carol was shown a single soul that inspired many throughout all of history to make the world a better place with love and charity.

Finally, Carol was shown Calcutta. Inside of a building she saw a short, thin, little lady, dressed in a white habit. The lady's face was weathered and brown, but with soft kindly eyes. "That is Mother Teresa," Carol thought.

Mother Teresa bent over a sick patient and smiled, offering comfort and a prayer. Other women, dressed in similar attire were doing the same thing. These were only a few of the many from The Sisters of Charity.

The old man nudged Carol, and said, "Let me show you Mother Teresa's history. The vision changed to when Teresa was the child of a well-to-do family in Albania. She was taken regularly to church and worked with her mother on charity work to help the poor or homeless. As a teenager, she felt a calling to go into "church work" full time and became a Catholic sister. She then felt a calling to go to India and volunteered for a teaching post there.

At the convent in Calcutta, Teresa enjoyed very lovely quarters and worked with wealthy patrons. She had beautiful accommodations that were surrounded by extravagant gardens, and taught in an attractive classroom. One day while living there for three years, she had to make a trip to the "poorer" part of town. When she walked through the streets alone, down the back parts of Calcutta, she saw something she had never seen before: human beings dying in the streets, and nobody paying any attention to them. When she inquired around, she found that this was quite common. Nobody had time for the dying; there wasn't any place for them to go. The young nun was haunted by this terrible situation. Teresa felt another calling, this time to serve the poorest of the poor: a call to minister not to the living, but to the dying.

289

This was such a strong call that she asked the Church to release her from her vows so she could start this ministry on her own. It took two years, but finally she was released. No longer a nun, she was sent out of the convent and into the streets of Calcutta. With only a few rupees, or pennies, in her pocket, she shuffled down the streets with no promise of a meal, and no promise of clothing from the church. She was on her own, and she prayed, "God, lead me to somebody dying all alone."

Two blocks away she saw a woman lying in the gutter on the main street. The living body was being eaten by the rats that were running there. She picked up the woman and literally dragged her to the nearest hospital. She was refused admittance. "But," she exclaimed, "this woman is dying!" She was told, "People die in the streets of Calcutta all the time. We cannot take her." Teresa refused to leave until they had taken the dying woman. She said, "If there is a God in heaven we love, nobody should die alone."

Shortly thereafter Teresa went to the city government and asked for an empty room, "A place where I can build a home for the dying." The civil authorities told her, "Well, we have this empty Hindu temple of Kali, if that would suit you." She accepted gratefully.

Two other sisters heard about Teresa's project, and helped to drag the dying from the streets into this Hindu temple. Without medicine, without money, without an organization, without any backing, they did what they could, and nobody died in their place without at least a touch on the cheek and a kind word. "We love you." "Go in peace with God." They did not die alone.

Carol wondered aloud for the first time, "But this was them, how could I possibly do all they did?"

She jumped when Mother Teresa actually looked at her, answering the question by repeating words that she had said to others in the past: *"In the choice of works, there was neither planning, nor preconceived ideas. We started our work as the suffering of people called us. God showed us what to do. We are neither big nor small, but what we are in the eyes of God, and as long as we surrender ourselves totally, then God can use us without consulting us. We like to be consulted, but letting him use us without consultation is very good for us. We must accept emptiness, accept being broken to pieces if need be, accept success or failure. I was merely a little pencil in God's hands."*

As Carol's vision faded, the old man stated somewhere in the distance, *"Believe in yourself and in who you are. Remember, you are never alone."*

Tears streamed down her face and clouded her vision as she awakened. It was suddenly clear to her just how simple everything was. Carol's old neighbor had made a difference just by taking her and her daughter into her home and loving them both. And, she was helped back because of it. Every single person who had ever made a difference for good, all throughout history, had acted as a single person initially. All of them had put aside their personal road blocks for the sole purpose that they cared enough to do what had to be done, and our world was a better place because of them.

Smoke from the campfires down in the valley below her, still rose from the small settlement of homeless families. Carol watched as a sheriff drove up, got out of his car, and strolled over to talk to them. It was obvious he was asking them to leave because of the argument that ensued.

Carol looked to the heavens, and then sighed. She had to smile because her goal was now clear and the obstacles gone. The words of Mother Teresa came back to her as she looked into the distance, and suddenly she knew what to do.

She walked to her bike, got on and rode toward the camp with the words lingering in her mind, "I am merely a little pencil in God's hands, and I believe in who I am because I'm not alone."

AFTERWORD
Living The Golden Rule

by Dr. Surya M. Ganduri

More than 2 years ago, Linda Forsythe, a friend of mine, a great mentor and now my business partner asked me to join with her, in The Village of Abundance group that she was founding with some other like-minded individuals and creative thinkers. At the time I said yes, I did not know I had been accepted into the University of Life for an advanced course, nor had the reality hit in full force. Thus began a time of growth, challenge, and discipline!

I learned so much through these experiences, of which many are applicable to what we do in our lives. Whether in corporate America as entrepreneurs starting new businesses, or as school leaders or nonprofit executives – the lessons are the same.

How did we create magic under challenging circumstances and overcome the obstacles?

1. Create a common vision and "manifest a mantra" to represent this vision.

We were taking on the stewardship of putting together a group, committed to laying a solid foundation to guiding us towards peace... indeed, many pieces of a puzzle patiently being woven together to create a Whole – a Village where wealth and prosperity are enjoyed by all. The group is unlike any other, in that there are many moving parts which are very reliant upon the other in a global environment and the health of the economy. We, as an organization, needed to come together as a collective whole, and partner with our extended villagers to ultimately put services together for our global beneficiaries. We have no staff or existing resources to help with the legwork or heavy lifting. 100% of all the work is completed by a team of volunteers, many of whom work full-time, have young children, or were facing their own hardships during this time (and many still do). We had to pull together to make this happen – there was simply no other way! Our tagline and vision for the group was to create something based on the "village mindset" of a "Stone Soup" (complete with everything earthly... healthy, balanced and tasty).

292

Our mantra went something like this:

This is the time of coming together.
We join hands with each other.
We extend hands to the community.
We give hands to our beneficiaries.
We will create fellowship and community around the table,
Break bread together,
And Celebrate with the "Stone Soup!"

This became the common thread which tied everything we did tightly together. This message and mantra became contagious and it certainly took on energy of its own which held our group steadfast to this vision.

2. Build, inspire and trust your team.

It goes without saying that nothing is ever done alone... period. This is exponentially true when speaking in terms of volunteer work. A key secret to us fostering magic was: finding diverse talent with passion toward a common cause and then nurturing this group as a collective whole. We had a dream team on every level: very diverse, creative in spades, fearless of hard work, and committed eagerness to contribute. Many had never done anything like this before, which proved to be another gift – as their virgin viewpoints breathed life into old perspectives and ideas. We blew on these embers and trusted them without reservation. What power!

3. Color outside the lines and have the courage to stand behind these convictions.

As mentioned, this group has no long history; and with this comes all the expectations of "how it can be done." However, times are different – and certainly times are changing rapidly. We knew we were going to have to "shake things up" to bring life to the overall project. In fact, we took the project into the 21st century with a website and a presence on the social media (Facebook, Twitter and LinkedIn), including the internet radio on Blog Talk Radio (Village of Abundance Radio Network), and brain-stormed ways to generating revenue to self-sustain the project. It is one thing to have the creative ideas; it is another thing to have the courage to stand behind these convictions. What I can say retrospectively, and confidently, is that these new creative approaches, and the bold courage to "color outside the lines" continue to inspire us even to this day.

4. Be authentic and maintain the integrity of the project.

The concept of authenticity is not new to my fellow villagers, being world class mentors and coaches. We believe in the power of authenticity, transparency, and vulnerability. This became especially true when building a cohesive team and gaining support of our constituents. We spoke candidly about the hardships we were facing, the lack of sponsors, and the reduction of technical support from previous individual donors. This honest openness allowed members within the team and the organization to share our concerns and join hands with us in raising awareness and potential new supporters.

Trust me; this takes courage in challenging times. Many wanted us to cut, slice and dice, or downsize. We made a conscious decision not to do so. We kept the authenticity of the village (our theme) while building the group. No corners were cut on any level and it was indeed 100% authentically and fabulously earthy.

Faith and courage helped us maintain integrity against the odds.

5. Details are the differentiators – take it seriously.

More than once some of us were accused of being anal. Yes, I earned that distinction. Yet, more often than not it paid off to be attentive to detail, especially when times are tough and people need and want to experience value. Every touch, every interaction, and every exposure with our participants was covered with compassion, care, and a healthy dose of earthly flair, through notes coming from the hearts and the personal calls the day before the meetings to make sure all is ok and understood. The personal touch is not out of style – it matters! People see through boiler plate; they recognize and appreciate the care and attention of the personal touch.

Sure, it is hard – and it takes a ton of time. However, with few exceptions, the feedback we continue to receive is all about the details – this is what they remember. Details ignite the overall experience, build the memorable brand, and create the lasting legacy. This is not only true in executing a project – this applies to product launches, advertising plans, and leadership team values. Details are the differentiators and we must take this seriously.

6. Flu shots are imperative.

Those of you who know me know I am not referring to literal "flu" shots. I am speaking about the votes of confidence, the accolades! We need to give these abundantly. Arguably, it is more difficult to lead teams of volunteers than teams that are being paid to "show up and work and have a vested financial interest." Our team was indeed incredible; yet, we all were being pulled in a myriad of directions: work, family, school – and then the voluntary obligations. There were many bleak moments through the course of the past 18 months. Everyone was in need of getting healthy doses of "flu shot" encouragement. We couldn't afford to give up or lose the faith. We and our incredible core committee were the leaders of this project. We had to boost each other and ourselves; if we had given up, our fate would have been sealed.

7. Recognize the weak links, compensate, and rise above.

Initially, I wanted to exclude the "ugly bits" by primarily focusing on the positive aspects rather than the negative. However, a wise friend encouraged me to show the whole picture, as that is what makes the story credible. Let's face it; there are always weak links when we are tackling something of this magnitude. There are volunteers that don't come through; there are individuals who are focused on "what is in it for them" versus the charitable or the voluntary objective, and there are political, unspoken currents that often threaten the spirit of the group and the ultimate outcome. What I observed and realized is that the only way to deal with these challenges is to face them. Ignoring them or hoping they will go away in time is not the answer. We need to recognize these obstacles and hurdles for what they are – and then find a way to navigate around them. We must rise above, lest we succumb to the lowest common denominator. The shining light for me was always keeping an eye on where we had planted the flag – the finish line – coupled with a tremendous support system of individuals who shared the heavy lifting and compensated for the areas of weakness. Those individuals are the unsung heroes of this group (who remain in the core group to this day).

8. It is not about you!

The single greatest wisdom whisper from this project (and basically any other initiative in life) is that it is simply not about you. Viewing any experience, whether it is a charity function, a business deal, or a relationship solely through the lenses that it will benefit you, will ultimately compromise the results. Purity of intention will always be rewarded and will always win.

The metaphor I will offer is this: if I have a pebble and I hold on to this pebble so tightly for fear of sharing credit or losing control or whatever reason I have conjured up in my mind, then my single pebble will be my only reward. However, if I choose to involve others, share openly, praise often and publicly, be willing to sacrifice my own personal short term gain for the benefit of long-term gain for the overall team, that pebble is tossed into a fabulous pool of water and the ripple effects continue on and on. This I know to be true.

Summary

The principles of creating magic are the same, whether it is creating a new company, a new product or service, a new book being written, curriculum being created, a school system being reformed, a non-profit capital campaign effort, re-energizing a nation, or unifying the world.

There are two final thoughts to consider. Creating this kind of magic will always be a time of coming together (people joining with others to achieve what often seems to be the impossible). And secondly, as with any magician or alchemist, there involves the process of transforming commonality into substances of great value. This unique magical process was present in our efforts in building this great village. Our team, our supporters and those present were indeed the alchemists.

As you read the earlier articles by my fellow villagers, you will find many golden rules that we follow in our Village. With the challenges we face individually and collectively, if I look for just one rule on which we could all focus – one that stands out to me in a macro sense – is not a "new" rule, but rather a "mantra" for living with a fresh attitude:

Do unto others as you would have them do unto you.

Words are cheap – and actions can be hard. Sounds easy; yet, we know from our lives to date… it isn't.

We have an incredible – an incredible – opportunity to take our tremendous challenges to completely CHANGE the energy around them.

We can learn from each other. We can unite and scale this financial, political, and global mountain together.

These are changing times – and a new opportunity for each of us, individually and collectively, to align our thoughts, words, and deeds to truly live up to the principle of treating others as we would want to be treated. That's what we are at the Village of Abundance and what we do with the VoARadio Network.

I invite you to join the Village (you will find the details on how to apply for the membership towards the end of the book) so we can truly make a difference – individually, collectively, organizationally, nationally, and globally.

Namaste!

*I*f you would like to join our
"Village of Abundance Family,"
You May Apply by Sending a Private
e-mail with your contact
information to:
Linda@mentorsdigest.com

or

Send a request to the private
"Village of Abundance" Group page
to become a member:
https://www.facebook.com/
groups/VillageOfAbundance/

MENTORS HARBOR HIGHLY RECOMMENDS
Allan Davis

Allan Davis is an Art Director who utilizes his talents in graphic design and advertising. This service includes brochures, business cards, banners, logos, ads, and many other marketing materials to visualize your selling point. The more powerful your advertising is, the easier it is to sell!

After being in the Graphic Design/Advertising business for almost twenty years, Allan has just opened his own company known as "**Pacific Creations.**" After years of working with celebrities, mentors and high-end corporate clients… that gave him a powerful reputation and customer base to get his company started.

The logos, magazine covers, advertisements , and cover that you see in this book are a small example of Allan's talents. He has a unique understanding on what type of graphics have the most powerful effect on the public.

"The key to successful advertising is knowing your audience. Who is going to buy your product or service? What kind of imagery, colors, and fonts will grab their attention? That is the start to visualizing your selling point."
~ ***Allan Davis***

Pacific Creations
P.O. Box 82211 San Diego, CA 92138
Email: ADavis923@aol.com
www.sdpacificcreations.com

SPECIAL THANKS
&
ACKNOWLEDGEMENT

It is with deep appreciation that the following individuals donated their time to help put this book together. Your generosity and "Village Spirit of Stone Soup" has warmed my heart. Ultimately, all the individuals from around the world reading this book are benefitting from your mutual cooperation. Thank You! ~ Linda Forsythe

- Dr. Surya Ganduri
- Benjamin Hur
- Patricia Dietz
- Allan Davis
- Luigi Peccenini (Pecce)
- Leyla Hur
- Dame DC Cordova
- Mark Iriks
- Amy Jones
- Jeff Crandall
- Jack Zellmer
- Dan Kennedy
- Gayle Carson
- Monique Blokzyl
- Dr. Joel Bomane
- Dr. Marilyn Joyce
- KC Kang
- Susan Gibson
- Cynthia Hayes
- Shannon Collins
- Mark Semple
- Jennifer Stoll
- Wayne Dyer
- Louise Hay
- Kurt Scholle
- Tony Rubleski
- Tee Crane
- Mike Henry

- Stuart Rosen
- Tiffany Flowers
- Jason Wright
- Nira Kohl
- Sharon Lechter
- Bob Proctor
- Dr. Stephen Roulac
- Matthew Stone
- Don Green
- Arianna Flowers
- Alicia and Lorette Lyttle
- Sri David
- Camryn Oliver Lemmon
- Lynn Pierce
- Ted Ciuba
- Sharon McWilliams
- Lydia Proschinger
- Jack Canfield
- Jordana Carroll
- Lee Milteer
- Cynthia O'Neill
- Larry Louzon
- Versie Walker
- Rosalee Dodson
- Helen Maria
- Jason Bour
- Julette Millien
- Caroline Newman

- Leila Marsha
- Susie Girskis-Escudero
- Jean Davis
- Taji Clark
- Louis Lautman
- Burke Franklin
- Glen and Darlene Curry
- Gray Elkington
- Rick and Jane Otton
- Ken Varga
- Les Brown
- Brian Tracy
- Loral Langemeier
- Tahir Shah
- Marshall Sylver
- Glenn Brandon Burke
- Douglas Goodey
- Michael Skowronski
- Nordine Zouareg
- Judy Hoffman
- Stan Harris
- Vic Johnson
- David Koons
- John Assaraf
- Adria Manary
- Erica Davis
- Dr. Hari Harilela
- Brad Courson

MENTORS HARBOR HIGHLY RECOMMENDS

Dr. Surya M. Ganduri

Surya Ganduri PhD. PMP is a REAL Physicist, who utilizes his understandings of Quantum Mechanics and vast Business Operations knowledge. Combined together, the application of these two disciplines create a powerful force for success.

Dr. Ganduri is the founder and president of **eMBC Inc.** a national firm specializing in strategic and executive leadership development processes that "Help People Succeed in an Evolving World." He is dedicated to helping organizations and individuals manage strategic change, innovation, cultural transition, and goal achievement. He also has a program called "The Quantum Physics of Beliefs" that teaches the importance of your mind and action working together with equilibrium.

Surya has over 26 years of business experience in management consulting, leadership development, executive coaching, process improvements, organizational development, and youth leadership.

eMBC, Inc.
124 Plymouth Court
Bartlett, IL 60103
Phone: 630.445.1321
Email: info2@eMBCinc.com

Mentors ~ Village of Abundance Radio Network

Become a Talk Show Host
for
The Village of Abundance Radio Network

- Do you have a passion to provide inspiring information on a regular basis?

- Do you enjoy teaching and helping individuals?

- Do you have a proven area of expertise that could change someone's life for the better?

If so, we would like to speak with you about becoming a radio talk show host!

Help us make the Village of Abundance Radio Network, a new library of inspiration for people all over the world.

www.mentorsharbor.com/radio-show/
or
www.blogtalkradio.com/voaradio

Contact Linda Forsythe at
linda@mentorsdigest.com

Mentors ~ Village of Abundance Radio Network

This radio show network, is a collaborative effort from members of the Village of Abundance Group.

Listen to instruction and inspiration from our global mentors, who are ALL experts in their niche of proven expertise. Most have a Doctorate Degree; such as Dr. Marilyn Joyce, Dr. Ted Ciuba, Dr. Joel Bomane, Dr. Surya Ganduri and many others.

A weekly show is broadcast over the internet on blog talk radio.

Celebrated Mentors from around the World... Teach how to THRIVE during hard Economic times.

The Village of Abundance Radio Network is also streamed LIVE on Mentors Harbor seven days a week!

www.mentorsharbor.com/radio-show/
or
www.blogtalkradio.com/voaradio

MENTORS HARBOR HIGHLY RECOMMENDS

Monique Blokzyl

Monique Blokzyl is a wholehearted entrepreneur who loves helping others rocket their business dreams into profit. Her **Business Launch Portal** offers you all the support you'll need, from finding your dream business idea, to laying a powerful foundation, to building your personal support team.

Monique has built several successful organizations. Prior to becoming an entrepreneur, Monique worked for more than 15 years as a Marketing and Change leader in some of the largest corporations worldwide. She learned what it takes to turn a business vision into profit. As an international public speaker, trainer and coach, radio talk show host and author, Monique inspires and supports founders in many ways to jump-start their business.

"First you jump off the cliff and build your wings on the way down"
~ by Ray Bradbury

If you are brave enough to jump, the **Business Launch Portal** will help you build wings while rocketing your business dream into enterprise!

Business Launch Portal
Phone: +49.157.859.220.87
Email: monique.blokzyl@gmail.com
www.moniqueblokzyl.com

The World Is Yours!

Mass Media for EVERYONE...

'TaJoya
.com